Psychoanalysis and Catholicism

PSYCHOANALYSIS

AND

CATHOLICISM

EDITED BY

BENJAMIN B. WOLMAN

Long Island University

GARDNER PRESS, INC.
NEW YORK

Distributed by Halsted Press
A Division of John Wiley & Sons, Inc.

New York　　•　　London　　•　　Sydney　　•　　Toronto

Gardner Press, Inc.
32 Washington Square West
New York, New York 10011

Distributed solely by the Halsted Press Division of John Wiley & Sons, Inc., New York

Library of Congress Cataloging in Publication Data
Main entry under title:
Psychoanalysis and Catholicism.

    Includes index.
    1. Catholic Church and psychoanalysis. I. Wolman, Benjamin B. II. Title.
BF175.P77   150'.19'5   76-10765
ISBN 0-470-15079-3

Printed in the United States of America

1 2 3 4 5 6 7 8 9

Content

Foreword

FREUD'S ATHEISM AND HIS QUESTIONING OF RELIGION AND OF THE Christian morals of his time could not avoid evoking a spontaneous opposition of the Catholics, especially because most of them had never read Freud's works.

Such an attitude tends to disappear with the passing of time, partly because some freudian psychoanalysts are Catholic believers (some of them are converts, others are priests). Moreover, a growing number of psychoanalysts, whether believers or nonbelievers, have enough respect for *human values* (including faith) so as not to confuse them with the neurotic or infantile practice of religious themes.

Today many theologians and pastors have a sound knowledge of Freud. Far from rejecting him as a whole, they are inclined to believe that the freudian treatment method and his metapsychology can enrich and purify their pastoral activities and their theology.

Priests, monks, and nuns have more and more opportunities to meet psychiatrists and psychoanalysts and to share their experiences and their work. It is in this way that they participate in the congresses of the International Catholic Association of Medico-Psychological Studies, as active members or not. At the same time, Protestant pastors and rabbis participate in the Academy of Religion and Mental Health of the United States; we must also not forget the various organizations in many countries that elicit and receive psychological assistance in the discernment of sacerdotal and religious vocations. This help is used in the training of the educators of future priests and monks.

Such encounters have resulted in the disappearance of many reciprocal prejudices, and we can only be pleased by this development.

It is also of note that contrary to the widely held opinion amidst the Catholic Church as well as by others, the church hierarchy never condemned Freud or psychoanalysis. To be sure, Pius XII has rejected "The pansexualist theory of a certain psychoanalytic school" (Discourse to Doctors of Neurology,

1952), but he also declared that "psychology of the depths must not be condemned if it discovers the contents of the religious psychism and strives to analyze and to reduce it to a scientific system, even if this research is new and even if its terminology cannot be found in the past" (Discourse at the Congress of Psychotherapy and Clinical Psychology, 1953). He asked only that "the spiritual values be taken into consideration by both the psychologist and by his patients" (Discourse at the International Congress of Applied Psychology, 1958). The *Monitum of the Holy Seat* (1961) did not condemn psychoanalysis, only its inconsiderate use, as it seems inconsiderate even from the point of view of psychoanalysis.

If it is true that the Council of Vatican II did not express its opinion on psychoanalysis, it wished on several occasions to call on the sciences of man, notably psychology. For example, discussing the harmony between culture and Christianity, it decreed in the pastoral Constitution of *Gaudium et Spes* (no. 62, 1): "That sufficient knowledge not only of theological principles but also of secular scientific discoveries, especially psychology and sociology be used in the pastoral; (a knowledge) of the sort that the faithful will in turn be brought to a greater purity and maturity in their life of faith."

One cannot say this any better without distorting the texts, one may apply to psychoanalysis what was said there of psychology in general.

Thus the Catholic Church, in its mission and its present need of having a dialogue with the world and with all sciences, is far from turning away from the questions posed by psychoanalysis. The church places only one condition: that this dialogue be conducted by competent and duly informed men. The church is only afraid of amateurism and of superficial and tendentious informations of the great press.

This is why we have willingly agreed to write a preface to this work in the hope that through its serious studies this book will help to abolish prejudices, and to encourage research and its judicious applications in the service of human equilibrium.

L. J. CARDINAL SUENES
Archbishop of Malines Bruxelles

PART ONE

Correlations between

Psychoanalysis and Catholicism

BENJAMIN B. WOLMAN explains in the introductory essay, A Dialogue Between Psychoanalysis and Catholicism, *that the purpose of this volume is to initiate a frank and honest dialogue.*

Christianity started as a rebellion against the mercenary Zeitgeist *of the Roman Empire, and its origins are "connected with the story of One Man who died willingly so other people should see that love is stronger than hate and greater than life itself. Psychoanalysis started as a protest against the hypocrisy of the Victorian era and its origins are connected with the story of one human being who lay bare his own wounds to enable other people to understand human nature."*

1

A Dialogue between
Psychoanalysis and Catholicism

by

BENJAMIN B. WOLMAN, Ph.D.

I

THIS VOLUME IS AN OUTGROWTH OF A DIALOGUE BETWEEN THE
editor and some psychoanalytic and Catholic thinkers. There was
no effort to make anyone acquiesce or to appease any school of
thought, nor did anyone try to build bridges doomed to collapse.
No effort was made in this volume to patch over disagreements or
to deny controversies. The differences are deep, and the basic
tenets are far apart.

The sole purpose of this volume has been to start a frank and
honest dialogue. Psychoanalysis and catholicism have been at
odds with one another for a long time, although both of them are
most earnest schools of thought deeply concerned with man's
problems and his destiny. They disagree on almost every possible
issue, but they are inseparably united in their effort to help man to
understand himself.

The Catholic religion, the older party in the dialogue, started
as a protest movement against the enslavement of men and as a
silent rebellion against the cynical opulent civilization of the
Roman Empire. It was the little Jewish sect of Essenians that
rebelled against the mercenary *Zeitgeist* and called for a
reevaluation of traditional social norms such as success, glory,

and wealth. The origins of Christianity are irrevocably connected with the story of one man who died willingly so other people should see that love is stronger than hate and greater than life itself.

This philosophy, often forgotten and rarely practiced, has been the essence of Christianity. The fact that Catholicism became a ruling religion, that the followers of Jesus established Ecclesia Militans and Holy Inquisition, bears witness to the frailty and deceptiveness of human nature, but that fact does not contradict the essence of this religion or its basic philosophy.

Catholic thinkers, among them St. Augustin and Thomas Aquinas, using the conceptual tools of Greek philosophy, tried to penetrate the mystery of human feelings, thoughts, and actions. Man's godlike love for the fellowman and his satanic wickedness in face of weak and defenseless brothers were discussed again and again by Catholic theologians and philosophers. A complex ritual of prayers, confessions, and forgiveness was erected, hoping to alleviate human suffering and deal with man's unstable and selfish nature and his feelings of guilt and repentance.

For centuries the Catholic church was guilty of suppressing freedom of thought and ignoring the achievements of science. With a few illustrious exceptions, leaders of the most powerful religion represented conservatism and opposed scientific progress. However, at the present time we are witnessing a profound revolution within the Catholic church. Old issues are being reevaluated, new issues raised; thinking Catholics are perplexed by the magnitude and complexity of problems they do not intend to evade or avoid. It is the new spirit of Catholicism that may enable this great religion to regain its cultural role and spiritual leadership.

II

Psychoanalysis started as a rebellion against the bigotry and hypocrisy of the Victorian era. The origins of psychoanalysis are irrevocably connected with the story of one human being who had the courage to lay bare his own wounds and perform a public vivisection of his own nature, to enable other people to see human nature in a true light.

Psychoanalysis is not just one more psychological theory. It is a mental tool as sharp as a surgeon's knife that cuts through centuries of prudish lies and bigoted conceit. Man is neither animal nor angel, neither crooked nor perfect; he is just a perplexed creature somehow hanging in midair, struggling with his animalistic impulses he can never be rid of and striving to reach a heaven he can never attain. Being as doomed as Augustin saw him and as climbing as Thomas Aquinas perceived him, man is torn by a conflicting earthly id and a heavenly superego. Morals and manner, instinctual impulses, and acquired concepts are combined in an exasperating complexity of human nature.

Did Freud open Pandora's box? Perhaps, but the truth was long overdue. Freud did not make men weak, but by exposing their weaknesses, he offered a ray of hope. Freud was critical of the wishful presentation of God as a Father who takes care of his infantile human flock. Life is not a nursery, Freud wrote, and adults cannot expect to be pampered. Ever so often mental patients use religious imagery as an escape from painful realty, and many a religious ritual resembles obsessive–compulsive neurosis.

However, the fact that some people use religion as a neurotic crutch does not necessarily mean that religion as a philosophical system and a sociocultural institution *is* a neurosis.

The time has come for the twain to meet and talk with one another.

III

The present volume started as an exchange of ideas. It is a *sui generis* dialogue written with the distinct intention not to solve any problems and not to offer any lasting solutions for human ills.

It is an effort to let in fresh air and let some stale ill feelings out. The authors have been invited to express their ideas on issues that might be discussed by Catholic and psychoanalytic thinkers. The editor carefully avoided prodding the authors to prove or to disprove anything, and his talks with and letters to the authors had the sole aim of stimulating a free expression of ideas. The only credit he wishes to get is to have this volume prove to be thought provoking.

All the essays of the volume have been briefly summarized in synopses that precede each essay. There is no need to repeat them here. Let the reader enter the house we have built and marvel at or criticize our work. It might be worthwhile, however, to point to the diversity of opinions and the refreshing atmosphere of a free exchange of ideas. For instance, one essay goes into a detailed and scholarly analysis of christianity defending Freud's cultural-historical philosophy, whereas another scholarly essay critically examines Freud's analysis of religion. Although one author counterposes Freud's ethical system based on law to the Catholics' ethical system based on love, another author finds Christ's self-sacrifice as a most convincing example of love in the psychoanalytic sense. Although most authors discuss Freudian psychoanalysis, one author offers a brilliant application of Jung's ideas.

United we stand? No, by no means, Our pluralistic approach to human problems does not make us "stand"; we are moving ahead, forging toward a mutual understanding and mutual respect of free human minds.

Obviously, the present book was not intended to be comprehensive; it is not a textbook. It is neither authoritative nor authoritarian, and the people who wrote for this book wrote as individuals and not as heads or representatives of institutions.

This book does not seek an approval by the Catholic hierarchy nor by psychoanalytic institutes. It is the sole responsibility of those who put their thoughts down in the following pages. This book is not a part of any establishment, clerical or secular. It is merely what it is: a platform in which a few Catholic and psychoanalytic thinkers said whatever they felt like saying to one another, sharing their doubts and wondering about the everlasting search of man for himself.

IV

The present volume is divided into two parts. The first part is devoted to correlations between psychoanalysis and Catholicism.

Drs. Ancona, Bartemeier, Beirnaert, and Cousins participate in this part. The second part analyzes cultural-historical and ethical issues with the participation of Drs. Coltrera, Dempsey, Ple, and Wolman.

H. E. Cardinal J. L. Suenens wrote the Preface. Drs. I. J. Ibor-Lopez, Noel Mailloux, and Edouard Morot-Sir offered invaluable help in planning this volume.

DR. LEO H. BARTEMEIER, Psychoanalysis and Religion, *explains psychoanalytic ideas concerning religion against Freud's educational background. Freud "conceived religion as a part of a social process (civilization) which was essentially utilitarian and hedonistic." Freud's atheism antidated his psychoanalysis, and he related moral norms to primitive taboos and prohibitions.*

Jung broke away from Freud and believed that religion, as an answer to deep-seated human needs, is a form of psychotherapy.

St. Thomas Aquinas, in a way, anticipated the psychoanalytic ideas. According to him, the "soul" is the source of unconscious functions and love and hate are often ambivalent.

2

Psychoanalysis and Religion

by

LEO H. BARTEMEIER, M.D.

FREUD WAS AN UNBELIEVER FROM AN EARLY AGE. HE REFERS TO himself in *The Future of an Illusion* as "an infidel Jew," apparently intending the reader to understand that he had ceased to believe in the religion of Judaism (Freud, 1927). While working under Brucke in 1876, he had already adopted a materialistic view of man. The spirit of Brucke's institute was that psychology was the study of the nervous system, and psychical energy was nothing more than physical energy supplied by the brain cells. All through the rest of his life Freud clung to the physical-mechanical analogue or model of mental life, although he retained the terminology of *psyche* and *psychical*.

It is interesting to trace some of the influences that may have contributed to his thinking on matters of religion. As a child he had a nurse who was a Catholic and who used to take him to church services. "She implanted in him the ideas of Heaven and Hell and probably also of salvation and resurrection. After returning from Church the boy used to preach a sermon at home and expound God's doing" (Jones, 1953). Freud studied under Brentano for two years, 1874–1876. This is significant because Brentano was a priest who had left the Catholic Church; he was a trained scholastic philosopher who founded modern empirical psychology, and who emphasized the notion of *process* (rather than *content*) in his act-psychology. Moreover, it was Brentano who recommended Freud to Theodor Gomperz as the translator of part of the works of John Stuart Mill into German, and Mill has been aptly named "the saint of rationalism." From Brentano Freud may have learned more than the basic concept of the unconscious and from Mill perhaps the essentials of utilitarianism and hedonism. Mill had found himself constrained by the facts themselves and went beyond the rigid and narrow hedonism of his father as early as his twentieth year (1826), just as Freud found himself constrained by empirical data and reached "beyond the pleasure principle." Human life could not be explained by a simple maximizing of pleasure.

It seems clear also, especially from Freud's way of dealing with the concepts of culture and civilization, that he was much influenced by "social contract" theories of society. He thought of society in an almost Rousseauesque way. It is difficult to maintain Rousseau's theory of man existing by nature in an idyllic condition, corrupted by civilization, and at the same time to maintain a Darwinian view of man's descent, plus Hobbes' view of the condition of man in nature as *bellum omnium contra omnes* (the war of every man against every man) and "the life of man, solitary, poor, nasty, brutish and short." But these are the ideas that seem to lie behind much of Freud's thinking about anthropology, prehistory, and religion. Thus we read, "But how ungrateful, how shortsighted after all, to strive for the abolition of civilization! What would then remain would be a state of nature, and that would be far harder to bear. It is true that nature would not demand any restrictions of instinct from us, she would let us do as we liked; but she has her own particularly effective method of restricting us. She destroys us—coldly, cruelly, relentlessly, as it seems to us. . . . It was precisely because of these dangers with which nature threatens us that we came together and created civilization . . . the principal task of civilization, its actual *raison d'etre,* is to defend us against nature" (Freud, 1927).

Freud conceived of religion as part of a social process (civilization) that was essentially utilitarian and hedonistic, even though the utilitarianism may have been ideal utilitarianism, and the hedonism may have been enlightened hedonism. It is important, therefore, in the logic of Freud's thinking to understand that the question he was asking himself was this: Does religion successfully subserve the temporal needs of man? Does it defend us against the dangers with which nature threatens us? On his own premises, as a scientific humanist, Freud had already assumed that there was no God, no afterlife, no revelation, so the question of the truth of any proposition of religion was not asked by him. It is very interesting to note, however, that Freud was not as final in his rejection of religion as some of his followers were later.

Thus while teaching, as we shall see, that "religion is an illusion," Freud was careful to point out that "an illusion is not the same thing as an error; nor is it necessarily an error" and in fact what constitutes a particular belief an "illusion" is not its content, true or false, but its *motivation*: thus, he says that "we call a belief an illusion when a wish-fulfillment is a prominent factor in its motivation, and in doing so we disregard its relation to reality, just as the illusion itself sets no store by verification" (Freud, ibid). He is therefore clearly saying that the truth or falsity of a religious belief is not established by psychological statements about its origin.

Freud's atheism antedated his studies in psychoanalysis, and he did not teach that psychoanalysis *disproved* the teachings of religion. His polarity pairing regarding religion was not truth-falsity, but helpful-unhelpful as a means to temporal welfare. He conceded the right of the believer to go on believing: "I still maintain that what I have written is quite harmless in one respect. No believer will let himself be led astray from his faith by these or any similar arguments (Freud, ibid). Earlier he had said: "Nothing that I have said here against the truth-value of religions needed the support of psycho-analysis; it had been said by others long before analysis came into existence. If the application of the psycho-analytic method makes it possible to find a new argument against the truths of religion, *tant pis* for religion; but defenders of religion will by the same right make use of psycho-analysis in order to give full value to the affective significance of religious doctrines" (Freud, ibid). It is interesting to note that this is precisely what has begun to happen within the Roman Catholic Church.

The Origin of Religion

Freud's theory about the origin of religion is contained mainly in three works, *The Future of an Illusion, Totem and Taboo,* and *Moses and Monotheism.* In his *Obsessive Acts and Religious Practices* he put forward the theory that religious practice and the behavior of a compulsive obsessional person have much in common; the compulsive obsessional person, he thought, was one who had not successfully overcome the obsessional neurosis of his childhood. Thus he could relate what he thought of as religion, through the neurosis, to what he had already come to understand of childhood. Religion originates, he thought, in man's helplessness before his own instinctive fears within and the threatening forces of nature without. It belongs to an early stage of human development before man learns to handle his own internal fears and impulses and the forces of nature outside him. The affective states generated by fears that well up from within or are provoked from without are coped with by the introduction of counteraffects: the function of these counteraffects is to suppress and control the fear-producing elements man finds he cannot cope with rationally.

It is at this stage that the "illusion" develops. The child, when he experienced danger or uncontrollable fears, went to his father as a source of reassurance, strength, and comfort. The father was also a source of authority, reward, and punishment. The child discovered he could win affection by obeying the commands of his parents. Above all, he had the guilt of the oedipal phase of development to cope with. The violation of the parricide and incest taboos demanded expiation. (Freud assumed that morals were not essentially different from taboos: they were for his thinking merely the expressions of taboos in developed societies.) "Religion" derived from the fact that the adult who could not cope rationally with his problems "regressed" to the level of infantile defense. Religion was a reusing of infantile behavior patterns, but with this important difference: because these infantile behavior patterns were inappropriate at adult levels, they came to constitute a neurosis. This is why Freud could say that on his own premises: "Religion would thus be the universal obsessional neurosis of humanity" (Freud, ibid). The illusion is the projected image of the father.

Underlying this theory of Freud's is a fallacy which has been called the fallacy of psychomechanistic parallelism formulated by Zilboorg (1962). It is the fallacy of assuming that, when two behavior patterns are observed to exhibit the same constituents or are reducible to the same component elements, they are due to the same psychological mechanisms. Fromm points out that Freud himself saw the invalidity of this kind of reasoning. It is also interesting to note that much of what Freud says about religion corresponds to the theologian's traditional teaching about the debased form of religion called superstition.

Since, for Freud, moral injunctions and prohibitions were so often related to primitive taboos and had a primary utilitarian value, ministering to our personal comforts or preserving order in society, the notion of an objective, "natural" moral order was foreign to his thought. Together with many psychologists and psychoanalysts, he used the word *guilt* nearly always with an emotional (and therefore neurotic) connotation attached to it. Religion, then, is a means of getting rid of neurotic guilt, on the one hand by placating "God"- the projected father-image—and on the other hand by ritual cleansing of the guilt incurred by violation of taboo.

The problem of the existence of God is not a problem in psychology but in metaphysics. Freud saw that his theory about the origin of religion did not prove the nonexistence of God. But it has thrown a flood of light on some important problems. We now understand a great deal more about the phenomenon of adolescent atheism, seen as part of a more generalized adolescent revolt. It may indeed represent the young person's attempt to escape the domination of a father or father figure. We can understand some of the neurotic patterns of behavior in religious practice and the subjection of religion itself to neurotic ends. The functions of ritual, liturgy, and the sacramental system take on deeper significance through the application of the insights of Freud.

But this took many years to achieve. At first most believers turned away from the "errors" of Freud's thinking. C. G. Jung had already broken with Freud on the question of sexuality and its role in infancy and the neuroses. He soon took up the question of religion, and was seen by many as teaching a more acceptable doctrine. Jung thought that religion was the answer to one of our most deep-seated needs. Thus, far from religion being a neurosis, he had never, he claimed, had a patient whose neurosis was not due to his lack of religion, nor had he ever cured a patient whose cure was not due to his return to religion. But Jung was using the word religion in a very special and personal sense. He meant by it a dynamism of the unconscious, essentially irrational in kind, which served as a unifying function or value system, around which or on which one might build a consistent life pattern. He prescinded from the existence of God and regarded the propositions of all religions as equally true, having what he called "psychological truth," that is, they were true for those that believed them. Jung taught that religion was a form of psychotherapy.

Some Catholic theologians (e.g., Victor White, O.P., and Martin D'Arcy, S.J.) seem to have accepted this point of view, and further research and better understanding have led to a clearer understanding of Jung's position. Religion is not essentially irrational, and it is not a form of psychotherapy. For Jung, soul and psyche were regarded as one and the same. Father Victor White taught that soul and psyche were in fact identical, and thought that this was Thomas Aquinas' teaching. But Thomas Aquinas[1] is quite clear that this is not so. There is a real distinction between the soul and its faculties. Psychoanalysis is now seen to be concerned with the psyche (the apparatus of processes of the psychophysical composite), whereas religion is concerned with the spiritual welfare of the whole man, but specifically the soul, in whose essence grace resides.

---

[1]St. Thomas Aquinas: *Passio proprie dicta non potest competere animae nisi per accidens, inquantum scilicet compositum patitur* (S.T. la 2 ae, QXXII al). (Trans.: Emotion in the strict sense cannot apply to the soul, except incidentally, in so far, in other words, as it affects the psychophysical composite.) This implies a clear distinction between soul and psyche.

St. Thomas and the Unconscious

Although Thomas Aquinas does not discuss the concept of the unconscious formally, the idea is not foreign to his thinking. In fact, it is intrinsic to his conception of man. Man is not a soul, but the psychophysical composite, the living organism. This doctrine St. Thomas defended strenuously against the surviving platonists or augustinists of his own day. The platonic-augustinian idea was that man was essentially a soul, dwelling temporarily in the body. This was also the heart of Descartes' theory, and is often confused with Christian doctrine (it is called the "official dogma" by Gilbert Ryle, 1950). St. Thomas would have none of this, contending, rightly, that this theory has destroyed the essential unity of man. St. Thomas had to oppose the doctrine of "plurality of forms," asserting that the soul was the substantial form of the body and that, like all substantial forms, it was the source of *esse*, *agere*, and *species*; that is, it was the source of the very being, as well as of all the functions, of the body, and made man the kind of creature he is.

St. Thomas teaches that the soul is the first principle whereby we are capable of all the various functions of generation, vegetative life, sensory life, and intellectual life. It is precisely these functions that constitute the "psyche" in the contemporary usage of the term. Thus the soul is the source of many unconscious functions. At the lowest level, the vegetative and some of the generative functions go on unconsciously, mental life continues during sleep, and some of our highest functions of intellect (e.g., the process of abstraction from phantasms or the *conversio ad phantasmata*) can occur unconsciously. In addition, St. Thomas would not have found Freud's doctrine on libido unacceptable. He would undoubtedly have added a great deal, especially the relation of *concupiscentia* to reason. But he taught explicitly that *objectum potentiae concupiscibilis est bonum vel malum sensibile simpliciter acceptum* (the object of the concupiscible power is simply sensible good or evil). This is much wider than sexual gratification in the narrower sense, and it coincides very largely with Freud's usage of the term libido.

Moreover, it is quite compatible with Freud's interpretation of infantile experience and behavior.

St. Thomas taught also that emotion in the strict sense did not apply to the soul, but only to the psychophysical composite (1a 2 ae QXXII art 1). He anticipated something of Freud's doctrine of ambivalence and the love-hate relationship: *"omne odium ex amore causatur"* (all hatred arises from love), and again *"aliquando videtur odium fortius amore"* (sometimes it seems that hatred is stronger than love). He distinguished sharply between the desires of libido that belong to the very nature of man and those that are acquired, corresponding, in part at least, to Freud's conception of innate sexuality and subsequent distortions of the psychosexual development. St. Thomas was aware of the nature of anxiety, speaking of fears that are grounded in our nature: *"timor de malo corruptivo, quod natura refugit propter naturale desiderium essendi: et talis timor dicitur naturalis"* (fear of corruptive evil which nature avoids because of the natural desire of existing: natural fear), and of the consequences of fear for the organism: *"transmutatio corporis . . . Ex ipsa imaginatione quae causat timorem sequitur quaedam contractio in appetitu"* (bodily change . . . a certain narrowing of desire flows from the very imagination which causes fear).

The Roman Catholic Church and Psychoanalysis

The Roman Catholic Church has not spoken officially for or against either the theory or practice of psychoanalysis, wisely regarding both as natural phenomena to be treated with caution and subject to the same criteria as any other body of scientific research and practice. However, in 1961 the Holy Office issued a document in which the practice and use of psychoanalysis by priests and members of religious orders was made subject to the norms of Canon Law governing certain occupations. Special permission must be obtained by a priest wishing to practice medicine or act as a member of a state legislature, and now such permission is required if he wishes to practice psychoanalysis. Similarly, priests or members of religious orders require the permission of their religious superiors to obtain psychoanalytic treatment. Such permissions are readily granted. Thus the 1961 decree is by no means a condemnation of psychoanalysis, and in fact is solely a matter of church organization for the clergy.

BIBLIOGRAPHY

Freud, S. (1927), The future of an illusion. *Standard Edition,* 21:5–56. London: Hogarth Press, 1961.

Gedo, J. E. and Pollack, G. H., Eds. (1975), *Freud: The Fusion of Science and Humanism.* New York: International Universities Press, 1975.

Jones, E. (1953), *The Life and Work of Sigmund Freud,* Vol. I. New York: Basic Books.

Ryle, G. (1950), *Concept of Mind.* New York: Barnes & Noble.

Zilboorg, G. (1950), *Psychoanalysis and Religion.* New York: Barnes & Noble.

BROTHER LOUIS BEIRNAERT, S.J., *in the chapter* Introduction to the Reading of Freud's Texts on Religion, *links the psychoanalytic ideas on religion with Freud's own unconscious, and especially with his relationship with Jung, as representative of the father (Freud) and son (Jung) relationship. Although Freud put Jung at the head of the psychoanalytic association, he "resented Jung as someone who desired his death and wished to efface his name, the name of the father." Freud's book,* Totem and Taboo, *reflects these unconscious connections. At a later stage Freud ascribed universality to the son-versus-father conflict.*

3

Introduction to the Reading of Freud's Texts on Religion

by

LOUIS BEIRNAERT, S. J.

WHEN ONE DEALS WITH FREUD'S REMARKS ON RELIGIOUS phenomena, one can understand them as tangential psychoanalytic concepts, and thus criticize them as not being a necessary part of Freud's discovery. The theologian may show that by viewing religion as an "obsessional neurosis," Freud has misinterpreted the main idea of religion, which is promotion of universal love. The exegete will notice, among other things, that in the texts, the Son, very far from taking the place of the Father, is "sitting at his right." He will also find a number of assumptions without proofs, and there are many such assumptions. Moreover, Freud himself was the first to notice them, but this did not prevent him from following his ideas.

Why? What was Freud looking for? One must be aware of the fact that Freud's work is self-contained and does not omit relevant issues, and that the understanding of religion is an integral part of Freud's work. The subject matter is always psychoanalysis; when it is applied to knowledge and notably to religious knowledge, it is the study of connections between knowledge and the unconscious. From this point of view, a critique of Freud's texts confined to the conscious discourse on religion would miss its target, for it would not touch on Freud's real interest. To be frank, the only possible critique of the Freudian enterprise must be a radical one. It must necessarily bear on the unconscious and proclaim its negation. If the unconscious is only a phantasm of Freud, all his research was in vain. One would think it possible to escape from this dilemma by making of the unconscious a pathological formation that would exist in certain cases only, and would contaminate this faith and their religious conduct, whence the idea of a purification of faith by psychoanalysis. But such a conception of the unconscious is not Freud's, for whom the unconscious processes are universal and form an integral part of knowledge. One may not realize how important they are, but they operate everywhere and always. If one admits with Freud, the existence of the unconscious processes, an inevitable question is posed: how do these processes operate in religious phenomena? No other response can be given from a single theological, exegetical, ethnological, point of·view within the framework which these different discourses elaborate without taking account of the dimension of unconscious from which they cannot possibly escape.

If psychoanalysis of religion is an integral part of psychoanalysis proper, it follows that one cannot delve into this problem without discussing the well-known atheism and irreligiosity of Freud. One must not, however, deny to the new science the right to apply its method to the study of religious phenomena. A psychoanalytic study of religion is no less valid than historical and exegetical studies. The believer and the unbeliever share here the same methodological atheism that belongs to all science. If there is something particular to the psychoanalysis of religion, it is that its research is not based on the principles of other sciences nor on faith, in the sense that what it discovers does not depend for its truth on the exactitude of such and such confirmation outside its own field. Freud does not rely on Darwin, Roberts, Smith, or the like, except where their discoveries agree with his own research. Thus the ethnological hypothesis of primitive totemism could be abandoned, but the primitive prohibition of incest and patricide remain because they are based on studies outside of ethnology proper.

We are thus invited to read the Freudian texts concerning the psychoanalysis of religion as works of psychoanalysis, and not as theological works or antitheological, exegetical, or ethnological studies. From this point of view, what do these studies say and how should one understand them?

One might assume that it is only in taking them in their context, that one can grasp the truth that they convey. But, in regard to psychoanalytic works, the only possible reading could not be any other than analytical. By that I mean that we can no longer read Freud today, in exegete, in the classical sense of the term, as we cannot read the scripture from the single perspective of exegesis. What goes for the religious discourse goes also for Freud's discourse on religion. And just as the psychoanalytic reading of religious texts is centered on the study of the rapport these texts maintain with the unconscious, the psychoanalytic reading of the Freudian text is also centered on the rapport that connects Freud's knowledge with his unconscious. One must not be mistaken about the meaning of such a reading; one could believe, in fact, that this is a matter of an easy and reassuring enterprise of taking account of Freud's remarks concerning his own neurosis. But in addition to our having learned from him to pay attention to neurotic disclosures, we must not forget that the inventor of psychoanalysis is not just a neurotic. Freud's discovery of the laws of the unconscious is not related to his own neurosis; he merely analyzes neurosis. Thus Freud's remarks concerning religious phenomena form an integral part of his work in the course of which, by successive stages, the discoverer has advanced further toward his objectives. His discoveries should fit together under the same title as the "Interpretation of Dreams."

How and by what processes was the psychoanalytic interpretation of religion introduced into the Freudian elaboration? Therein lies a major question, for in dealing with religious formations, Freud moved away from individual psychology and entered the field of collective psychology. Freud was fully aware of the leap he was making, and that the analogy which he discovered between the processes neurotic symptoms engender and those

religious phenomena engender corresponds to a "postulate."
Nevertheless, Freud shifted from individual to group psychology,
and he never doubted the legitimacy of this shift. One can
watch Freud bypass all his difficulties concerning the mode of
subsistence of the repressed material in group life and hold im-
perturbably to what he estimates to be "an inevitable audacity."
The necessity imposed on Freud to grapple with religion is the effect of what he himself calls "his unconscious connections."

Freud and Jung

Let us consider the single period from 1910, the year when
the International Psychoanalytic Association was founded, to
1913, the year of the publication of *Totem and Taboo*. This
period was full of events that have left considerable impact on
Freud and on the destiny of psychoanalysis. The freudian
discovery and its workings attained at that time an international
stature through the creation of a large association of
psychoanalysts which united the already existing regional
societies. The president of this international association would
rank as the successor of Freud, then aged 65. With Freud's
benediction, Carl Gustav Jung occupied this position.

It is beyond doubt that from their first meeting on September
27, 1907, Freud found himself in a rather peculiar relationship
with Jung. On one hand, Freud was impressed by Jung and expected that Jung and the Zurich group would contribute in
making psychoanalysis something other than "a national Jewish
affair." But, on the other hand, Freud did not cease reminding
this "pastor's son" of the importance of sexuality, the import of
which the latter minimized in neurotics. Here one can notice
Freud's ambivalent feelings that show through all of Freud's
correspondence with Jung. Jung's character occupies after 1907
the place vacated by Freud's breaking off with Fliess. Nothing is
more significant in this matter than the rapprochement effected
by Freud himself, between his fainting fit in 1912 at the Munich's
Park Hotel in front of Jung, whom he reproached for having tar-
nished his (Freud's) name when he published on psychoanalysis in
the Swiss journals, and a similar fainting fit a few years earlier in

Fliess' presence, exactly at the moment when they broke off completely. Freud has developed transference in regard to Jung in which his own neurosis was expressed. At the same time Freud was making Jung into his "prince" and putting himself in the place of Moses, comparing him to Joshua "destined to explore the Promised Land," he resented Jung as someone who desired his death and wished to efface his name, the name of the father. Several incidents bear witness at that time to Jung's opposition to Freud, and in particular to his refusal to acknowledge that he had a death wish toward the father, and to Freud's sensitivity when he tried to show Jung that this death wish was directed toward Freud.

This issue was played out in the crucial years. It resembles a dramatic succession from father to son, and in regard to the psychoanalytic society, it was related to the fact that psychoanalysis, until then a Jewish affair, had won recognition by the "Gentiles." But in this very drama, something else is implied that touches on Freud's unconscious and his own neurosis, namely his desire to immortalize his name, to be recognized forever as the father of psychoanalysis, and without the son's death wish having come through. Jung observed well, to be sure, that Freud's neurosis had some bearing on the relations they maintained with regard to one another. But things did not change. Freud's genius lies in having had the courage to understand "that the analyst always ought to be more occupied with his own neurosis than with that of others." That is precisely what he did in writing *Totem and Taboo*. This work, of which he said that it followed on the same track as Jung's *Metamorphoses and Symbols of the Libido*, is in reality a psychoanalytic enterprise that places the evidence of the forgotten drama of fatherhood in social setting. *Totem and Taboo* was written by Freud in the same manner as all his great works; after a period of several months, when he complained of being capable of nothing, he became involved at the beginning of August 1911 in a work related to the psychology of faith and religion. According to Jones, this was a "torturous route" in comparison with the ease in which Freud wrote his medical works. *Totem and Taboo* reflects the above-mentioned unconscious connections. Beginning from this moment, everything turned "completely Totem and Taboo." This will be, Freud wrote, "my best work." After completion of the work Freud experienced one of these periods of uncertainty so customary to him, but Freud never doubted his discovery.

The theme of the work is sufficiently known so that I am dispensed from recalling it at length here. This "interpretation by psychoanalysis of the social life of primitive peoples" resulted in discovery of the origin of culture, and notably of religion and of the murder of the primitive father as signified in the oedipal myth. People have forgotten that the father is dead and that they have killed him. Here is the unconscious drama that traverses all human history. All sorts of deformations and denials prevented its return to consciousness and it has reissued repressed and transferred, by some compromise, into neuroses. When Freud said that it was a question there of an "interpretation by psychoanalysis," it is necessary to understand that nothing else but psychoanalysis, as a method of discovery of the unconscious, could offer an access to these processes. But psychoanalysis does not consist in a pure and simple application of the discoveries made in the individual psychoanlyses to the phenomena of collective life. It is a new moment in psychoanalysis that Freud has been elaborating, and the emergence of this new approach concerned not only individuals, but the entire human society. Freud would not have found this new path if he had not himself been a participant in the drama whose theme and laws he unravelled.

In a certain sense *Totem and Taboo* raises the question of the origin of psychoanalysis and of its social destiny. One can read this in the perspective of fatherhood that Jung, the son and successor has denied to him, thus making him die. At the same time *Totem and Taboo* analyzes the question of fatherhood as such as the inception of social life. The drama of the origins of the analytic society is interlocked with the drama of birth of the human society.

This somewhat clinical reading of Freud's discourse in *Totem and Taboo* may seem necessary for the discovering of the processes that have produced and organized the human society. One cannot escape it. Nevertheless, the book does not solve all the problems. If it permits restoring the genesis of the apparition of the primordial myth bearing on the murder of the father, it says nothing, as such, about the structural necessity of such an elaboration as a function of the very development of the totality of Freud's work. In other terms, the clinical reading can well render an account of the moment of discovery as a function of the events of Freud's life, but it does not go far enough to locate the discovery in the overall context and its logical import.

We have somewhat hastily affirmed that in the drama of the human society was read into the drama that inaugurated the Psychoanalytic Society. The passage of one to the other can be questioned. We would have no objections if someone would make us notice that when Freud speaks of murder of the primitive father, it is perhaps because he could not communicate directly to his followership that they wished him to die. The displacement to the origin of all social life represents rather an insupportable truth. The central thesis of *Totem and Taboo* would thus be only a substitutive formation that would occupy the place of another murder accomplished by the effacement of Freud's name. In terms of the history of humanity, Freud would only have spoken of the history of the psychoanalytic movement. Such an interpretation of Freud's discourse is, of course, clinical. Consequently, would it not be necessary to conclude that in speaking of religion and of its origins, Freud tells the truth related to something else? Such a conclusion would tend to deny all import to the critical analysis of the religious phenomenon as such.

It is thus necessary to pose a new question: what logical need, culminating in 1911–1912, was served by *Totem and Taboo*?

It was in 1907, in an article entitled "Obsessive acts and religious exercises" that Freud described for the first time the obsessive events and the rites of the believer. At this moment it was only a question of registering some analogies and some differences that permitted qualifying the obsessional neurosis as a private distorted religion, and the religion as an universal obsessional neurosis. From this time on, Freud was involved in a search for the common roots of obsessive formations and religious formations. He noticed a fundamental analogy in the renunciation of expression of primitive drives. It was merely an analogy, for at that time Freud believed in a dualism between sexual drives and the ego drives. The first ones motivate the obsessional neurosis, the second ones motivate religion, whence a difference that he strongly underlines in this article.

This difference has disappeared with the new elaboration of the theory of drives which were to be expressed in 1914 in *The Introduction of Narcissism*. At this time we see Freud renounce the distinction between the sexual and the ego drives and recognize the existence of a sexual libido directed toward oneself. But let us project ourselves two years later and we find Freud's touching up of his theory quite revealing. The study of "A case of obsessional neurosis," reported in 1909, convinced him of the presence of a repressed desire of murder of the father. The ego drives of destruction were no less present here than the sexual drives.

Recapitualism

Everything indicates that the two different elements postulated by Freud were disappearing and the hypothesis of a common source was given more credit. This hypothesis was suggested for the first time in "A souvenir of childhood from Leonardo da Vinci" in 1910. On the subject of Leonardo's phantasm, with its combination of maternal and of masculine elements, Freud remarked that the Egyptian goddess Mout presented both traits. This concordance, he wrote, is due "to a common factor yet unknown." The infantile sexual theory of the penis of the mother seems to him to be able to be this common source. From then on, with the support borrowed from biology, Freud was ready to admit that the psychological evolution of every individual is a repetition of the evolution of humanity.

The important thing here is the appearance of the concept of recapitulation. At this stage of his research Freud felt compelled to conceive that what happened to the individual is but a new edition of what happened to the human race. Something like a paradigm proper to the entire humanity dominates the course of the individual events and regulates their succession. An identical structure reproduces and repeats itself in the course of history. At this point I am unable to explain the necessity of the emergence of this idea in Freud's thought. There is, certainly, the perception of the resemblances for one thing. Perhaps there is also the logically indisputable idea that events experienced individually do not suffice to explain what happens and that it is necessary to discover other factors besides experience. To be sure, at the time of discovery of the odeipus complex, in a letter to Fleiss, Freud alluded to the universal effect of Sophocles' drama. At that time Freud stated that every man passes through the oedipal crisis. But now Freud went further: the Greek tragedy, as well as the oedipal crises of individuals have only reproduced and repeated a mythical prototype which Freud placed in the prehistory of the human race. This was the central theme of the last chapter of *Totem and Taboo*. The oedipal myth, with the murder of the father, was viewed by Freud as the origin of cultural formations, notably of religion. It is worth noticing that it was the dead father who founded society, that is to say the father had ceased to be involved in rivalries and illusions in order to become in his very absence a symbolic and regulatory presence.

In summary, one cannot get a full grasp of the role and function of Freud's discourse on religion without placing the latter within the process of development of the psychoanalytic theory. The simple reading of Freud's works enables one to notice that far from constituting a sort of contingent application of psychoanalysis, Freud's remarks concerning religious phenomena are related to the events of his own life and to the internal logic of his evolving thoughts. Even if we could not adduce rigorous evidence to our point of view, we believe that one cannot dispense with our hypothesis or refuse to take the greatest account of it.

From the point of view of religion and of faith the entire question is one of knowing not whether one can accept the support or, as Freud says, the "contribution" of analysis to reflection on the origins of religion, but rather to what extent Freud's remarks offer an indisputable specificity; in other words, is it because Freud makes us recognize in religion the mechanisms of the obsessional neurosis and the unconscious knowledge of the murder of the father? Does not all this convey and carry the ultimate sense of man, which is to know the Lord? A reply to this question trangresses the boundaries of this chapter.

BIBLIOGRAPHY

Freud, S. (1900), The interpretation of dreams, *Standard Edition,* 4 and 5. London: Hogarth Press, 1953.

——— (10;7), Obsessive acts and religious practices, *Standard Edition, 9:* 115–128. London: Hogarth Press, 1959.

——— (1910),   Leonardo da Vinci and a memory of his childhood. *Standard Edition, 11:* 63–137. London: Hogarth Press, 1956.

——— (1913), Totem and taboo. *Standard Edition, 13:*1–161. London: Hogarth Press, 1955.

——— (1914), On narcissism: An introduction. *Standard Edition, 14:*73–102. London: Hogarth Press, 1957.

Schur, M. Freud: *Living and Dying.* New York: International Universities Press, 1972.

PROFESSOR EWERT COUSINS *draws parallels between Freudian and Jungian techniques and Catholic concepts of the soul. His essay on* The Many-Leveled Psyche: Correlation Between Psychotherapy and the Spiritual Life, *starts with Jung's dream of a multileveled house resembling* The Interior Castle *written by Teresa of Avila.*

Professor Cousins uses the method of correlation between human experience in psychotherapy and in spiritual life. He does not reduce spiritual life to "psychologism," but finds meaningful analogies between psychoanalysis and religion. He writes, "When we speak of Christ as an archetype or symbol of man's deeper self, we do not mean that he is 'nothing but' a psychic symbol and has no objective reality either in history of in the eternal life of divinity."

Dr. Cousins summarizes Augustine's, Bonaventure's, and Thomas' concepts of soul. Psychotherapy may help a Catholic discover the depths of his mental life. The first stage in therapy is '"purgation," followed by oral assimilation, identification with the parent and, finally, the Jungian discovery of the inner self.

4

The Many-leveled Psyche:
Correlation Between Psychotherapy
and the Spiritual Life

by

EWERT COUSINS, PH.D.

Jung's Dream

When Jung and Freud were traveling together to the United States in 1909, Jung had a dream which he recounts in *Memories, Dreams, Reflections* (1962). He describes the dream as follows:

This was the dream. I was in a house I did not know, which had two stories. It was 'my house.' I found myself in the upper story, where there was a kind of salon furnished with fine old pieces in rococo style. On the walls hung a number of precious old paintings. I wondered that this should be my house, and thought, 'Not bad.' But then it occurred to me that I did not know what the lower floor looked like. Descending the stairs, I reached the ground floor. There everything was much older, and I realized that this part of the house must date from about the fifteenth or sixteenth century. The furnishings were medieval; the floors were of red brick. Everywhere it was rather dark. I went from one room to another, thinking, 'Now I really must explore the whole house.' I came upon a heavy door, and opened it. Beyond it, I discovered a stone stairway that led down into the cellar. Descending again, I found myself in a beautifully vaulted room which looked exceedingly ancient. Examining the walls, I discovered layers of brick among the ordinary stone bricks, and chips of brick in the mortar. As soon as I saw this I knew that the walls dated from Roman times. My interest by now was intense. I looked more closely at the floor. It was of stone slabs, and in one of these I discovered a ring. When I pulled it, the stone slab lifted, and again I saw a stairway of narrow stone steps leading down into the depths. These, too, I descended, and entered a low cave cut into the rock. Thick dust lay on the floor, and in the dust were scattered bones and broken pottery, like remains of a primitive culture. I discovered two human skulls, obviously very old and half disintegrated. Then I awoke [pp. 158–159].

Freud and Jung gave different interpretations of this dream; in fact, it marked a stage in the growing break between them. Freud focused on the skulls and suggested that they concealed a secret death wish, whereas Jung was led by the dream for the first time to his concept of the collective unconscious. Although they approached the dream from different points of view and their interpretations implied diverse frames of reference, they agreed on the basic structure of the psyche. Jung (1962) writes, "It was plain to me that the house represented a kind of image of the psyche—that is to say, of my then state of consciousness, with hitherto unconscious additions" (p. 160). The house with its many levels—with hidden depths that can be explored—is an apt image for the way that both Freud[1] and Jung look on the psyche, and with them the mainstream of twentieth century psychotherapy. Like the house, the psyche has not only an outside but an inside, an inside that has many levels that at first are hidden from view. By opening doors, by descending stairways, by penetrating the darkness of the lower levels, we can explore this inner world and discover its secrets.

It is interesting to note that mystics and spiritual writers also conceive of the psyche or soul as a many-leveled or many-roomed dwelling. In the sixteenth century work, the *Interior Castle* (Peers, 1949), Teresa of Avila compares the soul to a castle with many

[1]In Jung's recounting of the incident, Freud did not interpret the house explicitly. Yet Freud's (1900) general approach to dream interpretation and to the dynamics of the psyche implies that the psyche is like the many-leveled house.

rooms and uses this image as the framework for her entire analysis of the spiritual life. She writes: "I began to think of the soul as if it were a castle made of a single diamond or of very clear crystal, in which there are many rooms, just as in Heaven there are many mansions" (I, c.l; p. 201). She conceives of the rooms, or as she says mansions,[2] arranged on various levels and in various relationships to the center, where the King dwells:

> Let us now imagine that this castle, as I have said, contains many mansions, some above, others below, others at each side; and in the center and midst of them all is the chiefest mansion where the most secret things pass between God and the soul]I, c.l; p. 202].

Just as Jung moves from level to level in his house of the psyche, Teresa moves from mansion to mansion in the *Interior Castle.* Like Jung, she moves to areas that tend to remain hidden. She writes:

> Many souls remain in the outer court of the castle, which is the place occupied by the guards; they are not interested in entering it, and have no idea what there is in this wonderful place, or who dwells in it, or even how many rooms it has. You will have read certain books on prayer which advise the soul to enter within itself: and that is exactly what this means [I, c.l; p. 203].

Having entered into herself, she moves to ever greater depths: from the periphery to the center— from the outer region of the first mansions to the inner chamber of the seventh mansion, where the soul consummates its mystical marriage with Christ, the heavenly spouse.

Although the images of Jung's house and Teresa's castle are similar in many respects, there are major differences. Teresa moves in what is equivalent to an ascent to spiritual heights, although it is described in terms of entering into a center. Jung moves in a descent: from consciousness to primitive depths of the past. In the end of the quest Teresa discovers union with God, in mystical marriage with the King. In the subterranean cavern Jung discovers relics of man's primitive past: broken pottery and two disintegrating human skulls. Jung's own interpretation of the dream (1962) underscores this movement towards the primitive:

[2]The Spanish is *moradas* from *morar*, meaning to dwell and does not exactly coincide with the English *mansions*.

The ground floor stood for the first level of the unconscious. The deeper I went, the more alien and the darker the scene became. In the cave, I discovered remains of a primitive culture, that is, the world of the primitive man within myself—a world that can be scarcely reached or illumined by consciousness. The primitive psyche of man borders on the life of the animal soul, just as the caves of prehistoric times were usually inhabited by animals before man laid claim to them [p. 160].

Jung's interpretation reveals the appropriateness of our using his dream image to depict a main direction of psychotherapy in the twentieth century. In exploring the inner world, psychotherapy has tended to make the descent into the primitive, the instinctual, the animal. Of course, it would be simplistic to emphasize this direction to the exclusion of others, such as the exploration of ego psychology in the Freudian tradition (A. Freud, 1936; Hartmann, 1939) and Jung's process of individuation (Jacobi, 1940). Yet a major direction in psychotherapy's journey into the psyche has been the way down into the instinctual basis of psychic conflicts and the primitive levels of psychic life. Psychotherapy penetrates into the patient's past and into his depths, and in so doing, like Jung in his dream, penetrates into the dark caves of experience where the primitive in man fades imperceptibly into the common biological substrata shared by man and the animal. At least in one of its major thrusts, psychotherapy plunges down into the darkness of matter; in contrast the mystics and spiritual writers search after the divine light that blazes at the summit of the spiritual mountain.

Are these two approaches radically different? Are they completely unrelated? Are Jung's dream and Teresa's interior castle so different in structure that they have no common design? We believe that there is a common design, a basic pattern they both share. This is the pattern of the many-leveled dwelling. If we take this concept, which is common to both, and extend it to include the contents and structure of each, we can begin to discover certain correlations between them. Teresa herself gives a hint of this possibility when she writes (Peers, 1949):

In speaking of the soul we must always think of it as spacious, ample and lofty; and this can be done without the least exaggeration, for the soul's capacity is much greater than we can realize, and this Sun, Which is in the palace, reaches every part of it[I,c. 2; p. 208].

Let us conceive that the soul has a range wide enough to encompass Jung's house with its dark foundations and Teresa's castle with its brilliant palace. Let us also conceive that within the center of the soul God dwells or can dwell as the light of the sun, illumining all the rooms and levels, even filtering dimly into the caverns in the darkness below. Like the mansions of Teresa's castle, these rooms are not "arranged in a row, one behind another" (I, c. 2; p. 207), but "some above, others below, others at each side" (I, c.1; p. 202). Furthermore the rooms and levels all share, in varying degrees, in some overall patterns and designs that give shape to both the primitive depths and the spiritual heights. Hence when one enters this house of the psyche through the doorway of psychotherapy and explores the rooms containing his personal past and perhaps the collective depths of his psyche, he goes on a journey whose stages and whose movement are remarkably similar to those of the journey through those other rooms charted by the mystics and spiritual writers. In fact, if the person is a believer leading a spiritual life, he may discover that his journey through the spiritual levels has been blocked because he has been locked within the rooms on a lower level. Or in the course of his therapy, he may have a deep religious experience, which breaks the locks on the doors of his childhood conflicts and through a far-reaching spiritual transformation resolves a problem that psychotherapy has been searching to cure.

The Correlation Method

With this multidimensional concept of the psyche as our framework, we will attempt to point out correlations between psychotherapy and the spiritual life. We do this by describing in a type of phenomenological way certain correlations a Catholic might make between his experience in psychotherapy and his religious belief. Before we embark on this, it would be wise to state certain cautions at the outset.

First, this type of correlation is grounded in experience and must not be looked on as purely abstract or conceptual. It is not an intellectual game or a cool observation of a detached spectator. It grows out of the intense and grueling experience of psychotherapy and the deep experience of a lived religious faith. It is born in suffering and crisis and comes to light after much groping through darkness. It emerges as the reflective awareness of powerful affectivity rather than as a purely intellectual grasp of logical relations between concepts and symbols.

Second, by looking for correlations between experience in psychotherapy and experience in the spiritual life, we do not wish to imply a philosophical position of psychologism, in which all spiritual realities are reduced to psychic functions. If the soul is, as we shall see, both the mirror of the external world and the image of God, it is not surprising that we can see reflected within it, on the one hand, the objectivity of material things and persons and, on the other, the objectivity of spiritual values and of God himself. Hence when we speak of Christ as an archetype or symbol of man's deeper self, we do not mean that he is "nothing but" a psychic symbol and has no objective reality either in history or in the eternal life of the divinity. On the contrary, we presuppose these two poles of objectivity and feel that it is only in searching the mirror of the soul that one can discover their full power and meaning.

If we do not wish to be accused of psychologism, all the more so we do not wish to be accused of biologism, the reduction of psychic states to biological functions. In seeing correlations between the higher spiritual levels and those of the primitive psychic depths, where the animal and the human converge, we do not imply that the highest spiritual aspirations of man are "nothing but" sublimated instinctual drives or displaced libidinal energy. There has been a tendency in psychoanalysis, especially in its earlier development, to devalue the religious level and reduce it to "nothing but" displaced sexual energy. The Catholic need not follow this path. He does not have to reduce the spiritual to the biological, but that does not mean that he has to consider them unrelated. On the contrary, he can see psycho-sexual conflicts reflecting, in their own way and on their own level, a larger law or dynamism of total psychic life that has its expression both on the biological level and on that of spiritual development.

Furthermore, this correlation method is not intended as a form of syncretism, concordism, or disguised apologia. We do not wish to mix together in one large melting pot the beliefs of a Catholic and philosophical materialism, determinism, and atheism, which at times have been associated with psychoanalysis. We do not believe that either the experience or the method of psychoanalysis is inextricably tied to such philosophical positions. How these positions, which were widespread in the scientific atmosphere of the nineteenth century, became entangled with psychoanalysis is both a complex and an interesting question we cannot pursue here (Dalbiez, 1936; Stern, 1954). For our present purposes we can simply indicate that a Catholic would not be impelled by the experience or the logic of psychotherapy to adopt a materialistic or atheistic philosophy. In fact, many have experienced just the opposite; they have been led by psychoanalysis to a more personalistic and spiritual philosophical attitude. Hence, although a materialist in psychotherapy might make reductionist correlations, reducing religious experience to purely material causes, a Catholic in therapy, since he holds different philosophical premises, could legitimately and appropriately make a different kind of correlation.

Because we imply a different philosophical framework, our use of correlation is not a simple concordism in which external similarities are pointed out without a deeper foundation. Concordism is as unsuccessful in psychology as it has proved to be in Biblical criticism. Simply to point out similarities between oral intake and the symbolism of eating in the Eucharist, even after one has avoided the charge of reductionism, would be mere concordism. It is necessary to bring to light the underlying philosophical concepts of the psyche that make the believer's correlation different from reductionism and that make the correlation coherent with the believer's religious traditions.

Finally, the correlation is not intended as an apologia for the validity of the Christian or Catholic belief, although it might provide some basis for such an apologia. The purpose is rather to illumine and clarify beliefs by indicating the resonance between the beliefs and the structure of the psyche and the dynamics of psychic life. That there is such a resonance might lead the believer to conclude that the soul is naturally Christian—*anima naturaliter Christiana*[3]—that the soul is so constituted that it has an affinity to Christianity and that Christianity is the fulfillment of its natural tendencies. Although the correlation contains the seeds of such an apologia, we will not follow this through. This is not our purpose and to pursue it would call for extensive study in the phenomenology, history, and philosophy of religion, as well as a critical evaluation of the role of apologetics in one's own theology and in an ecumenical perspective.

In a generic form this method of correlation is as old as Christianity itself. It is found in the New Testament in the correlation between classic Jewish beliefs and the emerging Christian message.[4] In the second century the apologists, such as Justin Martyr, drew on data from philosophy, science, and everyday experience for a deeper understanding of the Christian vision. The Greek fathers drew from the mystery religions of the hellenistic world and the philosophy of Plato, Plotinus, Aristotle, and the Stoics to enrich their understanding of the Christian mysteries (Jaeger, 1961; Wolfson, 1964). In the Middle Ages the method was developed by Anselm as faith seeking understanding (*fides quaerens intellectum*) and as the search for necessary reasons (*rationes necessariae*) and appropriate reasons (*rationes convenientiae*) for the dogmas of faith (Deane, 1962). In the thirteenth century Thomas Aquinas explored the correlation between Aristotelian naturalism and the Christian message (Chenu, 1954). In the present case, faith seeks a deeper understanding of itself by looking with the eyes of psychotherapy into the human psyche and the dynamics of psychological growth, and at the same time remaining within its own Christian experience and world view. In this way the Christian patient can gain a deeper understanding of his faith, and by seeing the correlation on the level of faith, he can at the same time reach a more profound awareness of his

[3]The phrase is from Tertullian, *Apology*, 17.6 (Daly, 1950): "O testimony of the soul, which is by natural instinct Christian" (p. 53).
[4]Although the New Testament presents the Christian message as something new, there is a constant theme that the Christian message is a fulfillment of the Jewish tradition.

psychological experience.

To employ the correlation effectively—without falling into reductionism or concordism—it is necessary to state clearly the philosophical presuppositions that stand behind the method. We will do this by drawing three basic concepts from the thought of Augustine, Bonaventure, and Thomas Aquinas, respectively. It is fitting that our presuppositions be clarified by the thought of these theologians, because they have played a major role in shaping Christian theology and because they are thinkers with whom the Catholic intellectual tradition has identified and from whom it continues to draw a large portion of its philosophical and theological concepts.

Augustine

From Augustine we draw the concept that the soul is the image of God. This seminal concept in the Christian message was developed by the Greek fathers in the East and by Augustine in the West and became the basis for Christian anthropology and spirituality for centuries (Ladner, 1959). In his treatise *On the Trinity,* Book VIII-XV, Augustine explored in detail the nature of the soul as the image of God. In a type of descent, which parallels in its major outlines Teresa's *Interior Castle,* Augustine moves from the outer to the inner and examines various levels of the psyche where the soul can be seen as the image of God. The soul is the image of God when it turns its gaze upon itself, when it reflects on itself as object, when it remembers, knows, and loves itself. Augustine writes (Sullivan, 1963): "Behold then the mind remembering itself, understanding itself, loving itself: if we perceive this, we perceive a trinity; not yet God, indeed, but already an image of God" (XIV, 8, 11; p. 124). Although on this level the soul is an image of God, Augustine (McKenna, 1963) moves deeper to the very ground of the soul, where the soul remembers, knows, and loves God. "Let it, then, remember its God, to whose image it has been made, and understand Him and Love Him" (XIV, 12, 15; p. 432). It is here, in what Augustine calls the memory, that we find the true image of God. By memory

Augustine means the ground of the soul, the point where the soul is open to the infinite, where the divine light shines as in a mirror.[5] It is this reflection of God in the mirror of the soul that constitutes the religious nature of man and provides both the alpha and the omega of the spiritual quest. The divine light filters through all levels of the psyche and is the ultimate source of all psychic power and the goal of all psychic activity.

Augustine's concept of the soul as image of God is given symbolic form in Teresa's castle, the seventh mansion corresponding to Augustine's memory.[6] Yet Jung's dream[7] and much of twentieth century psychotherapy acknowledge no equivalent of Augustine's memory or of Teresa's seventh mansion. The psyche is seen as imaging primitive forces rather than the divine light. However, one who holds as a philosophical or theological presupposition that the soul is the image of God can glimpse, as we shall see, the divine light shining even in the primitive levels of the psyche.

Bonaventure

Not only is the soul a mirror reflecting the divine light, it is also a mirror turned toward and reflecting the external world. Taking over Augustine's concept of the soul as image of God, Bonaventure (Boehner, 1956) explored more than his master the mirror of the soul as reflecting objects in the sense world. The outer world enters the soul through the five senses: "The world, which is called the macrocosm, enters our soul, the microcosm, through the portals of the five senses" (c.2, m.2; p. 51). The macrocosm of the universe and the microcosm of the soul are

[5]Memory, for Augustine, includes many levels, but at its deepest and most significant level there is the reflection of God. Gilson (1943) describes Augustine's concept as follows: ". . . memory means much more than its modern psychological connotation designates, i.e., memory of the past. In St. Augustine it is applied to everything which is present to the soul (a presence which is evidenced by efficacious action) without being explicitly known or perceived. The only modern psychological terms equivalent to Augustinian *memoria* are 'unconscious' or 'subconscious,' provided they too are expanded, as will be seen later, to include the metaphysical presence within the soul of a reality distinct from it and transcendent, such as God, in addition to the presence to the soul of its own unperceived states" (p. 229).

[6]At the very outset of her work Teresa (Perrs, 1949) relates the castle to the image of God (I, c.1; p. 201).

[7]Although Jung's dream does not, his concept of the archetype of the self as God image approximates Teresa's seventh mansion and Augustine's concept of memory.

both books through which, by reading them rightly, man can see reflected their ultimate meaning, which is God. Just as they reflect God, so also they reflect each other. In the book of nature we can read the meaning of the book of the soul. The book of nature enters the soul through symbolism. It is through symbolism that the outer world correlates with the inner. If we are to read these books, we must learn the language of symbolism, for this is the language in which they are written. Bonaventure's writing is rich in the language of symbolism as he reads the book of the soul through the symbols of the temple, the mountain, the journey, the tree, the fountain (Boehner, 1956). It is this concept of the macrocosm united to the microcosm through symbols that lies at the base of the elaborate sacramentalism and religious symbolism of the Middle Ages. This same concept can serve as a basis for the symbolism of dreams, fantasies, and the ritual of everyday life as these are explored in psychotherapy. A correlation between psychotherapy and the spirituality traditions is not difficult here because they both take symbols seriously and use symbols for expressing and exploring the psyche. It is not difficult to see a common philosophical base that can serve as the understructure both for the rich symbolism of religion and the symbols that well up from the unconscious in dreams. They both have this in common, that the symbol is the point of contact between the macrocosm of the outer world and microcosm of the inner world. What was a mere object in the outer world, such as tree, a room, a road, when it enters as a symbol into the inner world, can provide a language through which we can read the complexity of psychic life. This is true on all levels of the psyche. Jung's skulls and Teresa's palace may be poles apart in their meaning, but as symbols they perform the same function of revealing through concrete symbols the inner life of the psyche.

Thomas

Not only is the soul the image of God and the mirror of the material world, but each of its levels is so constituted that its structure reflects all levels above and all below. This metaphysics of participation plays a central role in the thought of Thomas

Aquinas. He sees the cosmos so structured that each level of being reflects the other: the physical reflects the biological; the biological reflects the psychological; and the psychological reflects the spiritual. Although this concept of participation is common to medieval neo-platonism, in Thomas' case it provided the basis on which he worked out a correlation between the natural philosophy of Aristotle and the tenets of Christian belief. Thomas was able to take the structures of biology and psychology from Aristotle's treatise *On the Soul* and apply them to the higher forms of the life of grace (Gilby, 1963). He was able to do this because the higher life of grace and the lower forms of physical life share in a larger principle of life that emanates from God himself; hence each level participates, in its own way, in this ultimate form of life. Consequently, it is possible to use structures from one level to understand those of another.[8]

In recent decades much study has been directed toward Thomas' metaphysics of participation insofar as all finite beings share in a limited way in God's dynamic act of existence. Also considerable attention has been given to his doctrine of analogy, whereby man acquires from creatures an analogical knowledge of God (Geiger, 1942; de Finance, 1945; Fabro, 1950). However, there has not been sufficient attention paid to Thomas' doctrine of participation and analogy within the created world. A study of this concept would throw light on correlations made in psychology and also on the growing use of the model method in the physical and social sciences (Kazemier and Vuysje, 1961; Black, 1962; Hesse, 1963). If one holds the participation of forms in the created world, he would not logically have to reduce the higher forms to the lower; rather he can see how the lower reflects the higher and to some extent contains the seeds of growth toward the higher form. Thus when one enters into Jung's house and explores the primitive levels of the psyche, he might discover many correlations with the mansions of Teresa's castle.

This brings us to the paradoxical implication—suggestive of

---

[8]This is a classical insight and is shared by many thinkers. For example, it lies at the basis of the world view of Teilhard de Chardin (1955), who sees in the attraction of the atoms the rudimentary form of the attraction of love among human persons.

Heraclitus' dictum (Burnet, 1930)—that the way down into the psyche is also the way up (p. 138). The three philosophical presuppositions given above lead to the fact that the proper logic of the psyche is the logic of the coincidence of opposites.[9] It is not the logic of atomism, in which each particle is separate from all others; nor is it the logic of division into classes according to genus and specific differences. Rather, in the house of the psyche, the logic at work is the logic of the coincidence of opposites because in the psyche opposites come together. If the soul is the image of God, then the soul is the place where the maximum meets the minimum, the infinite meets the finite, the absolute meets the relative. If the soul is the mirror of the external world, then the objective and the subjective meet in the psyche as the macrocosm-microcosm. Through the symbol we can read the subjective meaning of the object and the objective meaning of the subject. Finally, if the lower level participates in the form of the higher level, then when we descend to the depths, we contact in a raw and primitive way a form that emanates from the heights. Thus in proceeding to the depths of Jung's cave, one may be embarking on a path that could lead to the entrance of Teresa's castle.

Collective Extraversion

When a Catholic enters the house of the psyche through the door of psychotherapy, he may discover, to his surprise, that this house has an interior and that its corridors lead to sources of conflict and vitality he had not dreamed existed. Although driven by personal problems, he might be only slightly aware of the turmoil within, and like so many in our culture, he might see only his surface symptoms: difficulties in his work or in his personal relations. He may suffer the objectification and fragmentation of experience that is the malady of industrial culture. Swept up in a current of science and technology, Western man has become an

[9]The logic of the coincidence of opposites was explored at length by Nicholas of Cusa (Heron, 1954). The coincidence of opposites has played an important role in psychotherapy (Jung, 1955).

extravert facing nature. His consciousness is turned to observe the sense world and to develop theories to explain its structure. His practical sense is directed to projects. He thinks of what he can do and make, how he can use the objects of the world, how he can discover new possibilities, how he can make new and better instruments. In his everyday life he follows a schedule; he travels to work, keeps appointments, sells products. At home he plans his budget, pays bills, figures out his income tax, and looks forward to his vacation. Caught in the collective and personal extraversion of our time, he looks on himself as an object or a product. He sees his psyche as a thin facade with no inner depth. He is unaware of the dark power and the well springs of life within. Like those souls in the first mansions of Teresa's castle (Peers, 1949) he "may have no idea what there is in this wonderful place . . . or even how many rooms it has" (I, c.2; p. 203).

Yet the Catholic has not succumbed completely to this collective extraversion, because he has some interior religious life. He has faith in God and belief in the teaching of his religion. And he has some degree of spiritual development, nourished through the liturgy and the sacraments, and through popular or sophisticated devotion. Yet even in the area of his religious life he may suffer a type of extraversion. His religious experience may be shaped by forces that have been at work in traditional Catholicism since the late Middle Ages, leading to an objectification of belief. Certain juridical, externalizing, and conceptual tendencies in Catholicism became thematic at the time of the Protestant Reformation. The Catholic Church was suspicious of the Protestant emphasis on subjectivity in its several forms: personal conversion, personal experience of Christ as savior, and private interpretation of the Bible. In opposition to this, the Catholic Church emphasized faith as an intellectual assent to dogmas that were objectively formulated and defined by the church. Adherence to this objective creed assured protection from the danger of heresy.

Shortly after the impact of the Protestant Reformation, the Catholic community was confronted with the rise of rationalism, both as a philosophy and as the presupposition of the growing development of modern science. In its defense against rationalism, the Catholic community adopted the premises of rationalism to refute its anti-religious claims; at the same time it elaborated the rationalistic side of its own position to appeal to the tastes of the times. Thus there grew up in Catholic theology a strong intellectualist and rational trend that helped solidify the objectivist tendency of the anti-Protestant response. These tendencies were furthered in Catholic seminary education and college religion programs of the first part of this century. Thus a Catholic entering psychotherapy—especially if trained in Catholic higher education—is likely to be heir to these forces of intellectualist extraversion in the area of his religious experience.

In psychotherapy the Catholic may break through his extraversion—both cultural and religious—and discover his inner life. He may learn that he lives a rich symbolic life, that his history is not written in the events of the external world alone, but that its outlines are glimpsed in the unfolding of his dreams and the suggestions of his fantasies. He may discover that his psyche has many levels, but that the doors leading below are securely locked. However, with care and diligence, with courage and perseverance, with the aid of an experienced guide, he can explore the depths of his newly discovered inner world. In a similar way he may overcome the intellectualist extraversion in the area of his religious experience. He may discover that just as the lower rooms of his psyche are rich in interior meaning and filled with power and life, so, too, the higher rooms of his religious experience also have vital inner meaning. He may realize that what before were isolated answers to catechism questions are now woven into the symbolic fabric of his life. What were cold, abstract concepts in a creed or a theology treatise are now charged with that powerful affectivity that flows from the depths of the psyche. Often enough it is by a specific correlation of the level of psychotherapy with the religious that one discovers the inner meaning of a dogma. As we see later, a breakthrough into the inner meaning of identification with one's father in personality growth may cause a breakthrough to the meaning of identification with Christ. But before he can reach that point of positive correlation, he must pass through the fire of purgation.

Purgation

When the Catholic enters into his psyche and begins his inner journey, he realizes that he has undertaken a difficult task. The path is arduous and the journey grueling. There is no easy route; he must proceed through humility and suffering. In this negative phase of purgation and purification, he may see a correlation with the first stage of the spiritual life. He may recall the advice of saints to enter into one's self and to purify one's self of pride and illusion. In psychotherapy he must enter into himself and take with utter seriousness the saying: know thyself. He soon learns how difficult that is, because he discovers that he himself is his own greatest deceiver. He must strip away with the aid of the analyst, in the face of anxiety and even terror, layer after layer of defensive illusion. He must become as a little child, returning to his childhood to exorcise what is childish in him in order to reach authentic maturity. He must be born again; but first he must die, so that he can be reborn to newness of life.

In this early stage of purification he will come to unmask his religious illusions. He may see that what he thought was genuine religious motivation was a disguised sublimated wish fulfillment. Too, he may discover that what he thought was a conclusive argument against divine providence was really a disguised rationalization of his unresolved hostility toward his parents. At this point he must separate authentic religious issues from their entanglement in his personal conflicts and illusions. He must also remove obstacles to his spiritual growth. It may be that a sense of neurotic guilt has been preventing him from experiencing the love and forgiveness of God. If this purification is successful, the person can come to the point where he can confront his relation to God with directness and freedom, without carrying over the ghosts and shadows from his childhood complexes.

Gradually, as the obstacles are being removed, there is an awakening of the inner life of the psyche. When one discovers his projections are rooted within, he takes his inner life more seriously. He gradually discovers a number of positive correlations that throw light on his religious experience. Though still in the purgative state, he gets a glimpse of the illuminative stage. He begins to see that his dream interpretation on the level of his personal history—with its infantile references to his mother and father—has another level of meaning that corresponds to his religious belief. His identification with his father has its counterpart in the tradition of the following of Christ. His attachment to his mother has its counterpart in the problem of the attachment of the soul to material things. He begins to see his psychic life not as a static thing, but as a dynamic journey: an unfolding and a growth that has its laws and inner thrust that on their own level parallel those of the spiritual life. It is at this point that he begins to see the positive correlations between the many-leveled house of Jung and the interior castle of Teresa. Throughout all the levels of the many-chambered psyche there is a profound unity: a unity of the laws of growth or passage from one level to another. The laws—not in the sense of mechanistic laws, but in the sense of patterns of growth—that apply on the psychological level also apply on the spiritual. If one fails to develop on the psychological level, this will have repercussions on the spiritual; if one makes extraordinary progress spiritually, this may clear up psychological problems.

We now explore some of the positive correlations that a believing Catholic may discover in the process of psychotherapy. We discuss three phases of personality growth: (1) the infantile stage of oral assimilation, (2) the childhood stage of identification with the parent and (3) the mature discovery of the inner self as the true center of the personality. The first two stages are looked at from Freud's point of view and the third from Jung's. Throughout these stages we make correlations to the sacramental symbolism of eating the Eucharist, to the significance of identifying with Christ and of imitating him in his death and resurrection. We show that the growth process on the psychological level correlates with the death and rebirth process on the spiritual level and that the stages of psychological development, as seen through psychotherapy, correlate with the three stages of the spiritual life: the purgative, illuminative, and unitive.

Oral Assimilation

In treating the three stages of personality growth, we sketch their dynamics in broad and general strokes, without filling in the complexities of each stage. For example, the early stage of attachment to the mother has several distinct phases and is interwoven with aggression and hostility. Because of the brevity of our treatment, we do not go into detail here, although we believe that further correlations could be made very fruitfully within each of the stages. We have chosen our points of correlation with an eye to the growth process as a whole. With this overall perspective, we wish to highlight the most characteristic aspect of the beginning, the middle, and the completion of the process. Thus, while bypassing some of the intricacy of the process, we hope to throw light upon some of the most basic patterns of both psychological and spiritual growth.

In delving into the psyche the Freudian therapist attempts to explore that primitive level where the psychological converges with the biological. He attempts to penetrate to the psychic structures whose roots lie embedded in the early months of the infant's life. In this initial stage of personality development, the baby lives in a state of psychic fusion with his mother. Just as the baby had been physically joined to the biological life of the mother in the womb, so now he is fused with the psychic life of the mother. He lives submerged in the ocean of her feeling, the warmth of her body, and the security of her love. In this state of fusion, the baby experiences the world through his body, especially through his mouth in drinking in his mother's milk. As the baby drinks in his mother's milk, he is also drinking in his mother's feelings, his mother's love, his mother's personality.

Biologically, what the baby eats becomes the baby. His body digests the food and transforms it into tissue and bone. On the level of feeling and persons, however, the process is reversed. The baby becomes the people he eats and drinks. He becomes his mother and father and those near him. Thus eating becomes a symbolic act for the assimilation of another's personality. This is not merely a figure of speech or a metaphor seen, as it were, from the top of the head. On the contrary, psychotherapy shows how deeply embedded in experience this symbolism is; it flows from the roots of the psyche and emerges charged with powerful psychic energy.

The depth and power of this symbolism can be illustrated by a case history of a man whose mature development was hampered by an overidentification with his mother. When through counseling, he was able to reach the archaic level where the identification was lodged, he felt himself becoming physically ill and went through the motions of vomiting. In this spontaneous ritualistic act, he physically felt the attachment to his mother being coughed up from the pit of his stomach, where it had long ago been ingested. The case can be further illustrative. His problem had come about because of the death of his mother when he was three, at a time when he could not assimilate the horror of her death. Later in counseling, after the vomiting incident, he was able to accept her death by the fantasy image of his symbolically eating her body and realizing that her soul was living in heaven. Because of the traumatic shock of her death, he had not been able to assimilate her femininity into his personality; hence his development here had been arrested at an early stage. In both the ritualistic vomiting and in the fantasy are revealed the powerful significance that the symbolism of eating has for psychic development.[10]

A Catholic in psychotherapy who becomes aware of the powerful symbolism of eating could easily see a correlation with the eucharist. In Holy Communion the believer eats the body of Christ. As the infant does, he takes in physical food; and like the infant, he takes in also the person of Christ, for the Eucharist is looked on primarily as spiritual food that will nourish the soul of the communicant and further his spiritual growth toward assimilation into Christ. Karl Stern (1954) has pointed out how the theological tradition has been aware on the spiritual level of

---

[10]In the case cited, the breakthrough into the depth level of mother-identification which led to the vomiting occurred in a therapeutically oriented LSD session. Examples of the therapeutic effects of LSD can be found in the research of Masters and Houston (1966).

the same psychic law that psychotherapy has discovered in the primitive symbolism of eating (pp. 234 ff.). In the Patristic period Leo the Great (Migne, 1881) wrote: "Participation in the body and blood of Christ produces in us no other effect than to make us pass into that which we take" (Sermon 63; 12, c.7; col. 357). In the Middle Ages, Thomas Aquinas in his *Commentary on the Sentences* analyzed the Eucharist as follows (Moos, 1947):

> Bodily food is first changed into the one who eats it, and through this change it restores his losses and adds to his growth. But spiritual food is not changed into the one who eats it; rather it changes him into itself. It follows that the proper effect of this sacrament is the transformation of a man into Christ, so that he can say with the Apostle (Gal. 2:20): 'I live, now not I, but Christ lives in me' [IV, d.12, q.2, a.1; p. 524].

The same principle is expressed in *The Catechism of the Council of Trent* (Donovan, n.d.) which was commissioned by the Council and published in 1566:

> What bread and wine are to the body, the Eucharist is, in a superior order, to the health and joy of the soul. It is not, like bread and wine, changed into our substance; but in some measure, changes us into its own nature, and to it we may apply these words of St. Augustine: 'I am the food of grown men. Grow and you shall feed upon me. And you will not, as with the food of the body, change me into yourself, but you will be changed into me' (p. 165).[11]

The symbolism of eating throws light on the close link between the biological and the spiritual. Just as external objects such as trees and mountains can become symbols of the spiritual journey, so too the most elemental biological functions, such as eating, can become vehicles of grace. This close connection between matter and spirit lies at the heart of Catholic sacramental theology and indicates why the dim biological depths of psychic life can correlate with the highest level of spiritual assimilation into Christ.

---

[11] The quotation from Augustine is from *Confessions*, VII, c. 10. For this quotation we have used the English translation of Rex Warner (1963) pp. 149–50.

Identification

In addition to exploring the primitive levels of the psyche, where matter and spirit converge, the therapist also leads his patient through another level of assimilative mechanisms whose roots go back to preadolescent childhood, roughly from the ages of four to twelve. During this time the boy begins to identify with his father, who emerges as a hero in the boy's eyes. The father becomes an ideal he wants to imitate. The father is strong, resourceful, quick witted; the little boy is sure his dad can lick anybody on the block. The father must relate positively to his son: become his pal, play ball with him, talk his own language. He must stoop, as it were, to the child's level so that the child can rise to his. In the girl's development, a similar identification takes place with the mother, although this is more complex and less clearly defined. During this period the child's identification with the parent centers on ideal qualities and is less biological in its symbolism than was the case in the infantile stage. Instead of symbols of eating, we find the symbol of putting on clothes, the clothes of an adult or the clothes worn by the ideal person.

This stage of parent identification is very important for personality development. If a child does not pass through it successfully, his personality can be permanently affected. Karl Stern (1954) observes:

> In the case of male juvenile delinquents we not infrequently see that there has never been any wholesome identification with the father, or with any paternal figure. Deep down the patient is still strongly identified with the mother and is simply terrified of that tender core, and fights it with all his might. He becomes destructive and brutal. He "acts" tough and hard because, deep down, there is no genuine toughness and hardness in him (p. 220).

A boy who has not had a really deep identification with his father may go through life, as it were, looking for a father in his teachers, his employers, the clergy, or anyone in a position of authority.

This type of assimilation has a striking correlation on the spiritual level in the following of Christ. For the Christian Christ is the ideal, the model of virtue, the perfect man. He is the spiritual hero, the leader who will bring his followers to maturity and fulfillment. Solidly grounded in the New Testament sayings of Christ, this theme has been developed by spiritual writers throughout Christian history. In the second century Clement of Alexandria saw Christ as the *Paidagogos* or educator who teaches the Christian the way of virtue by his life and example (Wood, 1954). Bonaventure saw Christ as the tree of life on which has blossomed all the virtues (de Vinck, 1960). Thomas a Kempis' classical work bears the title *The Imitation of Christ* and is one of the most widely read of Christian books (McCann, 1954). This tradition was given dramatic expression in the *Spiritual Exercises* of Ignatius of Loyola (Puhl, 1963), where Christ is seen as the ideal king who makes an appeal to his men to join him in a noble cause. In the toil and the battle the king will be their companion, fighting at their side. They must be content to share his lot, to eat the same food, to wear the same clothes, so that in following him in suffering they may follow him in glory.

The followers of Christ are to meditate on the life of Christ and put on his virtues. The majority of Ignatius' meditations present us with scenes from the life of Christ in which examples of his virtues are held up for imitation. In the meditation on Christ's nativity, we are bidden to enter into the cave and observe Mary, Joseph, and the Infant. In the poverty of the cave we learn from Christ the lesson of humility and detachment. Throughout the scenes of Christ's life Ignatius prays "for an intimate knowledge of our Lord, who has become man for me, that I may love Him more and follow Him more closely" (p. 49). By meditating on Christ, we are to absorb his attitudes and become other Christs. We are to heed the words of Paul and "put on Christ" (Gal. 3:27) and "let this mind be in you, which was also in Christ Jesus" (Phil. 2:5). The followers of Christ, in the words of the Jesuit rule (*Rules of the Society of Jesus,* 1894), are to desire "to be clothed with the same garment and livery of their Lord" (Rule 11; p. 6). Yet this putting on of Christ must not be a mere external thing, a throwing on of a cloak from the outside. As we explore in the next section, it must go deep, into the very center of the person; but in going deep, it must not smother one's individuality.

At the same time that Christ manifests himself as the spiritual ideal, he also shows himself as a man among men. In his human nature he is one of us, our friend and brother. This parallels the relationship between the child and the parent. For the father to make contact with his son, he must first stoop to the child's level. He must leave behind his own adult world and enter into the child's world, where he must show interest in his son's hobbies. He must establish a warm, affective link between himself and his son, which will make the assimilation of the ideal possible. In this setting it is possible to see a psychological correlation for the Pauline interpretation of Christ's incarnation as an emptying, in which he assumes the form of a slave, to make contact with us to lead us to our fulfillment.

The following of Christ means not only that we put on the virtues of his public life, but as Ignatius (Puhl, 1963) indicates, that we follow him in suffering so that we may follow him in glory (pp. 81-98). We must die with Christ so that we may rise with him. Putting on Jesus Christ means that we enter into the mystery of death and rebirth.

When a boy identifies with his father, he must break with his infantile identification with his mother, who until this time has been the source of his well-being. To the little infant the warmth of the mother's body was the harbor of security, for the mother was the giver of life, supplying the infant with food and giving satisfaction to his desires. In this atmosphere the baby developed a passive, receptive, oral orientation, drinking in everything. As the child grows, he wishes to remain rooted in this security, to have all that he desires given to him by his all-loving mother, and yet the forces of growth are pushing within him. He feels the desire to break from this security, which he glimpses now as threatening. The nourishing mother archetype, as Jung (1939) says, can become also the devouring mother. The security of the womb can turn into the death of the tomb. If the child remains nestled in the security of this mother identification, his powers of personality will wither and die. Yet he is afraid to break loose, for everything ahead seems dark and unknown. The mother was life; to break with her means death. And so he stands poised on the brink of being and nonbeing.

It is at this point that he needs a savior, someone who will come and lead him across the passage, across the chasm of darkness. This role is played by the father, who gives the child the chance to develop his own powers, to turn from security to self-realization, so that the child can change from an oral-intake personality to a productive outer-oriented adult. In the process the child must obtain the courage to die to his past on a deep level and accept the responsibilities and implications of his new life. This death, like all death, is frightening. It can create deep-rooted anxiety, for it seems to mean utter destruction of himself and his world. Yet in a mysterious way it is a gateway to new life. If the child accepts the death to the mother, he will experience liberation. He will feel himself rising to newness of life, to a higher and richer state of existence, to the possibilities of adulthood. On the psychological level this is the mystery of life coming out of death, expressed in Christ's statement: "Whoever will seek to save his life, will lose it; and whoever will lose his life, will preserve it" (Lk. 17:33; 9:24; Mt. 10:39; 16:25; Mk. 8:35; Jn. 12:25).

The paradox of death and rebirth has its correlation on all levels of life, from the biological to the life of the spirit. At the moment of the dissolution of old forms, there is the sense of darkness and abandonment that Christ expressed on the cross: "My God, my God, why have you forsaken me?" At the moment of transition, two contrary attitudes are present simultaneously: the sense of accepting death as absolute and a faith that resurrection will come, but at the time of crisis that this faith is not experienced existentially. When we turn full face to the darkness and embrace death, we experience liberation and rise to newness of life. In this new state we look back and see how foolish were our fears. The youth sees that he really has not abandoned security in leaving the mother, but has found security in creativity. He has incorporated the mother into his own personality, assuming her as a vital principle of creativity within himself. In this context we can see a psychological correlation with the dogma of the assumption. If Mary is seen as symbolizing the mother aspect of the cosmos and the psyche, then the dogma of the assumption gives expression to the cosmic and psychological goal of recapitulating and integrating all lower forms in a higher synthesis. Just as Mary follows her son in bodily resurrection into heaven, so in the psyche the mother must be lifted up and assumed to take her place as the creative aspect of the psyche, in the new glorified life of the mature personality.

The Inner Self

We have explored two levels of the house of the psyche that have been charted chiefly by Freud. The first of these was the level of the infantile fusion with the mother and bears the marks of the most primitive and biological dimensions of psychic life. We climbed the next level, where spiritual ideals begin to emerge in the young child's identification with his father in his search for his own personal identity. We now investigate a third level, one which has been explored by Jung and which by its nature tends to correlate closely with the spiritual life. It is here perhaps more than anywhere else that the processes of psychotherapy and those of the spiritual life tend to converge.

After a person has broken free of his mother and begun to discover his personality by identification with his father, he must not allow this identification to remain extrinsic, but must integrate the ideals of his father into his own personality and discover his true autonomy and individuality. It is during adolescence that the youth should free himself from his parents and take his place as an independent member of society who can make a creative contribution of his own. But the process of growth does not stop when one becomes a social adult. Even after one has taken his place in society, he still has the powers and the imperative to grow. He must constantly move toward the deepening of his individuality, integrating his psychic forces and discovering his true self. In a way that parallels mystical wisdom in both East and West, Jung looks on the psyche as being composed of three levels: (1) the persona or mask, which is the image we wear before society; (2) the ego, which is the center of our conscious mind; (3) the self, which is the center of the whole personality, both conscious and unconscious (Jacobi, 1940). A person might identify himself with his more superficial aspects—his social image or his conscious ego—and think that this is all he is, or at least that this is the most important aspect of himself. But hidden under these layers lies his deeper self, which includes the unconscious and which gives form and order to the totality of the personality. Jung (1916) describes this self as follows: ". . . it is the completest expression of that fateful combination we call individuality, the full flowering not only of the single individual but of the group, in which each adds his portion to the whole" [p. 238]. It is not only the center of individuality; it is the center of organization of all psychic forces and includes this organized whole. Jung (1944) writes: ". . . the self is not only the centre but also the whole circumference which embraces both conscious and unconscious; it is the centre of this totality, just as the ego is the centre of the conscious mind [p. 41]. As the center of individuality and the focal point of organization of psychic forces, the self is both the alpha and the omega of psychic life. "The beginnings of our whole psychic life," Jung (1916) says, "seem to be inextricably rooted in this point, and all our highest and ultimate purposes seem to be striving toward it" (p. 236). Although it is most intimate, it yet remains mysterious to us. It "is strange to us and yet so near, wholly ourselves and yet unknowable, a virtual centre of mysterious constitution" (p. 235). In its deepest structure, the self has a religious quality and is closely associated with what the church fathers called the *imago Dei* or image of God. Jung (1952) writes:

But empirically it can be established, with a sufficient degree of probability, that there is in the unconscious an archetype of wholeness which manifests itself spontaneously in dreams, etc., and a tendency, independent of the conscious will, to relate other archetypes to this centre. Consequently, it does not seem improbable that the archetype produces a symbolism which has always characterized and expressed the Deity . . . The God-image does not coincide with the unconscious as such, but with a special content of it, namely the archetype of the self. It is this archetype from which we can no longer distinguish the God-image empirically (pp. 468–469).

Jung (1942) states: "One can, then, explain the God-image . . . as a reflection of the self, or, conversely, explain the self as an *imago Dei* in man" (p. 190). For Jung, the self as God image is the empirical side of what theologians and spiritual writers describe in theological concepts and mystical images. Interpreting Jung, Jacob (1940) writes:

> To depart for a moment from the language of psychology, we might call it the 'central fire,' our individual share in God, or Meister Eckhart's 'little spark.' It is the early Christian ideal of the Kingdom of God that is 'within you.' It is the ultimate in psychic experience and in man's knowledge of the psyche [p. 128].

If we take Jung's idea of the self and situate it in the Christian world view, we can see correlations with the imitation of Christ. It is through Christ that the Christian discovers his true self; it is through Christ, who is the image of the father, that the Christian realizes himself as image of God. He absorbs Christ through his body in the sacrament of the eucharist, and he puts on Christ's moral attitudes and ideals by identifying with Christ in the Ignatian way. To some extent these are extrinsic—a putting on from the outside. We reach a further stage when we discover that Christ is the center of our inner selves, the very source of our individuality, when we can say with St. Paul, "I live, now not I but Christ lives in me" (Gal. 2:20). At the very center of myself, at the root of my being I discover Christ, the base of my individuality and the source of my psychic unity. It is this mystery that is expressed in the symbolism of Teresa's seventh mansion, in which the soul consummates the mystical marriage with Christ, its heavenly bridegroom.

This is the discovery of the true self as opposed to the false self—just as Jung's process of individuation penetrates beyond the persona and the ego to find the archetype of the self. So often people identify with their social roles or their superficial egos. To do this sets limits to the personality and produces profound anxiety and hostility. The mystical and ascetical traditions emphasize the importance of the inner or true self as opposed to the false or illusory self. The false self must be unmasked; its pride and illusions must be dispelled. This distinction between the true and the false self provides a basis for understanding the harsh, sometimes shocking statements made by spiritual writers against one's self. We are told that we should die to ourselves, that we should die that Christ may live in us. Such statements are not intended as a threat to one's individuality or as expressing an antihumanistic bias. Rather, they point to the mystery of death and rebirth within the very structure of the psyche, where we must die to the superficial levels of ourselves in order to discover and live on the level of the deeper self.

When the Christian dies to his false self and rises to newness of life in Christ, he realizes that his deeper self is in a mysterious way identified with Christ. As divine logos dwelling in his soul, Christ gives the ultimate metaphysical support for his individuality. This is what Augustine meant by calling the soul the image of God, and this is what reaches its full flowering in the mystical marriage in Teresa's castle. As son of the father, Christ draws the soul into the life of the trinity, and in the light of the trinity, the true nature of the soul is revealed. The trinity is the divine archetype of infinite self-expressive, relational life. In the generation of the son from the father we have the metaphysical basis of all symbolism, for the dogma of the trinity asserts that at its core the divinity is profoundly symbolic. The son is generated as the perfect expressive image of the father. It is this eternal, self-expressive imaging that lays the foundation for the symbolic nature of the psyche and of the entire material universe. This is why the soul is the mirror of God and the mirror of the external world. Thus by glimpsing the mystery of the trinity reflected in his soul, the Christian can see the metaphysical basis for the multidimensional symbolic life of the psyche which is brought to the fore in psychotherapy. It is here that the light at the summit of the spiritual quest can illumine the winding paths below. Because the psyche reflects the eternal generation of the son from the father, it reveals in the depths of its inner life such rich, dynamic, and expressive symbolism. Because it shares in the mystery of the trinitarian circuminsession—in which the persons interpenetrate—its own inner structures and forms interpenetrate, so that one level contains within it the structures of another. Hence behind both the house of Jung's dream and Teresa's interior castle stand the ultimate mystery of the trinitarian God.

It is not surprising, then, that the stages in psychological development should correlate with the three traditional stages of the spiritual life: the purgative, illuminative, and unitive. In personality development the first stage of fusion with the mother corresponds to the purgative stage of the spiritual life. In the infantile stage the baby is fused with the mother and identified with her, is self-centered and desirous to drink in all good things. His mouth is the center of his experience; eating and the satisfaction of his desires are his chief concern. To grow the child must break this mother identification, become aware of ideals, and ultimately become creative and oriented toward others. The same is true in the spiritual life. To grow we must break our attachment to sense pleasures, to the world, and to material things; we must overcome our selfish desires and become aware of the ideals Christ holds before us.

In the context of growth the world, matter, and sense pleasures are symbolized by the once-nourishing mother who at a later stage of development becomes the devouring mother, for she holds us back, tempts us to remain in her security, and swallows us into spiritual death. But by identification with Christ, by the illuminative way of becoming aware of his virtues and his ideals, we can die to the world and rise with Christ. In this we do not reject the mother or matter, but assume the material, now symbolized by Mary, our spiritual mother, in the glorified state of maturity.

Finally, there is the unitive way. In the case of personality development, this is in Jung's perspective the realization of the self. The integrated person has discovered his deeper self and is in union with all things. The same is true in the spiritual life. The ultimate state of union with God brings about our own individuation and the discovery of our true self; it brings us into creative union with other men and with the entire universe.

These three stages of personality development are also three existential aspects of every moment of our existence. We must always be in the process of overcoming our infantile attachment to matter and of advancing toward ideals we incorporate into our true or inner self. The same is true in the spiritual life. We can see, then, that the purgative, illuminative, and unitive ways are three existential aspects of growth on every level—from the infant's first month to the mystic's ecstatic union with God.

In concluding, we wish to call attention to a problem. We do not want to give the impression that psychotherapy automatically leads to personality development, let alone spiritual development. Many have entered the door and penetrated very little. Others, more problematically, have been entrapped along the way. Having wandered the devious way down Jung's stairways, they remain locked within the lower regions, just as in the spiritual ascent some spend their lives in the purgative phase. For all its vastness, the psyche can be confining; each corridor—although leading to new levels and new expanses—can become a prison that can hold one for life. The believer's ultimate hope of liberation from the infinite labyrinth of the psyche is his deep trust in divine providence and his openness to God's grace. God's grace can break through the psychic structures to heal deep wounds, to purify one from attachment and pride, to illumine all levels from the depths to the heights, and it can ultimately lead to a creative union of all the forces of the psyche.

The psyche, then, is a many-leveled dwelling. In our personal lives and in human history it constantly reveals its vast scope and intricate complexity. In the twentieth century psychotherapy has explored its unconscious and has thrown light on its dark, primitive regions. This knowledge has enhanced the awareness of the believer, who can bring into correlation with it the spiritual wisdom amassed over centuries by saints and mystics who have lived intense spiritual lives. Although both modern psychotherapy and the ancient wisdom of religion have illumined the psyche, they have not exhausted its scope, for as image of the infinite God, the soul stands open to new complexities and new possibilities of growth. Within recent times new techniques have developed for exploring the psyche; as science and human knowledge expand, one glimpses ever-expanding possibilities on the horizon (Masters-Houston, 1966). Because both psychotherapy and religion face the future, they should keep in mind both their need for mutual cooperation and their need to be increasingly sensitive to new techniques for exploring the inner world of man. The psyche is too vast in its scope to be explored exhaustively by either. As modern man embarks on his spiritual quest, he needs—more than ever in the past—a sense of the richness of the psyche. When facing the future, he should be mindful of Teresa's words (Peers, 1949): "In speaking of the soul we must always think of it as spacious and ample and lofty; and this can be done without the least exaggeration, for the soul's capacity is much greater than we can realize, and this Sun, which is in the palace, reaches every part of it" (I. c.2; p. 208).

BIBLIOGRAPHY

Black, M. (1962), *Models and Metaphysics*. Ithaca, N.Y.: Cornell University Press.

Boehner, P. (1956), trans. of Itinerary of the Mind into God, *Works of Saint Bonaventure*, 2. St. Bonaventure, N.Y.: Franciscan Institute.

Burnet, J. (1930), *Early Greek Philosophy*. London: Adam & Black.

Chenu, M. D. (1950), *Toward Understanding Saint Thomas*. Chicago: Regnery, 1964.

Dalbiez, R. (1936), *Psychoanalytical Method and the Doctrine of Freud*. 2 vols. London: Longmans, Green, 1941.

Daly, E. (tr.) (1950), *Tertullian: Apologetical Works*. New York: Fathers of the Church.

Deane, S. (1962), trans. of *St. Anselm: Basic Writings*. La Salle, Ill.: Open Court.

Donovan, J. (n.d.), trans. of *The Catechism of the Council of Trent*. New York: Catholic Publication Society.

Fabro, C. (1950), *La Nozione metafisica di partecipazione secondo S. Tommaso d'Aquino*. Turin: Societa Editrice Intenazionale.

de Finance, J. (1945), *Etre et agir dans la philosophie de S. Thomas*. Paris: Beauchesne.

Freud, A. (1939), *The Ego and the Mechanisms of Defense*. New York: International Universities Press, 1966.

Freud, S. (1900), The interpretation of dreams. *Standard Edition*, 4 and 5. London: Hogarth Press, 1953.

Geiger, L. (1942), *La Participation dans la philosophie de S. Thomas*. Paris: Vrin.

Gilby, T. et al. (1963–   ), trans. of *St. Thomas Aquinas, Summa Theologiae*. New York: McGraw Hill.

Gilson, E. (1943), *The Christian Philosophy of Saint Augustine*. New York: Random House, 1960.

Hartmann, H. (1939), *Ego Psychology and the Problem of Adaptation*. New York: International Universities Press, 1958.

Heron, G. (1954), trans. of Nicolaus Cusanus: *Of Learned Ignorance*. New Haven: Yale University Press.

Hesse, M. (1963), *Models and Analogies in Science*. New York: Sheed & Ward.

Jacobi, J. (1940), *The Psychology of C. G. Jung*. New Haven: Yale University Press, 1962.

Jaeger, W. (1961), *Early Christianity and Greek Paideia*. Cambridge: Harvard University Press.

Jung, C. (1916), The relations between the ego and the unconscious, *Collected Works*, 7:141–239. New York: Pantheon, 1953.

——— (1939), Psychological aspects of the mother archetype, *Collected Works*,

9, Part I: 75–110. New York: Pantheon, 1959.

—— (1942), A psychological approach to the dogma of the trinity, *Collected Works, 11*: 107–200. New York: Pantheon, 1958.

—— (1944), Psychology and alchemy. *Collected Works, 12.* New York: Pantheon, 1953.

—— (1955), *Mysterium Coniunctionis, Collected Works, 14.* New York: Pantheon, 1963.

—— (1962), *Memories, Dreams, Reflections.* New York: Pantheon Books, 1963.

Kazemier, B. and Vuysje, D., Eds. (1961), *The Concept & Role of the Model in Mathematics & Natural & Social Sciences.* Dordrecht: Reidel.

Ladner, G. (1959), *The Idea of Reform: Its Impact on Christian Thought and Action in the Age of the Fathers.* Cambridge: Harvard University Press.

Masters, R. & Houston, J. (1966), *The Varieties of Psychedelic Experience.* New York: Holt, Rinehart & Winston.

McCann, J. (1954), trans. of *Thomas a Kempis: Of the Imitation of Christ.* London: Burns, Oates & Washbourne.

McKenna, S. (1963), trans. of *Saint Augustine: The Trinity.* Washington: Catholic University Press.

Migne, P. (1881), *Patrologiae Cursus Completus, Series Latina, 54.* Paris: Migne-Garnier.

Moos, M. (1947), editor of Thomas Aquinas: *Scriptum Super Sententus Magistri Petri Lombardi, 4,* Paris: Lethie-Lleux.

Peers, Edgar A. (1949), trans. of *The Complete Works of St. Teresa of Jesus, 2.* New York: Sheed & Ward.

Puhl, L. (1963), trans. of *The Spiritual Exercises of St. Ignatius.* Westminster, Md.: Newman.

Rules of the Society of Jesus (1894), Roehampton: Manresana.

Stern, K. (1954), *The Third Revolution.* New York: Harcourt, Brace.

Sullivan, J. (1963), *The Image of God.* Dubuque, Iowa: Priory Press.

Teilhard de Chardin, P. (1955), *The Phenomenon of Man.* New York: Harper & Row, 1965.

de Vinck, J. (1960), trans. of The tree of life, *The Works of Bonaventure, 1*:99–144. Paterson, N.J.: St. Anthony's Guild Press.

Warner, R. (1963), trans. of *The Confessions of St. Augustine.* New York: Mentor-Omega.

Wolfson, H. (1964), *The Philosophy of the Church Fathers, 1.* Cambridge: Harvard University Press.

Wood, S. (1954), trans. of Clement of Alexandria: *Christ the Educator.* New York: Fathers of the Church.

Jung, C. (1952), Answer to Job, *Collected Works, 11.* New York: Pantheon, 1958.

PROFESSOR LEONARDO ANCONA *in his essay,* Considerations on Christian Vocations Seen from the Point of View of Psychoanalysis, *explains that religious vocation can be viewed as consecration of oneself to God or as one's desire to make the best use of his talents.*

Traditionally, the concept of vocation has been interpreted as "a total consecration of one's life to the service of God implying celibacy and virginity." The opposite view, called by Dr. Ancona "technical subjectivistic," is based on the assumption that God's grace is gratuitous. This point of view grants everyone, including the priests, the right to change their vocation. Thus there is not much difference between religious and secular vocation, because both ought to serve the community.

The idea of psychological selection of priests was introduced in 1936 by Father Thomas Verner Moore in his book, Insanity in Priests and Religious. *Presently, anamnestic investigation of future priests and other religious candidates includes the use of the psychoanalytic method.*

Some people aspire for priesthood for status reasons; some seek escape from their fear of sexual impotence; some seek power and control over other people; some anxiety-ridden individuals seek affiliation with the church to feel that they "belong." The church represents a mother image and many immature and selfish individuals prefer to receive maternal care to giving love to others. Psychodiagnostic technique and psychoanalysis may help in discovering one's true vocation.

5

Considerations on Christian Vocations

Seen from the Point of View

of Psychoanalysis

by

LEONARDO ANCONA, PH. D.

THE SUBJECT OF VOCATION, WHICH COVERS BOTH RELIGIOUS vocations within the church, and personal vocations of a religious character but lived in secularity, is gaining both theoretical and practical importance. What is new in the growing interest for a subject that strictly belongs to the tradition of the ecclesiastical way of thinking, especially of the Roman Catholic Church, is the firm intention of viewing it in a wider psychological perspective or at least investigating it from that angle. This new orientation is easily discernible in all the acts of Vatican II whenever the vocation and the formation of priests is being dealt with. It also appears in Pope Paul VI's recent Encyclic: "Sacerdotalis Coelibatum," where the subject is approached in a way that may be considered daring, and a product of our times.

The reference to general psychology in this context has led many to suggest clinical and social psychology, and even psychoanalysis, psychoanalysis being a sort of revolutionary vanguard, often looked on with suspicion and fear by moralists and even by nonanalytic psychologists. It is in this perspective that this chapter has been written. Its aim is not to present a psychoanalytic approach of vocation, but to assess the present situation by describing the attempts made so far to find a solution of the problem in psychoanalytic terms. It is also an endeavor to draw up a first synthesis between the facts that contemporary culture and pedagogy are putting before us all the time and the traditional principles of the Christian way of thinking as set forth by the Roman Catholic Church in the past and in its more recent official acts and documents.

Before going any further, it is advisable to refer to the traditional concepts of vocation that have become crystallized in the process of time and the passing of generations, and which today's synthesizing of all Christian thinking has left behind. It is suitable to stress the merits of this synthesis and to point out that, despite the efforts in the last score or so of years by progressive theologians and thinkers, a large portion of the "faithful" have been left behind and still cling to obsolete conceptions.

On the other hand, all that we say here is mainly concerned with the psychological point of view disregarding all considerations of a moral, pastoral, juridical, or scriptural nature, for which the present writer has no adequate competence. Nevertheless, considering the psychic dynamic of man, which truly does not begin and end in itself but naturally opens out towards transcendence and the sphere of God, many theological concepts necessarily enter into the discussion.

It is precisely in reference to this limitation that only two traditional concepts of vocation are considered here, opposed to each other because they stand at either end of a unidimensional psychological continuum. They could, respectively, be described as the extreme of juridical extroversion and the extreme of subjective introversion. The same limitation has brought us to consider under the name of vocation both the vocation of the person who "consecrates himself to God," and the vocation stamping the life of every man who desires to put to use the talents alloted to him by nature and by God, according to the best interpretation he is able to give of the designs of God on him. Vatican II has repeatedly considered the many facets of vocation from the narrower to the wider meaning, speaking of vocation to the church, human vocation, vocation of the laity, vocation of Christian spouses, vocation to the service of the community. It seems that the stress is put on the second, wider, meaning as if it were a presupposition and a condition of the first.

Principles and Criteria of Vocation

The first and more general view of vocation we refer to here is the one that may be labelled as juridical moralistic. It is also the easiest to understand, being traditional in Italian culture, and the one by which the supernatural relationship that can be established between man and God can be described more concretely. This is also the concept prevailing (probably since the great re-organization that followed the Council of Trent) in the Western-Latin Church, even if, obviously, it is not limited to Italy, France, Spain, and Portugal. This way of considering "the call" is very alluring from a subjective point of view. It begins with the presup-position, theologically valid, that every vocation comes from God (Thomas Aquinas Summa Th. 11–119, 189 art 10: *propositum de ingresso religionis non indiget probationem utrum sit a Deo*) and comes to the conclusion, which is only psychologically certain, that a vocation is to be understood as a total consecration of one's life to the service of God, implying celibacy and virginity. Thus viewed, vocation materializes that "best part of all, that which shall never be taken away" (Luke 10:42) for those who have chosen it, bears witness to the future resurrection (Luke 20:36) and advances the consummation of the Kingdom of God to life on earth. In fact, the tradition of the holy fathers in the first place, then the provincial councils of ancient times, and last, the Council of Trent and the Code of Canon Law have extolled this concept of vocation against the ordinary life to the point that a consecrated life was considered as a supreme good which man can but accept when he has "signs" that it has been granted to him, just as it is well that a newly born baby should accept baptism even though he is not personally "able" to receive it. Thus a life of vocation is to be seen as an expression of God's will, no matter how the call reaches the ear of the "called," provided it has come through legitimate channels.

This view accepts the principle that God's call may reach a still unprepared person, one who may even be reluctant or inhibited by fears of his own unworthiness, but that the grace of God by its specific "healing" power will straighten the warped, strengthen the weak, and lend support to the faltering. The only thing that is required of the human being is a trusting disposition, a ready and generous answer to the voice of God whose call cannot deceive. Still, if it happens that in the course of his life and through the experiences he has lived, a man discovers that the way in which he has thus engaged himself is not really the one he was meant for, that the original, deeper, orientation of his life is another one, then, in the conflict that arises between the call to a life considered to be vastly superior to any other, and the actual subjective incapacity to live it, the command becomes "do as if you had been called" ("fac ut voceris"). The necessity of self-abnegation (Matthew 16:24 ff.) is presented with the warning that "unless the grain of wheat falling into the ground die, it remains nothing more than a grain of wheat; but if it dies, then it yields rich fruit" (John 12:24-25) because it is "far better not to have promised than to forswear oneself" as it would be like "taking one's hand from the plough" (Luke 9:62).

Such frame of reference implies the firm belief that to resist a vocation from the High or not to recognize it inevitably exposes the recipient to trials, dangers, and uncertainties of all sorts in both this and future life with unfathomable consequences. In short, it can but be a temptation from Satan. Furthermore, if the decision to stray from the path taken proves to be irreducible and it cannot be curbed, the cause attributed to the change is always implacably that of some resurgent factors of sexuality, or, in the most favorable hypothesis, of "having fallen in love"; in the most damning, of "having lost vocation" because of some serious fault.

It is in such an atmosphere of implicit menace, attribution to wrong causes, and pat diagnoses that the subject sees his own responsibility of decision questioned. He is repeatedly warned that the "others"—friends, advisors, confessors, and relatives—know better, have better lights by which to judge on the merits of his destiny, and that he must put his trust in them. Everything, anyway, can always find a suitable solution in a firm act of faith. It is not uncommon to hear, among priests and religious communities as well as novices and laymen consecrated to God, declarations such as: to turn back is tantamount to taking a passport for hell, or the moment when one decides to change confessor or director is the first step toward treason.

Technical-Subjectivistic View

Another way of viewing vocation is an alternative to the former and might be described as technical-subjectivistic. It starts from the presupposition that the grace of God is a gratuitous gift that raises human nature without destroying it or doing violence to it (gratia perficit naturam). The grace of God does not intervene therapeutically on a weak or unsuitable nature, not even when the trouble is of a psychopathological nature. It is true that a miracle—in the sense of a healing—is always possible, but it would be temerity to expect it as a matter of course, for this would be "tempting the Lord" and falling into a sin that the first Egyptian monks had stigmatized. To do away with this possibility, this concept of vocation gives greatest importance to the consideration of human nature, which becomes a visible pointer to God's will that would otherwise remain invisible and unperceivable in God's relations with man. God covered Moses' eyes when He passed in front of him so that he could only glimpse His back (Exodus 33:32 ff). The main "sign" that may reveal a vocation, if not the only one, is, therefore, one's body in its being and growing. The very best means to ascertain its presence becomes the expert and dispassionate look one turns inside oneself. This is a practical approach that has spread especially within the Roman Catholic Church in Latin America; it has also occurred to a remarkable degree in the Church in countries where there is a plurality of religious denominations. Actually, this view is rooted in an optimistic belief of man's capacities for self-investigation. It is pragmatic, admits to no dramatic inner conflicts, and is concerned above all with perfecting the techniques of self-observation, considered as a necessary and sufficient instrument enabling one to become aware of one's own "truth."

The intervention of grace is seen here mostly in an "uplifting" aspect, and the realization of a vocation is considered to be dependent more on a subjective availability than on a specific and determining intervention of God. Accordingly, "God calls everyone" but he does not elect everyone. The lack of other specific inclinations in the mind or heart, the discovery in one's self of a reassuring capability of overcoming loneliness at home and the demands of the flesh, a constant orientation toward a human destiny devoted to the priesthood or to a consecration to God, these are considered the fundamentals needed to recognize within oneself the existence of a religious vocation. The work of a director is seen here merely as a suitable approval of a direction already chosen by the subject that does not depend on his advice in the first place.

In this view great importance is given to vocational tests, to the analysis of motivations, probing deeper and deeper. When possible, psychoanalysis is suggested to remove all those defense mechanisms that may simulate a vocation by camouflaging the real, deeper inclination of the subject. The consequences deriving from a refusal of the vocation are not stressed as much as the results emerging from the always dangerous warping of one's natural bent and the psychopathological troubles inevitable in anyone who insists on living a life to which he is not suited. The whole issue is thus dealt with on a strictly human level of vocational guidance, leaving to each person a large margin for self-observation with the help of all the technical means offered by the progress of the different branches of psychological science. At any time a way of life already entered into following a suggestion obtained from a technical test may be abandoned by obedience to new and contrary advice received through the same means. There is no question here of a "hand taken from the plough," "treason," yielding to temptation proceeding from the devil. To abandon a vocation is no longer described as something fraught with fearsome consequences on both the worldly and the heavenly plane. It is, on the contrary, considered highly reasonable to respect human needs, to use one's intelligence with the help of all available instruments of research, and to safeguard self-determination and social responsibility, which may prevent one from taking a course that may cause mental troubles or, at least, impair one's general efficiency.

On the whole, this view grants full liberty to pursue or to alter one's way of living to everybody including priests, members of religious communities (to whom it recognizes implicitly the possibility of receding from the vows taken, especially as regards chastity), and consecrated laics. The latter are generally considered an objectionable expression of mental stiffness and masochistic self-punishment.

Both these concepts, reciprocally extreme and antagonistic, are, in reality, partial and therefore psychologically unsound. The problem of vocation is extremely complex, when viewed from a psychological angle, because both human drives and the particular action exerted by God must be accounted for. To be more precise: a psychological approach must identify the connection between the free and open attitude of a man and the personal intervention of a divine nature. It is when this connection is smooth a true religious vocation can be available. When the problem of vocation is viewed from one side only, either the theological or the human aspect is put on a subordinate plane or overlooked.

In the so-called Latin-Western frame of reference, a vocation becomes tantamount to the acceptance of a principle of authority without allowing for an adequate development and the use of personal responsibility, under menace of a temporal punishment or even of eternal damnation in the case of refusal or transgression. The pedagogical principle, imagining oneself on the point of death or at the last judgment and thinking of how one would like at that moment his own life to have been in the past, is an appalling, yet typical, example of abstractness and intimidation!

In the so-called Latin-American perspective, on the contrary, an exasperated "technicality" has reduced vocation to the mere possibilities of human nature, as if it were a question of solving an algebraical equation. The unhappy, albeit important results of the attempt made by G. Lemercier at Cuernavaca in Mexico, which failed because of the excessive importance attributed to psychoanalytic techniques, is a good example of the danger in one-sidedness. It seems to confirm the scriptural warning: *maledictus homo qui confidit in homine!*

As we have already mentioned, things are undergoing a deep change. The texts of Vatican II and the Encyclic "Sacerdotalis Coelibatus" are clearly overstepping traditional notions about vocation. They take into full account all the elements of spontaneity and truth that must be developed in a human being to make him qualified to answer God's call. They all contemplate the possibility of recognizing different vocations for different states of life, and they contain a bold acknowledgement of the trustworthiness of psychological science and of the personal responsibility of the individual. Never before have theological considerations been integrated in the official documents of the church, with psychology rather than with philosophy; never before have they revealed such optimistic views of human dispositions autonomously applied to the investigation of truth. It is in view of this evolution that we feel it is possible to draw a tentative outline of the concept of vocation, going deeper in the psychological investigation connected with it.

In the new outlook it is evident that every vocation is an explicit message of Christ's love, to which man can answer but with love; it is the voice that called young Samuel in his sleep and to which the prophet answered when not yet fully awake but having already decided to obey it (1 Kings 3:3.). When answering that voice man realizes himself fully, and this perfection of his own being is unfailingly put to the advantage of others. As another example, Elias was called upon as he lay sleeping and exhausted in the desert; the bread he received from the angel was not for the sustenance of his body (III Kings 19:5 ff) but rather to put him in condition to carry out the historical and social missions that God was to entrust him with in the cave of Horeb. If we were to translate these images into psychological language, we would say that God's call must be understood as an invitation to reach at once the highest personal efficiency and the best possible psychological attitude, to be able to exert charity all the time, an everburning charity so that one may be all to all (2 Corinthians 12-13) in the widest and most concrete manner. Only this possibility is truly in keeping with the tradition of the Catholic Church, to which the Encyclic "Sacerdotalis Coelibatus" explicitly refers, because it removes the danger of "limiting the free expansion of the deepest realities of nature and Grace" (41).

Seen in this view, vocation is no longer limited and privileged in the mere sense of a virginal and ascetical consecration of one's life to God. It breaks out of all fixed schemes, reaching out to all men, to every time in their lives, independent from what might have occurred in their life before. Moses was called by God when he seemed to be far from any possible design of predestination; he was, at that time, deprived of all public authority: an exile in a foreign country, keeping the flock of his fahter-in-law, devoting his life to his wife and children, and unwilling to carry out any mission whatsoever (Exodus 2 & 3 ff.). Yet his vocation was of no lesser import than the vocation of all the judges and priests, prophets and kings of the Old Testament. On the contrary, Moses anticipates the mission of the Savior.

We are entitled therefore to say that on the psychological level a religious vocation superimposes itself onto and blends intimately with a secular vocation from which it differs only on the qualitative level. Essentially, both have to be in the service of the community, and in this frame of reference every vocation comes from God. Also, it appears that vocation becomes "the best part of all" according to the natural inclinations of the individual called to fulfill it, because any form of compulsion in this sphere destroys the possibilities of improvement. If Martha had dropped all that she was doing to follow the example of her sister Mary, she would not have attained perfection, because for her the best part was to look after the house, even though she was not to have "too many cares and troubles" about it (Luke 10:40). Nevertheless, it is evident that the part attributed to Mary is ontologically superior to that given to Martha, and that Mary had very great personal merit in having accepted and even chosen it.

Precisely because of this responsible personal search for the

best way for oneself to carry out a vocation (a search that is entrusted to the ever-fallible energies of man), all hints of intimidation, menace, or condemnation should be banned from the
contemporary view on vocation. First, a change does not
necessarily correspond to taking one's hand away from the
plough; it may merely mean that the ploughman wishes to change
direction because he has met stony ground that would spoil the
ploughshare were he to continue in the same furrow; the furrow
will be straighter and deeper in the new direction, and the
ploughing will not be abandoned. Besides, God allows His
children to seek and choose their way freely. Whenever they may
make mistakes in their honest search, He does not punish them
for that; His charity abounds precisely where man fails, and the
Mass for the Holy Heart is full of references to this consoling
reality. Thus in the *Tractus* for *Septuagesima* it is said: "He does
not treat us as our sins deserve, does not exact the penalty of our
wrong–doing " (Psalm 102:10); in antiphon of the offertory for
Easter "Thou hast not found any pleasure in burnt sacrifices, in
sacrifices for sin" (Psalm 39:7).

In this modern view of vocation it would seem that stress is
laid on the exercise of "charity" as the human answer to God's
call and on a congruency between the two interlocutors, instead of
an aspiration to do "what is absolutely the best thing." Even if
the "best" in *itself* is pointed out by Christ, it is always bound to
be relative to each of us in *respect to our individual forces*. If this
elementary principle is overlooked, if anyone's powers are
strained to the utmost under compulsion to do what is "best"
against one's own nature, there is always the risk of bringing
about the very worst. This principle is very clearly set forth in n.6
of "Presbiterorum Ordinis" where it says: "The faithful are to be
guided by the Holy Spirit to develop each one of his own specific
call, according to the Holy Gospel, to practice operative charity,
to exercise the liberty wherewith Christ has made us free." In this
set of rules full importance is still being given to the exterior
"signs" of a religious vocation, but profound respect to be paid
to "the natural exigencies [of the subject] in harmony with God's
will" is underlined to make sure that it will be possible for anyone

to "carry out in a Christian spirit one's task in the community" (ibid).

There is great distance between the concept of vocation centered on the individual's private relationship with God and this new concept into which "the others" enter in their full right in the interrelation between man and God. There is a definite change toward a new mental attitude in which a religious vocation is seen not as a personal privilege but as a service, an alliance in a properly "ecclesial" dimension. Thanks to this rediscovery of the dynamic charitable nature of a vocation which is given by God and returns to God through one's self-donation to others, its realization cannot omit the most possibly precise evaluation of the physical and moral suitability of the subject, so as to help him adjust his own natural and psychological predisposition to the kind of vocation he will choose. All this, it is to be noted, has the character of a "very strict duty, under pain of damaging results for those who may believe they have a religious vocation, and for the Church itself" (Enc. Sac. Coe., 64).

The plan for a psychological selection of priests and members of religious orders, already boldly launehed in 1936 in North America by Father Thomas Verner Moore in his book *Insanity in Priests and Religious,* appears today to have been fully accepted, as already sanctioned in art. 33 of the *Statuta Generalis* of the Holy Congregation of Religious annexed to the Apostolic Constitution *Sedes Sapientiae* dated 31/5/56 and quoted in a more recent instruction of the same Congregation (2/2/61). In addition, it has developed into an actual vocational guidance centered on a psychological investigation carried as deeply as possible, which, as has been established by the Council, is to be made on the "right intention and the free will of the candidates, on their spiritual, moral and intellectual suitability, on their necessary physical and mental fitness [so that] if the worthy are accepted, those found unsuitable should be timely and paternally directed towards other professions, and helped to devote themselves to Laical Apostolate, in the full knowledge of their Christian vocation" (Optatamtotius 6).

The most important aspect of the consideration given to personality dynamics in the assessment and direction of vocations is clearly exemplified by the fact that although maintaining unaltered the principles of social and physical unfitness established in the Code of Canon Law regarding the ordainment of priests, the rules concerning mental health have been widened. Whereas in the past only serious states of psychosis were considered, it appears evident that the rules are now extended to emotional maladjustment, neurotic impediments and all those resistances that may not be apprehended at first sight, but which can be ascertained through a psychological diagnosis obtained through an investigation carried out not merely on the surface but also in the depth of the personality. This is what we are authorized to believe in art. 33 of the General Statutes of the Holy Congregation of Religious, where anamnesis is explicitly referred to as an instrument of investigation. Now, anamnesis is not only a collection of biographical and clinical data, but it became the main tool of depth analysis as well.

In actual practice, among the causes of impediment or invalidity of ordination, besides the concept of oppression from the outside (viz. of a social factor that may unduly sway a vocation) another concept is slowly gaining ground, that of oppression from the inside which takes into account the unconscious pressures exerted by psychoneurotic factors. This is the domain of psychoanalysis. The distortions these factors may originate, either in camouflaging a genuine vocation or in reifying a nonexistent one, the manner in which they operate in the light of psychoanalytic investigation, the precise limits such an investigation may not overstep when applied to a religious vocation that has already matured into ordination or consecrated secularity, all are the subject of the second part of this chapter. Some possible solutions of the problem are also discussed.

Results of the Analysis

Doubtlessly, psychoanalysis can throw light on the lines of mental processing along which a vocation, naturally oriented in one direction, has been unnaturally structured in another. It is unthinkable to make here a systematic description of all possible

alternatives, yet it is necessary and probably sufficie͟
two very typical manners of living a vocation that are, ͟
point, opposed to each other. These are the ways that, in ͟͟
wording of Summa Theologica, are called in religion and outside
the religious state.

The problem may be that of a person who, although
naturally inclined to matrimony, believes he has a vocation for a
life of religious consecration. To this purpose, we can see that
there are at least three dynamic lines that psychoanalysis can ob-
jectivate. We now describe them, starting from a very superficial
level and going progressively deeper. Of course, we are far from
thinking that all subjects can be sorted out strictly according to
these lines.

The first dynamic line appears to be mainly a motivation of
achievement, that is, the desire to be more successful than other
people, to rise higher in a scale of absolute values, to gain
superiority that is not assumed or destined to come to an end and
will endure to the end of time, thus securing for oneself, already in
this world, "a hundredfold" (Matthew 19:29). Having opted for
"the best part of all that which shall never be taken away" (Luke
10:42) may really be a strong incentive to choose a religious
vocation, even if it means thwarting a natural orientation towards
the so-called common life.

> One patient, who was troubled by a problem at this level and had
> chosen a "life of consecration", had a dream that he was among a
> group of people. He was on the shoulders of one of them, strad-
> dling his neck and looking down on all the others, making the men
> carry him where he wanted.

At n.58 of the Encyclic *Sacerdotalis Coelibatus,* this possibility of
unsuitability for a religious life is perfectly described as "pride of
being different from other people."

At a deeper level, the desire to emerge seems to find its roots
in a feeling of social inferiority. It is tainted with group rivalry
and a social prejudice. Not infrequently one finds in such subjects the oneiric image of groups of people dressed in white as a
mark of privilege, in contrast with others dressed in dark colors.

The subject views the former as a symbol of a life of consecration to God and feels it is a "status" superior to the lot of ordinary people.

Everybody knows how in the past "laics" were emotionally "lived" by the clergy as second-class people. In the Middle Ages, they were even considered as between animals and real men, people endowed with one right only: that of receiving the sacraments. This attitude, which has ceased to exist today, may, however, still account for a latent drive to social superiority connected with priesthood.

At a third and yet deeper level, the motivation to achievement may assume the negative aspect of an escape from failure. In such cases the orientation toward a life in religion may be founded on a deep, latent, yet very real fear of one's deficient virility. In fact, in today's dynamic civilization, a wider knowledge of psychological laws and the notion of matrimonial incapacity deriving from psychological causes have become generalized. Young men are often haunted by the fear of a possible impotence on their part, which is not the last motive prompting some of them to have premarital experiences they consider rightful and necessary to make sure of their own efficiency. There are other young men, however, who, doubting the legitimacy of such experimenting, withdraw into themselves and, by this introversion, magnify to themselves the impossibility of their fitting in suitably with the reality of facts. Thus they keep aloof from matrimony; their fears of impotence grow stronger and stronger and, for some of them, a religious life may seem a providential way out of a torturing, unconscious conflict.

One patient, a priest, had had to view in the course of his duties, the film by De Seta "un uomo a meta" (*Half a man*) in an unexpurgated issue. In this film the sexual inhibitions of a young man loved by a woman and unable to possess her are emphatically dwelt on. In the course of psychoanalysis the patient, when telling about this experience (which he had found very upsetting), stressed, with relief, the fact that, luckily for him, being a priest, he would not have to face such problems. Besides, it was precisely thanks to that that he had never had to worry about his own deficiencies.

A second line along which an abnormal mental process may proceed to the reification of a religious vocation on a defensive basis, can be referred to the motivation of power. At a surface level this motive takes shape as a possibility of exerting authority over or at least control of other people, giving one a higher position than would be granted by the person's own social, intellectual or even physical qualifications. This power libido undoubtedly could be better satisfied and therefore more frequently indulged in, in the past when the church, then exerting a temporal dominion, easily degenerated into a hierarchy of powers. Luckily this is no longer the case to the same extent and manner. Yet the striving toward a better and higher social standing by advancement in the church still exists. The mere fact that the title and status of "prince" goes with that of cardinal, and that there is an ever-present possibility of getting, through ecclesiastical promotion, to partake in organizational or financial administrative activity, may still be very alluring for anyone who has strong power motivations.

Through a more subtle dynamic—which also has been losing much ground in recent times—control over others can be exerted within the compass of spiritual direction. This pedagogical institution, created by the church after the Council of Trent, which, doubtlessly, has reaped plenty of good fruit, has also, unfortunately, enabled some individuals to satisfy their power drives. These drives, although deeply hidden and ignored by the "director" himself, motivated him to dominate the inner life of his penitents. The latter were fully aware of such dependence and, for those who accepted it with candor and humility, the outward results, in the past, were possibly good, as it sometimes offered the opportunity of fulfilling themselves in humble service in some social welfare activity.

A priest in a mountain village, an excellent parish priest by the way, a man of high spiritual qualities and remarkable pastoral capacities, had been for quite a long time acting as spiritual adviser to a young woman. It so happened that the penitent had a slight lapse in the moral order which caused her to feel very uneasy in her relations with the priest. At this point she had a dream that she was running away from the village, down along the road to the plain yet, when she had already gone a long distance, at a turning of the road, she suddenly saw the parish priest looking down at her from the top of the hill. He stretched an arm in her direction; the arm grew longer and longer till at last it took her up and brought her back to him.

It must be said that in actual fact the priest in question had no qualms in intruding into the most intimate level of the psychic life of the people he "directed," to the point of transforming confession, as my patient put it, "into a real psychoanalysis."

Another priest acted far more emphatically. He had made it a point to orient a group of young girls towards a medical career because he wanted them to go, later, as lay missionaries to the Far East, where the need for trained medical staff was indeed very great. The methods used by this priest with his flock were, however, extremely unorthodox: they ranged from hard driven dialectic insistence, to imposition and intimidation. Till at last, one day, madly out of patience with one of his penitents who revealed some reluctance to follow his advice, he slapped her face and knocked her about with fisticuffs.

At a deeper level, the drive to power is marked by an all-pervasive feeling of doubt, by the fear that other people may behave contrary to expectations, by a suspicion of betrayal. At a certain degree of intensity, still within the limits of normality, this motivation may shape itself as a systematic diffidence as regards the possibility of "holding" other people, therefore as a withdrawal from any situation that may expose one to this danger.

This orientation, too, may seriously jeopardize the possibility of being married and may, instead, push one toward a life in religion. Actually, the life of a couple, bound together by the formal seal of indissolubility, increases enormously the possibility of a subjective defection of the other party and everybody looks on marriage, at least at the beginning, as a chance to be taken.

Therefore, the hesitating person who is not sure of himself when faced by the problem of getting married, feel that he is absolutely unable to make up his mind. How can he trust himself to another person, giving her the whole of his life? Is it not much safer to avoid such a risk? And is it not true that one may seek refuge in a highly commendable way by entering into a definite relationship with God? A religious consecration is, in fact, "certain": it is a solemn covenant that will never be broken because the other party is always faithful. He is the one of whom Isaias sang "faithfulness [shall be] the strength that girds him" (11:5), and this certainty is reassuring.

> A young man, who functioned in this way, had been hesitating to consecrate himself to God in a life of celibacy, yet his doubts were suddenly swept away when his director told him that "all the men and all the women in the world were ready to betray him, the only one who never betrayed was Jesus!"

"Power," lastly, can be exerted, at a yet deeper level, following a dynamic that may seem paradoxical but which has been precisely identified by psychoanalysis, namely the fear of being crushed. Power libido can, in fact, be interpreted as a defense reaction to the intolerable pressure of other people's power. The power libido tries to attain its aim by pushing the subject to participate as much as possible in the life of those in power, thence to attain a place where he, too, may exercise authority. However, in many subjects this reaction mechanism fails, and in the face of failure a pervasive feeling of guilt sets in. The subject feels that he has to "pay" for something, that he has committed faults for which he has to amend. He finds relief in the repetition of expiatory actions he tries to perform with untiring zeal.

In such cases to enter into religion may seem to be the perfect, and perhaps the only means of atoning for one's guilt. In a large number of cases the motive that suggested the choice of a life of religious consecration shaped itself in this way, especially in the case of women. Sometimes the remembrance of sexual play performed in childhood, perhaps even only in imagination, causes such a "flight into virtue."

> A religious, who lived with great zeal his spiritual life, discovered, through analysis, that one of the fundamental reasons of his consecration to God was derived from a particular guilt-dynamic; his

parents lived for a long time away from the Church, in a relationship which, against their will, was that of "public sinners". At long
last they had been able to regularize their situation and had been
readmitted into the Church. The subject had then felt that he was
"compelled" to choose the most difficult and most meritorious
things to do, and he had offered himself to God to "pay the debt of
his parents."

Doubtfulness, which is well expressed by shutting and opening
alternatively as in a sphinteric action (Erikson); the experience of
a feeling of being crushed, which, unconsciously, shapes itself as
the treatment to which faeces are submitted to when being pressed
out of the bowels (Freud), appears to be condensed in dreams that
would otherwise admit of no explanation.

A nun was, in the course of psychoanalysis, investigating her
belonging to the Order she had chosen. At that time vows had to be
renewed, following a complicated ceremony, at the foot of an altar
placed in a very impressive little church. She was deeply troubled
because she kept on dreaming that she was in that very Church and
that a W.C. was standing where the altar should have been. . . .

Actually, the patient in question was living in an order where
diffidence and lack of sympathy reigned. The struggle for power
was intense, and in her deeper association she identified herself,
or parts of herself, with the contents of the bowels.

Lastly, there is a third parameter of mental functioning that
may induce one to choose the religious state instead of the more
usual one of matrimony. It is the so-called affiliation motivation,
the need to belong to someone or to something that may give
reassurance to the subject of his wretchedness. One seeks to
"belong" because one feels defenseless, threatened, lonely, and
misunderstood. The greater and the more imposing the body or
the person chosen as a protector, the better the longing for "affiliation" is fulfilled. Mother's womb offers and sums up in-
superably in its historical reality as well as in immediate perception, these protective functions.

Of all social groups that may offer similar characteristics the
church may appear the most reassuring. It presents itself to man's

eyes like a great and powerful society, backed by thousands of years of history, destined to last forever through all the vicissitudes of time. It has a divine origin and a theandric nature; what harbor may seem safer for anyone who is afraid of life? In addition, the church is viewed as a mother. One of its most eminent figures, one often taken as a symbol of the church itself, is Mary, the mother by definition. Obviously, all these aspects offer an important possibility of gratification to the affiliation motive, to the need of feeling safe. One may safely think that depth motivations of this kind have moved some priests, such as the Don Abbondio so masterfully described by A. Manzoni in his famous novel *The Betrothed,* to enter the church.

At the level of superficial symbolism, affiliation is satisfied by participation in the life of a community, especially in an atmosphere of cooperation, by choir singing, church music, liturgical ceremonies, and so on. All these things exert a powerful suggestion, so much that some people, at times, feel in a sort of ocean of bliss, and feel merged with the other participants and at one with the divinity. Nothing can, they think, compare with this blissfulness approaching Nirvana, and certainly not a family life!

Affiliation is, besides, fulfilled in anticipation by the perspective of belonging one day to the number of the white-robed blessed "these are the Lamb's attendants, wherever he goes" (Apoc.14:4.); because they "were ransomed from the earth, these have kept their virginity undefiled by the touch of women" and they are, therefore "the first fruits of mankind"—a highly suggestive prophecy, which goes well with the parable of the wise virgins that escorted the bridegroom to the wedding (Matthew 25:10), in contrast with the foolish ones that were left out.

The dynamic of affiliation is, however, much wider and deeper than might be expected. The findings of psychoanalysts of the Melanie Klein school, repeatedly corroborated by clinical experience, have proven that the need of a mother-relation that lasts into adult life always includes hidden elements of hostile feelings and reveals libidinal impulses that have failed to merge with the hostile ones (splitting). Even at the very beginning of mental development the mother is the object of both love and hatred and the feeling of safety that she gives is mingled with the fear of losing her love so that she is in never-ending succession entirely good and entirely bad.

This splitting process may still be operating in the link that is established between an adult and the church at least in part, and as in early childhood. In such cases the church is lived as a mother: sometimes good, sometimes bad, at times loved and other times feared and opposed.

Only when this splitting has been overcome, does the process of mental maturity begin, and the individual passes from the state of body–ego to that of relational ego. The persistence of an "unfused" emotional relationship with the church may, therefore, cause some form of mental regression.

There are people who despise married life because the only emotional value they can appreciate is "belonging" as closely as possible to the church, which seems to them easier if they remain unmarried. Not unlike those who do not marry so as not to break up with mother, who, they feel, offers much safer moorings than any wife, they strive to be ever more fully accepted by the church. This desire of approval is, in reality, essentially egoistic.

Actually, however, real progress for any member of the church can only be achieved in terms of a spiritual identification with Christ. This implies an ever-growing charity and loving care for others. In the above regressive dynamic, on the contrary, the main preoccupation of the subject is with himself; progress is seen only as stepping up in the hierarchy of the church or in the acquisition of an attitude of uncompromising, strict, observance of the letter of the law and in exacting undeviating conformity in other people, all of which implies lack of charity.

It must also be mentioned that the persistence of both the ego as body and of splitting have the unpleasant consequence that some part of the body or the whole of it, may become the representation of the "bad mother"—of all that is bad in contrast with the rest of the body or with the spirit, the latter seen as the seat of all that is good. Thus we have those penitential excesses, described in psychoanalytic literature as moral masochism, to be interpreted as a furtuer instrument of regressive mother seeking, as Mara Palazzoli Selvini has so well proved in her works on mental anorexia and dysmorphophobias.

> One patient had consecrated himself to God in the state of secular celibacy; not long before that he had had to undergo medical treatment for some patches of psoriasis which had broken out on his arms. These seemed to have been put under control. When talking about his future with his spiritual adviser, it appeared that he was firmly convinced that "he knew what to expect if ever he was to be guilty of defection"; he had no doubt that his body would be covered all over with psoriasis!

The mental and practical attitude of the Pharisees repeatedly condemned by our Lord, the acts of fanatics of all times, the inconceivable abuses of the Spanish Inquisition and the excesses of asceticism censured by Pope Benedict XIV are many instances of the ambivalence of those who enacted them while belonging to the Church. Their asserted faith to the creed and their declared purpose to preserve the integrity of it were in reality intermingled, blended with, and contradicted by homicidal aggression against the church in the person of its founder, its members or themselves. The obstination with which such lines of action are generally justified and pursued is, moreover, a confirmation of the strange pleasure and the emotional gratification they grant to those who follow them, strengthening them in their conviction that they are thus carrying out a mission entrusted to them by God's call.

These things are no longer possible nowadays, and Vatican II has definitely closed the door to their return. Deep inside some subjects it is still possible, however, to discover feelings of hostility accompanying a too primitive affective adhesion to the church. A religious consecration structured on such lines has tokens of deep fear of the church, of the ecclesiastical hierarchy, of God Himself insofar as they all become the targets on which to transfer by projection one's own hostile feelings.

This fear, of course, has nothing to do with the filial reverence offered as a tribute to God, which is *initium sapientiae*. The former is of a neurotic nature, and may lead to the most unexpected developments in which the sacred is amazingly mixed with the profane. One of the most interesting of these developments is that which may be termed a challenge to God through revenge-submission. One submits to God as one would to one's despotic and very severe father, who forbids all sexual activities, that is, a castrating father; yet the adhesion to the church, which implies a celibate life, is, by reaction, "libidinized" to the point of constituting a revenge, on the level of male competition between father and son. The life of consecrated celibacy, thanks to the spiritual fecundity it confers, becomes the life of a super-father when compared to that of one's natural father, and this is achieved all the better the more exactly it is performed. However, to be thus a super-father is also like openly challenging God the Father and taking the Mother away from Him.

It is also strange, but consequential, to see how this challenging attitude may at times materialize in a marked interest for women who are or who have been in religion, or for members of the Catholic Action, all of whom may become extraordinarily interesting on the affective level.

> A doctor, specialized in gynaecology, had privately consecrated himself to God; yet he was mainly interested in becoming medical adviser to cloisters and, in general, in having patients that were virgins. He was very zealous from the professional point of view and actually also very able. Analysis revealed that he got a very high "secondary gain" from his work which was for him an unconscious but very real instrument of challenge; he had, in this way, gathered together for himself what may be termed a real harem of "brides of the Lord."

Things may not be very different when the challenger is a woman. In that case the objects of libidinal interest are priests or religious.

Needless to say, on this level we find in all the mental dynamisms described above that challenge implies also competition and desire of achievements, power, and fear of retaliation. The affiliation motive seems here, instead, to have faded out. However, challenge has been included in our description because it synthesizes a primitive, deep compromise, containing in a nutshell the different motives where they receive color and qualification from an intense hostility of oral character, which could be traced to the archaic relationships with the mother.

Discussion

Psychoanalytic depth investigation lays bare the roots of human motivations, both of everyday actions and of the drives that underlie the important choices in life. In the preceding pages we have mentioned the results psychoanalysis may attain when it boldly undertakes the study of a religious vocation. We have seen that it is thus possible to evidence some defense structures, namely, its artificial character. In fact, the motives of achievement, power, and affiliation correspond, respectively, to the phallic, anal, and oral mechanisms in the psychoanalytic theory.

These or similar processes may cover up a true religious vocation, leading the subject by reaction-formation to a matrimonial destiny that is not the real one he was meant for. We want, however, to focus on the value of a religious vocation that reveals itself, through analysis, as the result of an unconscious compromise. In such cases we have a religious vocation structured around a neurotic axis. Can we come to the conclusion that such a vocation is essentially spurious, and therefore, it is *not* a religious vocation? It is impossible to answer this question in the affirmative.

As we pointed out in the introduction, a religious vocation must not and cannot be considered as a process in which only natural psychic forces are concerned; it must be viewed as a meeting point between human availability and divine intervention. The discovery of distortions, even deep ones, on the human side does suffice to solve the problem, insofar as it would imply a judgment on, and a decision about, that supernatural variable which cannot be compared, either on the ontological or on the technical level (Mailloux-Ancona), to the psychological variable.

In other words, the presence of a genuine religious vocation is not at all incompatible with some elements that may markedly deform it on the psychological plane and consequently create the impression that it is not genuine. The church does not ignore this occurrence, which it has known from its very beginnings. It was, in fact, a desire to *"sit in glory"* above all others that prompted James and John to make a bold and irresponsible request (Mark 10:35 ff). The thirst for *power* was lurking in the hearts of the apostles, disappointed because through their doubting they could not cast out the devils, that is, exert power over them (Matthew 17:20). Their repeated, uncomprehending demand of restoring an earthly *kingdom* (Acts 1:6), Peter's impertinent expostulations (Matthew 16:23 ff), and Judas's finding pretexts to justify his inordinate love of money: all these are plain traits of a neurotic character that set in *after* an unmistakable call from the Lord.

We can hypothesize that at the beginning the apostles had answered God's call prompted by such human motives, but then the Holy Ghost intervened to set order for those who, unlike Judas, had made possible His operating in them through "prayer and fasting" (Mc.9:28). This possibility seems to be even more clearly confirmed by the parable of the marriage of the King's son (Matthew 22:3 ff) where the invited guests failed to come and therefore were found unworthy. Those that "are on the highways," who have to be brought in, are really "called," even if they are not perfect. All they have to do is show their willingness to cooperate by donning the suitable garment which gives them full right to partake of the wedding feast.

Not even the discovery, through psychoanalysis, of a natural orientation toward heterosexuality is sufficient to solve this problem. Fundamentally, the problem concerns a reality that it is not merely psychological. Therefore, even when light has been thrown on it at that level, it still has to be solved at the source of subjective dynamic; namely in the light of the principle of charity which, as we have seen, dominates the modern concept of religious vocation.

To sum up, psychoanalysis allows us to identify, sometimes with brutality but always efficaciously, the defense structures built around the vocational orientation of a subject that mask, warp, or simulate its genuineness. This work can be carried out boldly by a believer without fear that he will find himself compelled to interfere with some extremely delicate processes of conscience tuned in with a supernatural dynamic. The only warning that seems to be reasonable is that the secular research should not take place without an accompanying progress in the spiritual life through prayer and the exercise of charity. When in this inner atmosphere of perfect balance all defensive structures have been outflanked and left behind, the subject is able to reach out to the very bottom of himself. In the stark silence of all things, he becomes able to recognize the true vocational orientation of his life, and he is really free to follow the destiny he feels is his.

In this careful examination, into which no one can presume to interfere because it takes place as a dialogue between the subject and his conscience (by now cleared of all spurious matter) and in his search of God, the way the subject intends to follow may be precisely the one on which he was already set: the very life of religious consecration followed so far, although *then* weighted down with neurotic deformations of compromise, which have *now* been swept away. We are then called to witness the wonderful event, which one would not know whether to consider natural or supernatural, of the subject who resumes and accepts fully the old plan which he recognizes as fully valid, and integrates it in a manner that has all the distinguishing marks of liberty, inner contentment, and readiness to comply. Life is taken up again with renewed energies and genuinity, above all with a progressive development in the domain of charity.

The result of the analysis may, of course, be totally different. Having got rid of all tethers and deforming illusions, the subject can be led to realize that the orientation he had thus far followed was altogether contrary to his existential reality. He may recognize himself as oriented toward rearing a family, not because he has discovered he possesses unmistakable heterosexual traits, but because he finds in the deep recesses of his being a clear native matrimonial vocation that had long been stifled and hidden even to himself. At this point his possibilities of action are still, necessarily, to be placed in function of a definite plan of charity, as has been pointed out in the first part of this chapter.

In fact, in the restrictive and judicial frame of a vocation centered only on a private relationship with God and viewed as a great privilege to be preserved at all costs, the way begun in a "religious" direction and then discovered unsuitable, was, in the past to be followed nonetheless to the bitter end (*fac ut voceris*). On the contrary, according to a conception of vocation inspired by charity, which implies living one's life as a donation to other people, not only is a change considered possible, but it is, in all fairness, bound to happen.

Obviously, "to follow on" may mean giving one's formal adhesion to an abstract loyalty, open to the acceptance of many defense compromises. It may mean wanting to keep the secret sources of very high secondary gains of a neurotic nature so as to manage for oneself an escape from the reality of a life fully lived, beginning with the risk inherent in a total change of old schemes. Obstinacy to keep to the old ways may be the result of a process of regression and therefore culpable. It may be tantamount to keeping buried many, sometimes even all, one's talents, at the very moment when the church has great need to be able to make use of all its followers. It would therefore seem that the scriptural warning *sapientis est mutare consilium* fits very well in this case!

Evidently, the possibility of such change is easier, and the duty to perform it more acceptable, when the person involved is only privately consecrated to God, when he is a member of some secular institution, is a novice, a student in a theological seminary who has not yet received major orders, a nun who has taken only temporary vows, and, generally speaking, any of those whose state is not considered irrevocable.

The whole question is far more complex when it concerns a priest or the member of some religious order whose consecration has had a public character and whose life is lived in a wide net of pastoral duties and connections stamping him in a way that the faith of many people finds a prop in their loyalty to the vows they have taken. Here the common good enters into play, and charity has one more variable so that a new integration is needed to untie the knot. It is evident that such integration can take place, basically, only with the juridical intervention of the Ecclesiastical Authority who, alone, has power to "bind and loose" (Matthew 16:19 ff). Still, some considerations can be made also on the level of psychic dynamics.

In the first place, the church maintains the inalienable right to say the last word in the solution of such delicate problems, because it is, at this level, the only authorized interpreter. Only the church is entitled to judge and is in possession of all the elements needed to do so in each particular case. Only the church may know the pastoral opportunity of granting a dispensation from priestly duties. The Church's present orientation in this regard shows, it must be said, an admirable sensibility in understanding, accepting, and dispensating as the case may be. As it is said in the encyclic "Sacerdotalis Coelibatus," the "investigation of the motives" of ordination has been extended to "other very serious causes, not provided for in the existing Canon Law, and which may leave room for real and well-grounded doubts as regards the full liberty and responsibility of the candidate to the priesthood and to his fitness to that state, so as to set free all those whom a careful judicial trial may demonstrate to be really unsuited to the office" (84).

Therefore it can be said that the church today is ready to recognize the possibility of a "past evaluation which was not sufficiently prudent in assessing the qualities of the candidate to the priesthood" (ibid, 83), and it is certainly not held back from carrying out this intention by a possible "penury of clergy" "Optatam Totius" (6).

Now, if a mere psychodiagnosis suffices to discover the mistake that has been made, we can presume that even better results could be obtained by a correct psychoanalysis that, besides its therapeutical effects, has unequalled *diagnostic values*. Within this pastoral and juridical framework, at the very root of it, it is now possible to consider the human, the individual problems existing deep inside the personality of those who, invested with priestly dignity, are brought, in the course of a well–conducted psychoanalysis, to discover that their existential orientation is another one. They may be made fully aware that their original vocation was, unmistakably, directed towards family life.

How will it be possible for them to realize all the same the greater charity? How will they be able to give all its due weight to the common good? It seems to be altogether impossible to give an answer that may be systematically "releasing" on the psychological level. The extension of the sphere of the pastoral activities of the subject, his capacity to keep a sufficient balance even in a permanently frustrating situation, the efficiency and quality of his activities as a priest so far (no matter how structured from the point of view of depth psychology), all may have had such results that it might be advisable for the subject to hold on faithfully to the old course, even if he does no longer feel that that was the life he was really meant for. In such cases, it goes without saying, charity will not be attained directly through the full and best application of one's energies and personal responsibilities as in the family; but it will be attained indirectly, but as surely, through the loyal acceptance of a way of life that will, inevitably, offer an example to many and prove full of very high spiritual values. Thus the parable of the marriage feast of the King's son to which his servants brought in "all they could find, rogues and honest men together" (Matthew 22:10) and all were welcome, as long as they wore the wedding-garment, finds its full realization.

It is also evident that in all such cases the decision must be absolutely personal and freely taken, and that it must come before any contacts are made with the church's authorities, who are thus greatly helped by being exempted from the duty of pronouncing a judgment which, necessarily, can only be made from the outside.

Conclusion

The church, as it presents itself today, renovated and as the true bride of Christ, is determined to sympathize with the many needs of modern man, and prefers in our times to use "the medicine of mercy, rather than the scourge of strictness" (opening speech at the first session of Vatican II). For this very reason, although maintaining unaltered faith to the principles and directions of its founder, it will endeavor, more than it ever did in the past, to understand both on the surface and in depth, the human promptings of its followers, both priests and laics. Therefore, it looks benignantly with trust and hope toward "the profane sciences, psychology and sociology in the first place" (Gaudium et Spes, 62).

It must also not be forgotten that the opportunities offered by psychological diagnosis, particularly by psychoanalysis, have not always existed and that even today few are those who can avail themselves of these services. There are even some who would altogether debar analysis to the religious. In fact, although the council has more than once emphasized the suitability of cultivating the germs of a religious vocation "in harmony with the rules of a sane psychology" (Optatam Totius, 3) and despite the fact that it has said "psychology offers to man the possibility of a better self-knowledge" (Gaudium et Spes, 5), still not many are ready to accept a systematic use of psychodiagnostic tests, which are considered suitable only in very few cases of "unmistakable necessity" (International Congress of the H. Congregation of Religious, Rome, December 10th-16th, 1961). This applies even more strictly to analysis.

On the other hand, the teachings of the Gospel, such as those we have quoted, show very clearly how similar problems were dealt with in the past. Humble personal cooperation and recourse to "prayer and fasting" have authoritatively been described by our Lord as the most suitable instruments to bring about the adjustment of a vocation which might be imperfect because spurious on its human side, an adjustment which psychoanalytic technique cannot bring about if it is used alone.

In this way analysis appears to be a most valuable instrument for the knowledge and advancement of man, particularly suitable to render more easy the dynamic of a spiritual vocation, but unable to oppose it, and absolutely needless only when the spirit overflows in a psychologically well-balanced subject. It has, instead, to be considered an indispensable instrument in all those cases, more and more numerous nowadays, where adjustment appears more or less difficult to attain.

It is, therefore, highly desirable, and fitting that psychologists and analysts should answer, precisely in this perspective, to the overtures the church is ready to make to them. They must meet the Church halfway, recognizing the precise limits that cannot be overstepped of the scope of their instruments of investigation when applied to problems touching on the inner life of the church, as is the case with the religious vocation of the "folk of God."

BIBLIOGRAPHY

Erikson, E. H. (1963), *Childhood and Society*. New York: Norton.

Fornari, F. (1963), *La Vita Affettiva Originaria Del Bambino*. Minalo: Feltrinelli.

Gemelli, A. (1957), La Psicologia a servizio del discernimento delle vo cazioni e della direzione spirituale dei seminari sti. *Rivista di Ascetica e Mistica, 1 & 2:* 1–27.

Gutierriz, M. M. (1968), Il contributo psicologico nell'orientamento vocazionale, alla luce dell'enciclica "sacerdotalis coe libutiis." *Orientamenti Pedagogici, 15:* 69–82.

Klein, M. (1950), *Contributions to Psychoanalysis* 1921–1945. London: Hogarth.

Mailloux, N. and Ancona, L. (1958), Unostudio degli atteggiamenti regigiosi ed un nuovo punto di vista nella psicopatologia. In *Contributi dell'Istituto di Psicologia XXI*. Milano: Vita e Pen siero, 102–111.

Moore, Th. V. (1936), Insanity in priests and religious. *Ecclesiastical Review, 95:* 485–498, 601–613.

Nodet, Cn. (1950), Considerations psychonalytiques a propos des attraits nevrotiques pour la vocation religieuse. *Supplement de la Vie Spirituelle,* 14: 280–906.

Palazzoli-Selvini, M. (1963), *L'Anoressia Mentale*. Milano: Feltrinelli.

——— (1965), Contributo alla psicopatologia del vissuto corporeo. *Archivio di Psicologia, Neurologia e Psichiatria, 26:* 344–369.

Zani, L. (1967), Vocazione sacerdotale in adolescente. *Archivio di Psicologia, Neurologia e Psichiatria, 28:* 545–550.

PART TWO

Cultural-Historical
and Ethical Issues

FATHER ALBERT PLE *counterposes* Christian Morality and Freudian Morality. *According to Father Ple, evangelical morality is based on love and mercy. "Be merciful as your heavenly Father is merciful" (LC 6: 36), in contradistinction to the insistence of the Pharisees on law and commandments. According to Freud, "morality is first and foremost a cruel restraint, imposed by civilization." It is based on "constraint imposed from outside by parental or cultural prohibitions."*

Thus the conflict is between lois et amour *(law and love). Christian morality stems from love, whereas Freud seems to believe that morality is based on law and "composed of prohibitions, restraints of the instincts and a source of obsessive guilt."*

Ple believes that a rediscovery of moral principles leads to St. Thomas Aquinas, for St. Thomas' morality was opposed to legalistic concepts. Progressive humanization of mankind is the essence of St. Thomas' moral system.

6

Christian Morality

and Freudian Morality

by

FR. ALBERT PLE, O.P.

SIGMUND FREUD HAS THE REPUTATION—ESPECIALLY AMONG THOSE
who have not read him—of being the perfidious and dangerous
advocate of a most radical immorality. He is often described as
the partisan of a total liberation of the most base sexual instincts.
Freud (1923) often had to defend himself against this accusation.
Obviously psychoanalysis, as practiced and taught by Freud, does
not preach or practice immorality. Moreover, Freud's own life
sets an example of decency. One must, nevertheless, admit that
Freud's concept of morality is hardly acceptable for a disciple of
Christ. Must it, then, necessarily lead to a complete rejection of
Freud's teachings as incompatible with the Gospel? It seems to
me, quite to the contrary, that Freud's views can stimulate the
reflection of Christian moralists, and that psychoanalysis could
even enrich the work of theologians at the same time, fostering a
healthy moral growth in Christians.

A Catholic theologian like myself can adopt the remark
which Pastor Pfister confided to his friend, Freud, after reading
Freud's *Civilization and its Discontents:*

> What I experience upon reading your book is similar to the im-
> pressions one receives on an excursion into a mountainous coun-
> tryside. There emerges a gorge that one doesn't explore and, behind

it, a vast valley opens. At many a laconic sentence one feels pushed to look further and one feels certain of discovering an important "terra incognita" (Freud, 1966, p. 186).

I would like to advance here some reflections of a theologian, as a party to the discovery of this "terra incognita" perceived by Pfister.

Evangelical morality and the moral concepts of Freud appear to be far apart and irreconcilable. It is, possible, however, for these two moral systems to embark on a dialogue in a climate of scientific honesty that, ultimately, might prove fruitful.

My personal conviction has been strengthened by the Second Vatican Council, which solemnly expresses the wish that "specialists in the sciences, notably those biological, medical, social and psychological...by a concerted sharing of their studies" (Concile Vatican, no. 52) bring their contribution to the task the Catholic church has undertaken, namely, a dialogue with the world and science.

Evangelical Morality

The man who becomes a disciple of Christ is invited to change his habits and their underlying motives. He is supposed to love God and his neighbor as himself (Mc 12: 28-34; Lc 10: 25-37).

The "new commandment," says St. John (John 13:35) is at the same time "the old commandment which you have received from the beginning" (1 John 2, 7), since it was already prescribed from the beginning of revelation (Leviticus: 19: 18: Deuteronomy 6; 5; 24; 19-21; Os 6;6). On this point, as on the others, Christ has not come to abolish the old law, but to complete and fulfill it (Matthew 5:17). It is this love of God and of neighbor that permits the accomplishment of the Law "in spirit and in truth" (John 4:24).

This importance is given to such a love, because God is love incarnate (1 John 4:24) and man has been created "in his image and likeness" (Genesis 1:26), that is, it is in loving as much as is possible for a creature in whom the Spirit of God resides, that man responds to his vocation: "Be merciful as your heavenly Father is merciful" (Lc 6, 36), which is to say "perfect" (Mt 5, 48).

The mistake of the Pharisees was to go one better than the written law, by multiplying the prescriptions and thus stifling this spirit of love, which alone give life, wheras "the letter kills" (Corinthians 3:6).

If the Pharisees are condemned—and how severely—by Christ, it is not because they have acquitted the tithe to the minute details, but for their having neglected "justice and love of God" (Luke 11:42). Their legalistic zeal aimed, unconsciously no doubt, at a self-satisfaction, coupled with a scorn for others that, blinding them to their misery and their state of a sinner, shut them off from the gift of divine mercy, the sole source of salvation (Luke 18:9–14). Thus it is that, to reuse the very expressions of St. Paul, ex-Pharisee, "it has happened that the precept, made for life, leads me to death (Romans 7:10).

On the contrary, the "new" commandment reattaches all the law to love of God and neighbor (Matthew 22, 40, etc.). There is no life unless there is love: "He who loves not remains in death" (1 John 3, 15), and mutual love is the criterion of true disciples of Christ (John 13, 35).

To be sure, there are other commandments (those of the Gospel, but also of the apostles and of the ecclesiastical community). To practice them in reality, one must love: "If you love me, keep my commandments" (John 14, 15).

Thus Christian ethic condemns the written law as a fundamental reference and places the accent instead on the interiority of the human heart (Matthew 15, 19), that is, on love of God. It is an ethic inspired by the Holy Sprit: "The fruit of the Spirit is charity, joy, peace, longevity, goodness, confidence in others, gentleness, self-mastery; against such things, there is no law" (Galatians 5:22-23).

It would be useful to recall this fundamental and specific truth of Christian life in order to understand well what Freud may have to tell us on morality.

Morality According to Freud

Freud's idea of morality seems, on the one hand, to be related to what he observed of the morals of his patients; on the other hand, it is influenced by Kant's concepts of morality, widespread at the end of the nineteenth century. Undoubtedly, Freud's moral concepts are related to his own personal problems, especially in regard to the connection between morality and religion.

For Freud, morality is first and foremost a cruel restraint imposed by civilization. Its source is external to the subject. Whether it is a question of the superego or of the ideal self, morality is rooted in the renunciation of instincts, in the constraint imposed from outside by parental or cultural prohibitions. The renunciation is primary:

> The situation is usually presented as though ethical requirements were the primary thing and the renunciation of instincts followed from them. This leaves the origin of the ethical sense unexplained. Actually, it seems to be the other way about. The first instinctual renunciation is enforced by external powers, and it is only this which creates the ethical sense, which expresses itself in conscience and demands a further renunciation of instincts (Freud, 1924, p. 170).

This exogenous constraint may render an account of the cruel character of morality as much through its demands as through its sanctions:

> After sublimation the erotic component no longer has the power to bind the whole of the destructiveness that was combined with it, and this is a released form of an inclination to aggression and destruction. This defusion would be the source of the general character of harshness and cruelty exhibited by the ideal—its dictatorial "Thou shalt" (Ibid, 1923, p. 54-55).

This dictatorial "Thou shalt" is found sanctioned by a superior being as clairvoyant as he is unrelenting: "But even ordinary normal morality has a harshly restraining, cruelly prohibiting quality. It is from this, indeed, that the conception arises of a higher being who deals out punishment inexorably" (ibid, p. 54).

This morality, based on renunciations of impulses, is not only the work of the superego but also of the ideal self, the one which "comprises the sum of all the limitations in which the ego has to acquiesce" (ibid, 1921, p. 131).

This freudian morality is by reference sociological; it "is based on the inevitable demands of human coexistence and not on the order of the extra-human universe" (ibid, 1966, p. 186). Incidentally, it may not be inferred from science: "To demand of science that she establish an ethic is unreasonable—ethics is a type of order to march in use for the intercourse of men among themselves" (ibid, 1928, p. 178).

Is that the entire meaning of morality? Freud forbade himself to be a moralist, and on this subject his correspondence with Pastor Pfister is revealing. He wrote to Pfister, for example, that ethics scarcely interest him and that moral beliefs do not make people better.

> Ethics is foreign to me, but you are a shepherd of souls. I do not bother my head much over the subject of good and evil; however, as a rule, I have discovered very little of "good" among men. From what I know of them, they are for the most part only rabble, whether they advocate one ethical system or another, or none at all. You may not dare say that aloud, perhaps not even think that way, although your experience of life cannot be much different from mine. If it is necessary to speak of an ethic, I profess for my part a lofty ideal, from which all other ideals known to me, deviate, as a rule, in a most distressing manner (ibid, 1918, p. 103).

Freud has scarcely elaborated his lofty ideal, not even in his self-analysis. One may wonder, nevertheless, whether it is possible to find in Freud's writings the principles of a morality that surpasses that of "average" men.

To be sure, the Christian can only be deceived by the overly easy manner in which he extricates himself from an ethic based on love of neighbor as oneself (ibid, 1930, p. 109). Indeed, Pastor Pfister was justified in declaring: "I suffer a great deal that the theologians prove to be so lamentably feeble" (ibid, 1926, p. 155). It remains that the friendly and trusting correspondence of Freud with Pastor Pfister (the only theologian who conversed with him and declared himself his disciple) is misleading: In this correspondence Freud seems totally inaccessible to the evangelist morality so dear to his friend the pastor who, alone, seems to have made headway toward Freud.

Although Freud does not appear to have tried to understand the evangelist Pfister, he does not seem to ignore a morality that goes beyond that of present day man, an ethic that is the expression of an adult ego, a morality which (quoting Auguste Comte) is not at the level of the animistic stage, nor even at the "religious" stage, but which is at the "scientific" stage: "the stage at which an individual has reached maturity, has renounced the pleasure principle, adjusted himself to reality and turned to the external world for the object of his desires" (ibid, 1913, p. 90).

This "adult" morality is undoubtedly to be sought in his ego. It seems to us, in fact, that the function Freud attributed to the ego suffices as a foundation for an authentic morality (although Freud does not seem to conceive that the basic role of the ego can have a moral character), as one may judge for example from this paragraph:

> Its (the ego) psychological function consists in raising the passage (of events) in the id to a higher dynamic level (perhaps by transforming freely mobile energy into bound energy, such as corresponds to the preconscious state); its constructive function consists in interpolating, between the demand made by instinct and the action that satisfies it, the activity of thought which, after taking its bearings in the present and assessing earlier experiences, endeavours by means of experimental actions to calculate the consequences of the course of actions proposed. In this way the ego comes to a decision on whether the attempt to obtain satisfaction is to be carried out or postponed or whether it may not be necessary for the demand by the instinct to be suppressed altogether as being dangerous (ibid, 1940, p. 119).

When one reads, for example, Pfister's letter of February 20th 1928 and Freud's response dated the following day, one sees that Freud does not reply to the Pastor's question on "the nucleus and the substance of evangelism" (Ibid. pp. 177-179).

I am inclined to think that it is in this sense that a freudian morality could be elaborated, without repudiating anything a priori of the premorality of the superego and of the ideal ego. Such a morality would establish an adult morality as a function of the ego. But it is absolutely necessary to notice that Freud has not done it and did not seem to have invested much interest in this problem. Freud's disciples however, are not forbidden to continue his work and engage in a more complete analysis of the functions of the ego.

Morality of Love or Morality of Law

The morality of the Gospel, as we have recalled, requires that one should be animated by love, by a love that responds to God's love ("He has loved me first" I John 4:19), by a love that is a source of life ("We are passed from death to life because we love our brothers" 1 John 3:14) and by a love that liberates us from sin ("Love covers a multitude of sins" 1 Paul 4:8; Luke 7:47, etc.). Morality according to Freud appears, to the contrary, to be a morality of law, composed of prohibitions, restraints of the instincts, and a source of obsessive guilt.

These two concepts of morality as love and morality as law are, by fact, incompatible. Thus it is that Paul, in giving his faith to Christ, has rejected the morality of the law based on enforcement:

> What is to be said? Could Law be a sin? Certainly not. But I have only known sin through the law. Thus I would not have known covetousness if the law had not said: "Thou shalt not covet". Seizing the opportunity, the sin produced in me all kinds of coveting, based on the commandment of the law. For, without a law, a sin is a dead thing. Formerly, in the absence of law, I was living. But the commandment came; the sin is alive but I am dead: for me, the commandment which must lead to life has been found to lead to death. The sin, seizing the opportunity, has seduced me by means of the commandment, and through it, has given me to death (Bible, 1967).

One will have recognized in this morality that leads to death Freud's ideas on morality. Now "he who is in Jesus Christ" is "liberated from the law of sin and of death" (Romans 8:2): his ways of life change and they are inspired by faith and love. And yet, it is a fact that many Catholics—not to mention Protestants (Crespy, 1967)—adhere to moral principles that seem to be closer to Freud's notions than to the evangelical morality of John and of Paul.

Where does such an infidelity come from? Undoubtedly it stems from human misery and mediocrity; one does not escape from them even though he has given his faith to Christ. Which disciple of Christ is not forced to recognize that part of himself is not yet evangelized? But there is more to it: it is a fact that the teaching of morality in the Catholic church (catechism, manuals of morality in use among seminarians, preaching, confessions, etc.) presents itself, as it has for several centuries, as a morality of the law and that it is conceived more in reference to the Ten Commandments than to charity.

The history of ethics (so little studied, alas!) can shed some light on this regrettable "involution." It is necessary to notice first that the Stoic ethic, present in the Greco-Roman culture of the first Christian centuries, has influenced the thought and the comportment of the Christian world. It is incontestable that the legalistic conception, often joined to a scorn of the human body, has played an important role not only in the platonism of the first centuries, but also in Manichaeanism, Puritanism and Jansenism.

At the beginning of the fourteenth century the ethic of the law and of duty permeated Christianity, and even today, we are still the tributaries of this influence. The first systematic synthesizer of such a conception of morality was William Ockham. For this religious theologian, whose position anticipates those of Kant and Sartre, there is no nature, neither in man, nor in God; there are only liberties. God is an absolute and unconditioned liberty (a divine nature would limit him) and man has as his destiny to conquer his liberty. Because there is no nature, morality only has as its foundation the obligation made by God to man. It is an irrational obligation without any justification in nature and in the natural desires of man (Vereecks, 1958, pp 123–143). An act has moral significance only because it is commanded, arbitrarily, by God; it is moral because it is obligatory, and this obligation is totally extrinsic to man; it is a constraint imposed by God on human liberty.

This system of Ockham has gained extraordinary vogue and acquired numerous disciples, from Gerson to Gabriel Biel (whom Luther often cites). This attitude was undoubtedly a reflection of the collective anguish that marked the fourteenth and fifteenth centuries when the black plague, the Hundred Years' War, the anarchy of political and religious institutions, and the like raged (Mollat, 1966, 218:229). Thus it is that this legalistic, casuist, formal, scrupulous attitude has prevailed and has been transmitted to our days. Freud developed his ideas of morality from this tradition, from the Kantian and bourgeois mentality of his era, and from his own observations.

It is an historical coincidence that Catholic theologians are beginning to develop the conscience and to liberate themselves, not only by a return to the sources of revelation, but also by a dialogue with the experts of the multiple sciences of man. Certain of these theologians are searching for inspiration equally from Christian moralists prior to the fourteenth century. It is my personal conviction and hope for a rediscovery of the thought of St. Thomas Aquinas .

The morality of St. Thomas is indeed radically opposed to the legalistic mentality. Inspired by Revelation and the tradition of the Greek and Latin Fathers, it rests rationally on Aristotle. I will only mention the broad outlines here (Ple, 1966). For St. Thomas, man's life is a movement, an advance: departing from God, it returns to God through acts in which he finds himself. These acts have to be specifically free, this is to say, self-determined, being enlightened at their source by a rational intelligence and an affectivity of the intelligence (which Aquinas calls the will). Thus man is a "cause of himself" and he gets his bearings from within, according to his nature. And, on the contrary, man acts in a servile manner if he is motivated by constraint or fear (of God or of men) and when he follows his (uncontrolled, not humanized) passions or his habits. There cannot be a fully moral act unless there is intelligence, love and personal involvement.

Man attains this moral level only on the day when "deliberating on himself," he finds his own way, with intelligence and love toward the absolute end he chooses for himself as a *raison de vivre*. If this end is the true one (that is, specifically human), he acts well, and this act has all the qualities of moral goodness. On the contrary, if this end is false, he sins. This absolute end that determines man's morality is the object of his love (God, himself, and neighbor) and this is also his manner of loving. Fully human love—and thus morally good—does not have for its ultimate goal the well-being or the pleasure of the one who loves. He loves because he is in love with the goodness and the beauty of that which he loves. There is an overcoming of the primitive narcissism, a relative gratuity of a love that has for expression the reality of the person.

In brief, according to St. Thomas, morality has for its dynamism, criterion, and expression the full humanization of our affective capacities. Morality consists in loving that which is good. This is to say that morality necessarily includes the search for happiness. Satisfied love is beatifying. Moral man seeks his happiness—not that this happiness, which is always subjective, is the ultimate expression of his love: it finally rests itself on the extra-subjective reality of the loved person. The fact remains that the search for one's own happiness is morally good as long as it is not the ultimate expression of one's desire. There is for St. Thomas a "beyond the pleasure principle" and this is the reality of the beloved person. Thus understood, happiness is the object of morality (St. Thomas, Commentaire).

The moral law is essentially an inner law of human development, a law inscribed in the source of his being, which is not without analogy to the DNA messenger molecule whose structure carries in it the coded principles of the future evolution of a living being. To be sure, there do exist some moral laws that are written and exterior to the subject. They are useful sociologically and individually as pedagogues are useful to children. Laws are needed to make life possible for members of a society, for educating men while facilitating their discovery of the demands of their interior law. It is necessary also to restrain "carnal men" by fear. But the *raison d'etre* of laws is to bring men to the perfection of the new law, to the law of liberty, which permits them to accomplish the prescriptions of the written laws not by obedience but "as free men, by the interior instinct of the Holy Sprit" (St. Thomas, Somme).

In this perspective, the moral offense, the sin, is not first an infraction of the written law, a refusal of the obligation imposed on man from outside (God or society). If there is sin, which is to say offense against God, this is because there is offense against man, who deliberately does not satisfy the inner obligation to wish himself to be a full man: "God is only offended by us by the act that we act against our welfare" (St. Thomas, Contra).

This welfare of man is not only that of his spirit; it is that of all his being. For St. Thomas man is not an accidental agglomeration of two heterogeneous and enemy substances: a spirit and an animal. Man is an animated body; he is substantially one. He is born an animal and he humanizes little by little. Before he is capable of acts authentically human—and thus having fully moral value—he prepares himself for it, he approaches it progressively.

Even when he has arrived at a sufficient humanization of his behavior, man remains an animal. His most superior activity remains tied to the physiological state of his body, which is even more true of his passions. Good in themselves, thinks St. Thomas, it is up to man to fully humanize them, that is to say, to integrate them (and not to kill them) by the dynamism of a superior love (that of an intelligent affectivity) on which man regulates his passions in which they participate while remaining passions.

Many other points of St. Thomas' morality ought to be added here. The reader will have noticed, I hope, St. Thomas' concern and his "health." It has a double quality. On the one hand, it lends itself to the best penetration of the evangelical leaven in human dough. On the other hand, because it starts from man, such as he is and is called to become, this morality seems to me to offer a solid base for a dialogue with Freud and his disciples.

In any case, this conception of St. Thomas manifests with force (is he not called the "common Doctor" in the Catholic church?) that one can be Catholic without adhering to a legalistic morality like that which prevailed for several centuries. It allows meaning be recognized in and given to Freud's observations and to his conception of morality, and at the same time, it permits that along with the collaboration of his disciples, a search be made as to how to devise a more authentically "human" morality that surpasses, without denying it, the primitive or neurotic determinism analyzed by Freud.

In his extraordinary study on Leonardo da Vinci Freud wrote: "It is possible that in these figures Leonardo has *denied* the unhappiness of his erotic life and has *triumphed over* it in his art" (Freud, 1910, pp 117-118). He added: "We must recognize here a degree of freedom which cannot be resolved any further by psychoanalytic means" (Ibid, 135).

This possibility, pointed out by Freud, of a victory and of a certain liberty beyond psychic determinism, seems to me an invitation to a dialogue between Freud's disciples and the Christian moralists. Such a dialogue would have a chance of being fruitful only in accepting, to be sure, the existence of infantile or neurotic morals among too many immature Catholics, but also in seeking the meaning, the place, and the development of a morality truly inspired by Christian revelation, which is summarized in this sentence of St. Paul: "A single precept contains the whole Law in its fullness: "Thou shalt love thy neighbor as thy self" (Galations 5:14).

The morality of St. Thomas Aquinas could furnish, it seems to me, an anthropological base for this dialogue between Christians and disciples of Freud.

BIBLIOGRAPHY

Constitution *L'Eglise dans le monde Concile Vatican* No. 52.

Grespy, G. (1967), *Introduction a l'ethique, Recherche d'une problematique. Etudes Theologiques et Religieuses, 2:* 91–108.

Ecumenical translation of the Bible. Alliance Biblique Universalle et Editions du Cerf, Rm 7: 7–12.

Freud, S. (1910), Leonardo da Vinci and a memory of his childhood. *Standard Edition, 11.* London: Hogarth Press, 1956.

———(1913), Totem and taboo. *Standard Edition,* 13: 1–164. London: Hogarth Press, 1955.

——— (1918), Letter of October 9, 1918 to Pfister. In *Correspondance de Sigmund Freud avec le Pasteur Pfister.* Paris: Gallimard, 1966, p. 103.

——— (1921), Group psychology and the analysis of the ego. *Standard Edition, 18:* 67–143. London: Hogarth Press, 1955.

———(1923), The ego and the id. *Standard Edition,* 19: 12-68. London: Hogarth Press, 1961.

——— (1924), The economic problem of masochism. *Standard Edition, 19:* 157–172. London: Hogarth Press, 1961.

——— (1928), Letter of February 24, 1928 to Pfister. In *Correspondance de Sigmund Freud avec le Pasteur Pfister.* Paris: Gallimard, 1966, p. 178.

——— (1929), Letter of February 16, 1929 to Pfister. In *Correspondance de Sigmund Freud avec la Pasteur Pfister.* Paris: Gallimard, 1966, p. 186.

——— (1930), Civilization and its discontents. *Standard Edition, 21:* 59–145. London: Hogarth Press, 1961.

——— (1940), An outline of psychoanalysis. *Standard Edition, 23:* 144–207. London: Hogarth Press, 1954.

——— (1966 *Correspondance de Sigmund Freud avec le Pasteur Pfister.* Paris: Gallimard, 1966.

Mollat, M. (1966), Le sentiment de la mort dans la vie et le pratique religieuses a la fin du Moyen Age. *Supplement de La Vie Spirituelle, 77:* 218–229.

Pfister, P. (1926), Letter of September 10, 1926, to Freud. In *Correspondance de Sigmund Freud avec le Pasteur Pfister.* Paris: Gallimard, 1966, p. 155.

——— (1928), Letter of February 20th, 1928, to Freud. In *Correspondance de Sigmund Freud le Pasteur Pfister.* Paris: Gallimard, 1966, PP. 177–179.

Ple, A. (1966), *Chastity and the Affective Life.* New York: Herder and Herder.

St. Thomas, *Commentaire de l'ethique a Nicomaque d'Aristole,* Book VII lec. 11.

——— Somme theologique I a II ae 108, 1, 2 m., 106, 107, 1, 2m. etc.

——— Contra Gentiles III a 122.

Vereecke, L. (1958), L'Obligation morale selon Guillaume d'Ockham. *Supplement de La Vie Spirituelle,* no. 45, 2nd Trim. pp. 123–143.

In a brief Note on the Phenomenon of Pharisaism, *P. J. R. Dempsey describes the Pharisees as representatives of a harsh and negative superego morality. "Pharisaism is not just an ecclesiastial phenomenon. It can come into existence in any social or political group that, starting with an idealistic purpose and enthusiasm, thereafter becomes mechanized and institutionalized."*

7

A Note on the

Phenomenon of Pharisaism

by

P. J. R. DEMPSEY, PH.D.

SEPARATEDNESS AND SPIRITUAL SUPREMACY WERE THE MARKS OF the original Jewish sect of the Pharisees. Their zeal for the exact observance of all the detailed prescriptions, oral and written, of the biblical and rabbinical code set them apart from their less-observant Jewish brethren, from the rural dwellers and people of the land, and from the Gentile pagans. It also provided them with an acknowledged title and claim to superiority and precedence.

The essentials of Jewish morality were contained in the Decalogue, a common possession of Judaism and Christianity. In pharisaism, however, these essentials were heavily overladen with innumerable prescriptions that legislated for the smallest details of individual and social life. There were rules (Friedlander, 1921), for instance, concerning dress, the food of a Jew and non-Jew, the immersion of utensils, the manner of morning washing, the use of the Tephillim and the interdiction of no less than thirty-nine forms of work on Saturday. There was, for instance, a prohibition against writing.

The work of writing which is forbidden consists in writing with ink or with any substance, upon parchment, or upon any substance, even if one wrote no more than two letters of any language. Moreover, if one wrote but two marks, it constitutes the work of writing which is prohibited. It is likewise forbidden to trace any letter or picture, even in the beverage upon a table, or in the moisture upon a pane of glass, or in sand. It is even forbidden to make

marks upon a sheet of paper with one's nails. Whatever it is forbidden to write, it is also forbidden to erase. Hence it is forbidden
to break sugar-tarts or rolls on which there are coloured pictures,
but if the pictures were only impressed with a rubber stamp without
paint, it is permissible to break them. If wax was dripped upon letters, it is forbidden to remove it. It is forbidden to tell a non-Jew to
open for him a sealed letter. If a sealed letter was delivered to him,
he should not tell a non-Jew to open it for him, but he might hint to
him that he cannot read it, so that the latter should understand.
Even this should only be done in an emergency, as aside from this
prohibition, it is forbidden to read a letter concerning business on
the Sabbath. It is forbidden even to look at the writing without
reading it, unless ignorant of its contents, in which case, it is only
permitted to glance at it " (Ibid, p. 298).

Veneration for one's father is a very noble thing, but the rabbinical code prescribed that

"one must neither stand in the place appointed for one's father according to his rank, nor in the place reserved for him to pray. One
should not sit in the place of one's father's seat in the house. One
must neither contradict one's father, nor corroborate his words in
his presence even by saying: It is obvious that father is right. If the
son were attired in costly dress and presided over a meeting, when
his parents came and rent his garments and struck his head, and
spat in his face, he should neither insult them, nor feel aggrieved in
their presence, nor display anger towards them, but he should
remain silent, and fear the king who is the King of Kings, the Holy
One; Blessed be He who has *thus* decreed" (Ibid., p. 179).

In the Gospels, two of which were written by Galilean fisher-
men and one by a Galilean tax official, the Pharisees are depicted
as a class of men extremely observant of the letter and externals of
the law, severe in judgement of their fellow men, quickly cen-
sorious, easily shocked, disdainful and superior in their attitude
toward people, eager for honor, hungry for precedence, con-
centrating on appearances, washing the outside of the cup, and
crucifying the prophets of new vision and new life.

Paul of Tarsus, however, reared and trained in the sect, was
proud of his membership and vocation. He boasted that he was a
Pharisee of the Pharisees. Conversant with and observant of every
title of the law, persuaded that salvation lay in those minute ob-

servances, he confessed that he had been an intolerant inquisitor, participating in executions, ruthless in his persecution of deviants—until Damascus.

Thrown from his horse and blinded by light, he understood that he had been persecuting not men but their Saviour, not Christians but Christ. Thereafter, to live, for him, was simply Christ, to be filled with his Spirit, and the harvest of that Spirit was love, joy, peace, patience, kindness, generosity, forbearance, gentleness, faith, courtesy, temperance, purity. These things transcended legal prescriptions. They were essential. There was but one law, the law of an enlightened and understanding Love.

Anyone, with even a slight acquaintance with analytic thinking, will see in pharisaism all the obsessiveness, the paralysing restrictiveness of a super-ego morality—harsh, negative, cruel, and categorically imperative. The Pharisee wore a mask, played a role, was avid for dominion and homage, was intolerant and ruthless, was devoid of understanding of himself or people; he was a barren legalist empty of the love of God or man.

Originally the Pharisees as a group were idealists, but they became institutionalized. This led to a loss of contact with reality, to a blindness about essentials, to a need for continuing power, to pretence, to the multiplication of heroics, to hostility to those who raised basic questions of meaning and purpose, to persecution and elimination of the innovator and the visionary.

Pharisaism is not just an ecclesiastical phenomenon. It can come into existence in any social or political group that, starting with an idealistic purpose and enthusiasm, thereafter becomes mechanized and institutionalized. Its members, then, must habitually wear darkened spectacles, rationalize continually, and realize that honesty is a quality perilous to survival.

BIBLIOGRAPHY

Friedlander, G. (1921), *The Laws and Customs of Israel,* London: Methuen.

In BENJAMIN B. WOLMAN'S *essay,* Why Did Jesus Die on the Cross?
*"Christ is viewed not as a historical figure but as the image of a
willing martyr as remembered and worshipped by millions."*

Dr. Wolman *modifies Freud's theory and introduces the concept of* lust for life *as the overall motive of all human behavior,
that branches off into love (eros) and belligerence (ares).
Although all living organisms fight for survival, there are some
people who are willing to sacrifice their life for others. Christ was
not a masochist, but his love for people was stronger than his love
for himself.*

*Professor Wolman distinguishes three types of human at-
titudes, namely, selfish (instrumental), selfish-unselfish (mutual)
and unselfish (vectorial). Maternal love for a helpless child is vectorial. Vectorial love is nonsexual and unrewarded; it is pure love.*

*Jesus died to prove that love is stronger than hate. His
messianic mission was void of power, for Jesus was not an omnipotent father but a helpless son. Most religions have been based
on awe; Christianity started with compassion and love. The
"other cheek" morality meant a refusal to participate in any
violence.*

*"Christ's death and resurrection speak louder than life and
death, for He overcame both in the name of love." Was His
mission a failure?*

8

Why Did Jesus
Die on the Cross?

by

BENJAMIN B. WOLMAN, PH.D.

THE ISSUES INVOLVED IN THE VOLUNTARY DEATH ON THE CROSS CAN BE dealt with in a dual perspective. From a cultural-historical point of view Jesus' death is a part of a sociomoral rebellion against Hellenism and especially against its Roman offshoot and hedonistic-parasitic way of life. The death on the cross represents a turning point in the development of moral concepts, although it was hardly a turning point in human behavior.

The second vantage point is psychological. If offers an opportunity to analyze the tragic death on the cross in the perspective of human drives, feelings, and ideals. Jesus is viewed here as an individual who practiced the idea of self-sacrificing love and, instead of fighting for survival, accepted death willingly.

This chapter is concerned with the psychological rather than with the sociocultural aspects of the problem. Whether Christ's true life history does correspond to the story told by the New Testament or to the Dead Sea scrolls (Stendhal, 1957), is of little importance here. The subject matter of this study is not the crucification as a historical detail but as a symbol, and Christ is viewed not as a historical figure but as the image of a willing martyr, as remembered and worshipped by millions.

Theory of Instincts

All living matter resists destruction and fights for survival. Breathing, drinking, eating, fighting, and hiding from enemies serve this overall purpose.

The greatest fear is the fear of death, and all forms and types of fears are derived from this basic and fundamental biological reaction. The fear of darkness is related to one's inability to see approaching enemies; the fear of being alone is related to the inability to have allies in the fight of survival; the fear of falling, slipping, or being hurt, wounded, mugged, drowned, or choked are basically the same fear of death. The fear of want, poverty, hunger and thirst are other forms of the same fear. Fear of losing face, status, and prestige are symbolic forms of fear to be perceived as weak and defenseless and, therefore, more vulnerable.

And yet Freud has assumed an innate drive toward death, derived from his "constancy principle" which resembles Newton's law of inertia. According to Freud, an organism is in a state of equilibrium unless exposed to inner and outer stimuli. Stimulation causes tension or disequilibrium; this disequilibrium is a self-terminating process, for all organisms tend to return to their former state of balance through a discharge of energy. Stimulation causes tension, and tension elicits actions bringing relief and equilibrium.

The tension and discharge of energy are regulated by two forces. The first facilitates discharge of energy, and the other inhibits this discharge. The driving forces are called instincts; the inhibitory forces are the ego and superego.

The instincts arise from biochemical sources within the body and operate as a constant, ever-present force. According to Freud, instincts have an impetus, a source, an object, and an aim. The impetus points to the size of the driving force; the source is the excitation inside the organism caused by deficiency, or deprivation such as hunger; the aim of instinctual activities is a discharge of energy that brings about a reduction of excitation and restoration of the inner balance. All instinctual activity can be pictured as a certain sum of energy forcing its way in a certain direction.

An instinct is "an expression of the *conservative* nature of living substance." It is "a compulsion inherent in organic life to restore an earlier stage of things which the living entity has been obliged to abandon under the pressure of external, disturbing forces; that is, it is a kind of organic elasticity, or, to put it another way, the expression of the inertia inherent in organic life " (Freud, 1933, p. 47).

Freud wrote:

The instincts are mythical beings, superb in their indefiniteness. Our first step was tentative enough. We felt we should probably not go far wrong if we started by distinguishing two main instincts, or species or groups of instincts—hunger and love . . . We are here overshadowed by the immutable biological fact that the living individual serves two purposes, self-preservation and the preservation of species . . . In accordance with this view, we introduced the 'ego-instincts' and the 'sexual instincts' into psychoanalysis (1983, p. 73).

As indicated in the above quote Freud divided all instincts into self-preservation or ego instincts and sexual or libido instincts. The sexual instincts are more flexible than the self-preservation instincts; they can be disturbed, perverted, held in suspense (aim-inhibited), sublimated and diverted into new channels.

With the discovery of narcissism (1914) Freud had to abandon his distinction between the libido and the ego instincts. The ego instincts became a special case of the libido cathexis, namely, an investment of one's libido in himself. Thus Freud's interpretation of the instinctual life became monistic, limited to one instinctual force— the force of love, eros, and the mental energy at its disposal, called libido. In pathological cases this balance of libido cathexes is disturbed.

Freud now put together under the name eros all the forces that increase vitality. Eros included all sexual and selfish drives, and libido was the name of all energies that serve eros.

Thanatos

For several years Freud saw no need for another interpretation of hostile behavior. Hostility to others was explained in terms of extreme self-love. "Self-love works for the self assertion of the individual," Freud wrote.

However, some phenomena of aggression could not be explained by self-love, and among them were (1) cruelty, (2) sadism and masochism, (3) suicide, and (4) death. None of these phenomena could be interpreted by excessive self-cathexis of the libido. German atrocities in Belgium in World War I were not acts of self defense; German soldiers apparently enjoyed being destructive and cruel to the civilian population. Freud had to revise his theory to account for these facts.

Freud explained the evolution of his theory as follows:

"To introduce it (the death instinct) into the human condition seems impious; it contradicts too many religious prejudices and social conventions. No; man must be by nature good, or at least good natured. If he occasionally shows himself to be brutal, violent and cruel, these are only passing disturbances of his emotional life, mostly provoked, and perhaps only the consequence of the ill-adapted social system which he has so far made for himself (1933, p. 142).

And later on:

After long doubts and vacillations we have decided to assume the existence of only two basic instincts, Eros and the *destructive*-instinct...The aim of the first of these basic instincts is to establish ever greater unities and to preserve them, thus-in short, to bind together; the aim of the second, on the contrary, is to undo connections and so to destroy things. We may suppose that the final aim of the destructive instinct is to reduce living things to an inorganic state. For this reason we also call it the death instinct (1938, p. 20).

According to Freud instincts are "directed toward the reinstatement of an earlier state of things. We may assume that as soon as a given state of things is upset there arises an instinct to recreate it, and phenomena appear which we may call 'repetition-compulsion . . .'" (1933, p. 145). This principle of constancy applied to the interpretation of destructiveness and death, gives the following picture.

If it is true that once in an unconceivably remote past, and in an unimaginable way, life arose out of inanimate matter, then, in accordance with our hypothesis, an instinct must at that time have come into being, whose aim it was to abolish life once more and to reestablish the inorganic state of things. If in this instinct we recognize the impulse of self-destruction of our hypothesis, then we can regard that impulse as the manifestation of a *death instinct*.

Thus instincts are either *erotic* that try to collect "living substance into larger unities," or *death instincts* that "act against this tendency and try to bring living matter back into an inorganic condition" (1933, p. 147).

Organic nature is a continuation of the inorganic nature. With the onset of life, the death instinct was born, aiming at the destruction of life and return to the inorganic state. The death instincts bring living matter back into inorganic condition. "The cooperation and opposition of these two forces (Eros and Thanatos) produce the phenomena of life to which death puts an end (1938, pp. 146–147).

The balance of libido and destrudo cathexes determine human behavior:

We may picture an initial state of things by supposing that the whole available energy of Eros, to which we shall henceforward give the name of *libido,* is present in the as yet undifferentiated ego-id and serves to neutralize the destructive impulses which are simultaneously present.

So long as that instinct operates internally, as a death instinct, it remains silent; we only come across it after it has become diverted outward as an instinct of destruction. That that diversion should occur seems essential for the preservation of the individual; the musculature is employed for the purpose. When the superego begins to be formed, considerable amounts of the aggressive instinct become fixated within the ego and operate there in a self-destructive fashion. This is one of the dangers to health to which mankind became subject on the path to cultural development. The holding back of aggressiveness is in general unhealthy and leads to illness. A person in a fit of rage often demonstrates how the transition from restrained aggressiveness to self-destructiveness is effected, by turning his aggressiveness against himself: he tears his hair or beats his face with his fists—treatment which he would evidently have preferred to apply to someone else...Thus it may in general be suspected that the *individual* dies of his internal conflicts but that the *species* dies of its unsuccessful struggle against the external world, when the latter undergoes changes of a kind that cannot be dealt with by the adaptations which the species has acquired (1938, p. 22–23).

Freud assumed that "we have to destroy other things and other people in order to protect ourselves from the tendency to self-destruction" (Freud, 1933, p. 145).

Freud's theory implies that suicidal tendencies occur ontogenetically and phylogenetically earlier than the genocidal tendencies, and masochism comes earlier than sadism.

Was Jesus a Masochist?

Masochism is a desire to suffer in order to obtain pleasure. Masochism is a perverse hedonism, for it aims at pleasure. In its pure sexual form masochism in an inability to derive sexual pleasure unless the sexual act is accompanied by pain. Masochists wish to be hurt in order to enjoy sex, and some of them are unable to get sexually aroused unless they are hit, pinched, bitten, and hurt. One male masochist asked his partner to choke him with her hands; he could not get erection in any other way.

"Beat me but love me," this is the motto of masochists, based on their childhood experience. A masochist expects to evoke love by suffering, for he has learned that pain was the only way he could force his parents to love him.

Masochistic tendencies are most often associated with the manic-depressive disorder and paranoia. Several authors link these two disorders, finding the same etiologic background in both; they view paranoia as one of the syndromes of the manic-depressive disorder and a defense against overwhelming feelings of depression (cf. Kanzer, 1952; Kraepelin, 1921; Lacan, 1952, Wolman, 1965). The "cinderella complex," the idea of victory through suffering, seems to be the core of the manic-depressive disorder and paranoia (Wolman, 1969).

According to Mark (8:31) Jesus could have saved his life but refused to do so. He believed that his death would bring atonement and he would attain immortality and come back, resurrected, as a Messiah (Mark 10:35-45). Small wonder that several psychiatrists hypothesized that Jesus suffered paranoid delusions, believed himself to be sort of a sacrificial lamb, and hoped through his sufferings to become the Messiah (Binet-Sangle, 1911-1915; Hirsch, 1912). Schweitzer (1948) defended Christ's sanity and concluded that "the only symptoms to be accepted as historical and possibly to be discussed from the psychiatric point of view—the high estimate which Jesus has of himself and perhaps the hallucinations at the baptism—fall far short of proving the existence of mental illness" (p. 72).

One may add that Christ's thoughts were not necessarily new. They were a continuation of the Jewish tradition of self-sacrifice (Kiddush Ha'shem), especially in the Essenian version and related to the Hellenistic-Oriental mysticism (cf. Baron, 1955; Klausner, 1925; 1946; Greenstone, 1926).

Christ's ideals and ideas were to a large extent culturally determined. In Christ's time history was, as usual, on the side of the big battalions. All nations around the Mediterranean succumbed to the superior Roman power, to its military genius and organizational talent, and to its ruthless efficiency. Roman legions carried their eagle emblem victoriously from the Euphrates to the Nile, from Gibraltar to the Black Sea, from the Danube to Great Britain. *Pax Romana* was never very peaceful, and often oppressed people raised their swords in a futile rebellion against the Roman Empire.

The idea of redemption through suffering was shared by millions of people subjugated to Rome. Mystical cults spread around the Mediterranean, and great Roman poets Ovid and Virgil gave literary expression to human yearnings for salvation.

Although millions of people *thought* of acceptance of pain as the sole solution, Christ implemented the idea of self-sacrifice. Several issues must be clarified before one interprets Christ's willingness to suffer and to die on the cross.

The first issue that needs clarification revolves around the instinct of death. Was Christ suicidal *because* he did not want to hurt anyone? Must people either murder or kill themselves?

The conservative nature of the living organisms implies conservation of life. Following Freud's main idea (and I believe I am more consistent on this point than Freud was) I hypothesize that all instincts serve conservation of life. Destruction and death instincts do not conserve anything, and the idea of thanatos violates Freud's principle of constancy. All instincts serve survival, and they can be put together as the urge for survival or lust for life.

Life is a process of oxidation, disgestion, incorporation, metabolism and so on. The entire behavior of organisms is aggressive-defensive, for all organisms either devour other organisms or protect themselves against being devoured. No organism can survive without food; thus life is a never-ending struggle aimed at the destruction of the prey by the predator or of the predator by the prey. Men have always been painfully aware of this continuous struggle and preoccupied with the problems of destruction and death. All religions have good and bad gods; the good gods protect the believers, and bad gods side with the enemies. Ancient Egyptians had Set, Greeks had Ares, Romans had Mars, Jews had Satan, Persians had Adriman, and so on. The dichotomy of God and Satan, good and evil, creativeness and destructiveness, virtue and sin, life and death has preoccupied humanity forever.

Men have always feared the influence of bad gods and spirits and ascribed to them the talent to induce human beings to evil behavior, to hostile deeds and feelings. Zoroaster and the Manichiests internalized the struggle of good and bad gods. They believed that the fight between the forces of light and darkness was raging in every human heart and that man alone carried the responsibility for victory or defeat of the gods.

Freud's theory of eros and thanatos corresponds to this life and love versus death and hatred dichotomy. However, Freud's death instinct is primarily self-directed and suicidal, analogous to the narcissism of libido. Freud's own writing supports the hypothesis that *object-directed destrudo,* that is, the fight for survival is the true source of hostility:

From the earliest times it was muscular strength which decided who owned things or whose will shall prevail. Muscular strength was soon supplemented by the use of tools: the winner was the one who had the better weapons or who used them the more skillfully. From the moment at which weapons were introduced, intellectual superiority already began to replace brute muscular strength; but the final purpose of the fight remained the same (Freud, 1932, pp. 274–275).

Primitive societies are not a paradise of love and peace but clans and herds dominated by physical violence or by cunning. Cave men did not hate themselves; they were in love with themselves and hated their enemies. "Thou shalt love thy neighbor as thyself," the Scripture said, because there was no doubt in regard to self-love, but the love for the neighbor has always been a dubious assignment. There was no instinct of death, but there has been a continuous fight for survival. Let us call the driving force behind this struggle lust for life.

At certain evolutionary levels part of this force is directed to procreation; protozoa procreate by splitting and the preservation of the life of the species is, as it were, a continuation of the individual's life. At higher levels of evolution, procreation becomes sexual and the lust for life drive splits into ares and eros, the drive of war and drive of love, respectively.

Thus we postulate one universal drive, the lust for life, associated with one general mental energy, a derivative of the biochemical energy or organisms. The discharge of mental energy can go in any direction; it can be libido in search of eros and in support of life; the libido can be invested into self or in others, in a sexual or a desexualized, sublimated way. Whenever life is threatened, ares, the other instinctual drive, activates its energy, the destrudo.

Ares is the name for the destructive arm of the lust for life; ares, like eros, serves the same purpose of survival. To face the threat to life, a balanced love for oneself and for others suffices ares are two channels of the same drive of lust for life; they are activated in different situations; they basically serve the same goal, the survival of the individual and, in some situations, the survival of the species.

Ares is probably the more primitive and phylogenetically

earlier drive than eros. In case of inner conflict usually ares prevails. No animal can copulate when his skin is burned or bones are broken.

When one is hungry, thirsty, exhausted, or sick, he is hardly in a mood for love. Hurt people are likely to act in an irritable, hostile, and destructive manner. Libido seems to be sort of a "higher" energy, the destrudo a "lower" one; when there is no threat to life, a balanced love for oneself and for others suffices for survival. In emergency states and in cases of exhaustion of libido, destrudo takes over. In emergencies people act as if they had a new supply of energy; the more basic energy, destrudo, is put to use.

Eros and ares are the two channels for the general drive for life; they "release" mental energy. Ares, like eros, has an impetus, source, object, and aim. The impetus is the amount of destructive energy (destrudo) that the ares activates; its source is threat to one's own life; the aim of ares is a complete or partial destruction of enemies; the object of ares' hostility can be anything, including oneself.

Hostile, aretic behavior originates in threat to life. No one hates unless he fears. Immortals do not have to fight for survival, and an omnipotent being does not fight with anyone. Only a God can forgive all his enemies, because he does not fear them. But animals and human beings fear death and hate their enemies because enemies inflict injury and may kill. The ultimate fear is the mortal fear, the fear to perish, the fear of losing all men have: life.

Self-Sacrifice

To put the blame for Christ's death on some cruel Romans or ignorant Jews is tantamount to a denial of the symbolic role of the Golgotha. Were Christ an average man, the search for those guilty of his death would be an item of interest in the annals of criminology, persecution, and judicial murder. But, according to the tradition, Christ has had the choice. Like Socrates, he could escape if he only wished to. Unlike the unaware infant Isaac, Jesus willingly accepted the idea of sacrifice and turned it into self-sacrifice. As a human being Jesus made his own decision and did not seek to evade death.

Was Christ's decision suicidal?

In some situations the destrudo can be turned inwardly, against oneself. The child's resentment against his parents becomes internalized in the superego, and, later on, it may be activated against the ego. Suicidal tendencies are often a product of such a self-directed hatred, originating in child-parent relationships.

Nothing of the kind has been traced in Christ's life, whether as described by historical or by traditional sources. Whether the various authors labeled Jesus as a fanatic and megalomaniac or treated him as a teacher and spiritual leader of the Essenian sect (cf. Binet-Sangle, 1911–1915; Danielou, 1962; Gaster, 1956; Klausner, 1925; Renan, 1863; Schweitzer, 1958; 1961; Stendhal, 1957; Werner, 1911), they did not find an indication of suicidal or parricidal tendencies in Christ (cf. Freud, 1900; Kroeber, 1920). When he was nailed to the cross, Jesus complained to the God-Father about having been forsaken by him—but there was no rebellion or hatred. Whatever one could derive from the New Testament and historical studies, Jesus was neither the rejected nor the rebellious child, nor did he show any particular desire to die.

The idea of self-sacrifice and willing death is not limited to the Jewish and Christian religions; it came up in Greek mythology. The story of Antigone, the daughter of King Oedipus and his mother Jocasta, is a case in point. Oedipus and Jocasta had four children, two boys, Polynices and Eteocles, and two girls, Antigone and Ismene. After King Oedipus put out his eyes and left Thebes, his son Polynices rebelled against his uncle Creon, the new ruler. When the two brothers were killed in a fratricidal fight, Creon ordered a state funeral for Eteocles, and forbade the burial of the body of Polynices. Creon said. "His body shall be left to be devoured by dogs and fowls of the air" (Sophocles *Antigone,* transl. by G. Young 1948, p. 103).

No one in Thebes dared to violate Creon's harsh order, for Creon threatened to punish with death anyone who would bury Polynices' body. However, Antigone, Polynices' sister, decided that it was *her* moral duty to save her brother's dead body from the dogs and protect his soul from eternal suffering. According to the Greek mythology, the soul of an unburied man was doomed to wander forever, never finding peace and rest.

Antigone was neither masochistic nor suicidal, yet she accepted willingly the mortal punishment. She was engaged to Haemon (Creon's son) who described her as a noble human being who "for noblest acts dies by the worst of deaths" (Ibid., p. 115). Antigone did not want to die. She sang her beautiful last song full of desires to live and to be married to the man she loved.

> Behold me, people of my native land:
> I walk my latest way
> I gaze upon the latest light of day
> That I shall ever see;
> Death who lays all to rest is leading me
> To Acheron's far strand
> Alive, to me no bridal hymns belong
> For me no marriage song
> Has yet to be sung; but Acheron instead
> Is it whom I must wed.

(Ibid, p. 118)

Antigone was torn in a conflict between her desire to live (narcissistic love for herself) and her commitment to her brother.

Unselfish Love

One can distinguish three types of human relationships: selfish, selfish-unselfish, and unselfish. Whenever an individual sees in the relationship a means toward the satisfaction of his own needs, this relationship is, as far as he is concerned, selfish or instrumental. His aim is to *receive* whatever he needs. The prototype of such a relationship is the infant-mother relationship, with the infant receiving milk with love and care. An infant is a helpless creature that needs narcissistic supplies in order to survive. He is a taker. Instrumentalism in adults can be sexual or nonsexual, but is always selfish. Many men practice sex on this selfish and infantile level, trying to get satisfaction for themselves. Some men, unable to relate to women, go to a prostitute; of course they must pay, but certainly they do not go in order to support a poor call girl or to satisfy her emotional and physiological needs.

In a *mutual* or selfish-unselfish type of relationship each participant wishes to satisfy the needs of the other (s), assuming that they feel the same way about each other. It is a *giving* type of relationship combined with the conviction that the other partner is also willing to give. It takes years of growth and learning before an individual is able to enter such a *give* and *take* relationship. A man marries a woman because he wants to protect her, to take care of her, and to make her happy; he must, however, be sure that she feels the same way about him.

This mutual relationship can be sexual or nonsexual. Close friends have a "giving" and "receiving" attitude. Several religious and ideological organizations develop such a "mutual" intragroup relationship of solidarity and reciprocal responsibility: all for one and one for all.

The *vectorial,* unselfish relationship originates in motherhood, in the unconditional support of a child irrespective of the child's looks, abilities, or graces, but it is not limited to motherhood only. Vectorial love is the only truly unselfish love, for it is giving without expecting anything in return. It is a nonsexual relationship, in regard to people whom one protects and cares for, and towards one's ideals. The (vectorial) love for a person or the devotion of the ego to the object cannot be distinguished "from a sublimated devotion to an abstract idea," wrote Freud (1922, p. 75). Both types of relationships contain the element of unconditional support and giving and readiness for sacrificing one's own life for one's beloved person, country, or ideal.

Freud wrote in *Group Psychology and the Analysis of the Ego*

> When we are in love a considerable amount of narcissistic libido overflows on to the object. It is even obvious, in many forms of love choice, that the object serves a substitute for some unattained ego ideal of our own . . .
> If the sexual overestimation and the being in love increase even further . . . the tendencies whose trend is toward direct sexual

satisfaction may now be pushed back entirely . . . the ego becomes more and more unassuming and modest, and the object more and more sublime and precious, until at last it gets possession of the entire self-love of the ego, whose self-sacrifice thus follows as a natural consequence . . . Traits of humility, of the limitation of narcissism, and of self-injury occur in every case of being in love (1922, pp. 74–75).

Martyrdom

It is one thing is to kill oneself and another to accept the inevitable. Apparently, there is more than one kind of death wish; one may wish to destroy himself because he hates himself; one may commit suicide in order to punish others, especially those who do not love him as much as he wants to be loved; one may also commit suicide out of fear to live, or out of feelings of despair and hopelessness.

But there have been individuals who wanted to live, yet accepted death willingly. Jewish history is full of cases of people who did not wish to die but in certain circumstances preferred death to life. Consider the story of Eleazar and of Hanna and her seven sons on the eve of the rebellion of Judah Maccabeus; consider the heroic struggle of Jerusalem against Vespasianus and Titus; consider the defense of Massadah and the torturing of Rabbi Akiba; consider the long story of Jews persecuted by Christian kings, crusaders and the Holy Inquisition. Throughout centuries of persecutions, expulsions, and tortures the Jews refused to abandon their faith and have been loyal to the tenets of the tradition they loved (Baron, 1955; Greenstone, 1926). This *amor dei,* this love for God, was the driving force that inspired them to accept death willingly.

Human history is, to a large extent, a history of oppressors and martyrs. Consider Prometheus; consider Christians thrown to beasts by Roman emperors; remember Quo Vadis, Domine? Recall John Hus, the Waldenses and Albigenses, the Duchobors, Subbotniks, the Quakers, and other dissenters persecuted by the religious and civil establishments. Consider Giordano Bruno and Galileo Galilei, the defenders of the Warsaw ghetto, London under the blitz, and Stalingrad.

Christ was not a coward who, afraid to live, sought escape in suicide. Nor was he a masochist who looked forward to the pleasure of pain. In the times when the opulent, affluent, corrupt Roman Empire subjugated the entire world, when millions were enslaved by Roman arenas, when the upper classes of Rome idly basked in wealth as "beautiful people," and the lower classes refused to work and demanded (with riots) *panem et circenses* (bread and entertainment), Christ's voice was a voice of love and hope. Christ reflected the idea of salvation through self-sacrifice that had spread at that time among Jews and non-Jews (Segal, 1950; Tarachow, 1955). To kill the oppressors meant to perpetuate their method. A defeat would have led to a massacre, a victory could have proven that God is on the side of bigger battalions.

Christ *had* to die to prove that love is stronger than hate. Haters kill; a stick, a sharp rock, and a knife can kill. A snake, a bull, a mad hound and a crazy man can kill a genius and a saint. To kill is easy; ares is primitive and stays primitive forever. The techniques of murder progress, but murderous impulses have not changed much from the caveman era. Ares is unchangeable; it may be restrained and inhibited, but it remains the arch-drive. But eros does change. It starts from sex but, ultimately, it transcends sex.

Nonphysical Love

It was quite late in the process of evolution when procreation became interaction. Even when procreation required two partners, it could still be performed in some species without physical contact between them. Courtship has often been associated with pursuit on the part of the male and some degree of resistance on the part of the female. According to Tinbergen, males pursue females because "one male can fertilize more than one female" and females play a more important role in feeding and protecting the young (Tinbergen, 1953, p. 22).

There is no reason to assume that sexual intercourse in lower species is accompanied by affection. Insects procreate sexually; one can, however, hardly ascribe to them any emotion. However, at a higher evolutionary level, mating becomes associated with care and protection of the mate, usually the female. Protection of females by males and the mutual aid in search for food are more frequent among primates than among lower species. Sexual intercourse in higher species becomes gradually less of a rape and more of a courtship, less a mechanical motion and more a considerate emotion. On highest evolutionary levels the male-female relationships last longer and become more and more friendly.

Sexual attachment usually excludes or at least mollifies hostility. Certainly this rule has a great many exceptions, yet the process of evolution brings increased cooperation between the mates and the libido gradually counteracts destrudo.

This evolutionary process introduced new possibilities for the libido. At the beginning there was only selfish love, love being a part of the urge to live. At a certain evolutionary stage this love branches off; one part of the libido remains and will always remain self-invested; another part of the libido is invested in sex and procreation; and still another part becomes desexualized and invested in the care for others. Loyalty, affection, and kindness originate in sexuality, but they transcend the sexual urge.

Lower developmental forms do not disappear in evolution. They persist in many ways, sometimes subordinated to the higher level. For example, as mentioned before, the oral zone, the mouth, always remains an erotogenic zone, albeit subordinated to and incorporated in the adult genital sexuality. On higher developmental levels, sexuality becomes more refined, more sophisticated and combined with admiration. Yet human sexual love always retains the elements of selfishness.

Human beings give love in hope that their love will be reciprocated. When a man loves a woman or a woman loves a man, they expect to be loved in return. This rule applies specifically to physical love, that is, to sexual love. To obtain and to give satisfaction is the natural aim of sexual relations. Sexual relations must be selfish because they are associated with sensual excitement and pleasure; they are selfish-unselfish to the extent that one gives pleasure to his (or her) love partner.

Love must be nonsexual to become unselfish. Such a love is the vectorial love of parents for their child, of a patriotic man for his country, and of a pious man for his religion. The idea of immaculate conception contradicts hedonism. Motherhood without sensual love and love without sensual pleasure are a prerequisite for nonselfish, vectorial love. The story of Christ's birth represents a radical departure from the extreme hedonism of Roman life. Christ's love for humanity is vectorial—thus there could be no sensuality in his life.

Messianism

The messianic idea, as an idea of salvation that comes from without, is a derivative of childhood experiences. It reflects the wish to be helped and, as such, it carries elements of transference like the transference in psychoanalytic treatment.

Adulthood does not imply complete cessation of behavioral patterns of childhood. Consider the above mentioned orality. Oral patterns may remain unchanged and prevail in pathological adults; in normal adults, who practice genital sexuality, oral elements do not dominate but become included in mature sexual behavior.

Dependence on outside help is certainly part of childhood behavior, but no adult can entirely rid of it, especially in difficult situations. A continuous parasitic and overdependent reliance on others is pathological, but even normal adults may depend on others in certain difficult situations. Even well-adjusted adults cannot be completely self-sufficient; they seek help of dentists, physicians, lawyers, accountants, and travel agents whenever they need such help. To "doctor" oneself is not a sign of maturity, and adults do accept the authority of competence. Normal adults do not want to be enslaved to anyone, but they agree to vest part of their rights in their leaders. They follow the guidance of people whom they trust, and they expect leadership from the leaders.

It seems quite natural to assume that fatherhood is the prototype of leadership. Father's image, however, does not invariably correspond to the image painted by Freud in *Totem and Taboo*. Comparative histories of family (Engels, 1902; Murdock,

1949; Radcliffe-Brown, 1950) do not corroborate Freud's hypothesis and do not prove that all primitive families followed precisely the same pattern. The monophyletic idea of the origin of the human species as an offshoot of a certain herd of primates is as mythological as the story of Adam and Eve. It is probable that humanity evolved gradually in several places on earth, such as Australia, Java, and Neondethal, out of a variety of subhuman species in polyphyletic evolution. Certainly, there has been more than one pattern in family life.

It seems, however, that the ancient Mediterranean family was primarily patriarchal. It was so, at least, among the Semitic, Greek, and Italian communities. The father was the indisputable head of the family, the protector and provider. Although the Old Testament has its share of oedipal mythology, especially in the rebellion of Absalom, the fathers were there described as firm, trustworthy, and reliable leaders.

Moses is certainly one of the most outstanding leadership figures in Judaism. Freud's hypothesis of allegedly Egyptian origin of Moses (Freud, 1937) lacks definitive evidence; it is, however, not of any special relevance for our discourse. Whether Egyptian or Israelite, Moses was a specatcular charismatic leader of the Israelites, who liberated them from slavery and led them toward the Promised Land.

All messianic ideas in Judaism follow in the footsteps of the myth of Moses who led the Chosen People toward salvation. The messiah figure in Judaism has been painted as a father figure, that is, as an omnipotent and omniscient yet benevolent leader. There has been no meekness, no softness in messianic myths in Judaism (Greenstone, 1926; Klausner, 1946; Scholem, 1954). It may seem, therefore, surprising that the idea of a son as a savior has emerged and become almost generally accepted. Moreover, the son could have easily become a symbol of rebellion and fight against paternal authority.

Nothing of the kind can be ascribed to Christ.

Elevation of the Son

Freud's interpretation of religion is closely related with man's helplessness in life and his tendency to regress to infantile dependency on paternal protection. Religion is "born of the need to make tolerable the helplessness of man and built out of the material offered by memories of the helplessness of his own childhood and the childhood of the human race" wrote Freud in *The Future of an Illusion* (1928, p. 32).

The child's attitude toward his father is rather ambivalent. The first emotional attachment goes to mother, the source of milk and love. Then, the child's love shifts to father, who is stronger and can offer more protection. But strength may be threatening. Strong forces may become dangerous, and the child's attitude to father is a fusion of love and fear. Jehova, who personifies the father, is both God of Mercy (El Rahum Ve'hanun) and Lord of Legions (Adonai Zvaot).

In ancient times fathers exercised an absolute authority over their children. In Rome the father, *pater familias,* had unlimited powers over his children and their lives. His right was *ius vitae necisque* (right of life and death). Though fathers did not make much use of the right of killing their children, there have been cases of sacrificing of children all around the Mediterranean Sea.

In Freud's *Totem and Taboo* (1913), the sons rebel and kill the father. This killing was a preparation for eating his body in the spirit of cannabilistic introjection and indentification with the father. Totem and taboo were linked by Freud with the origin of religious awe, a combination of love and fear. Awe is the prerequisite of superego formation, and religion develops out of an objectification of child-father relationship.

People admire power and detest weakness. All polytheistic and monotheistic religions praised the unlimited powers of their gods. Mediterranean mythologies are full of dramatic battles among the gods; in Greek mythology. gods fought among themselves and with people. In the Persian religion the God of Light and the God of Darkness fought forever, but the stronger one has a better chance to win.

The forces of light in enslaved Judea did not have a fighting chance. In an act of despair a handful of Jews rebelled in 66 A.D. against the Roman might and were crushed after 4 years of suicidal defence. But most people in Judea and elsewhere did not put much hope in military power.

The head god of Greeks and Romans was Zeus (Jupiter), father and head of family. Also the God of Israel was a father. The idea of God-Father in pre-Christian era represented power and omnipotence, but the idea of the Son was associated with humility and devotion. As an Essenian, Christ advocated poverty, simplicity, and weakness, with a promise of ultimate reward after a long road of suffering.

Pre-Paulistic Christianity did not convey the idea of power. It was thoroughly Essenian (Danielou, 1962; Gaster, 1956; Klausner, 1925; Renan, 1803; Stendhal, 1956; Tarachow, 1955) and was opposed to power, wealth, glory, victory, and other cultural values of the opulent Roman society. Christ blessed the poor, the suffering, the discriminated against and promised them the Heavenly Kingdom.

The fact that people flocked to Christ and trusted him led inevitably to his death. Rejection of earthly pleasures was the essence of Christ's Gospel. Although all around people struggled to amass wealth and power, Christ repudiated them. Wealth and power are weapons in the struggle for survival; the more wealth and the more power, the more one feels secure. Christ rejected wealth and power; they belonged to the corrupt oppressors. The rejection of the struggle for survival could be justified only by rejection of the goal it has served—that is, survival itself. Christ *had* to repudiate life to show the valuelessness of greediness and oppression.

To put the son in a role of deity was, indeed, a major psychocultural revolution. In the Old Testament Abraham was willing to sacrifice *his* son. In Christianity, the son became his savior, for self-sacrifice became the only evidence of the new philosophy. Some of the Jews were the first followers of Christ. Instead of the Judaic belief in the *coming* of the Messiah, they believed that the Messiah had come. Christ, the Son of the Lord, was the Messiah. These early believers made the Son, Jesus, equal to the Lord the Father, because his weakness became equal to the Lord's power.

St. Paul displayed hostility to the Jews who made the Son

equal to the Father (Tarachow, 1955). It seems that St. Paul could never forget this and remained, all his life, anti-Jewish, though he himself stressed the role of Christ, his self-sacrifice and death.

The shift from God-Father to Son-Father is a shift from power to weakness, from authority to sympathy. One respects and admires the omnipotent and omniscient father, but one feels compassion for the suffering son. Most religions are based on awe; Christianity started with love instead.

But here, again, the necessity of Christ's willing death cannot be overestimated. In face of death all men are equal, a king and slave, a millionaire and a beggar. Hatred brings visible results—dead corpses loudly praise the victorious murder. Self-sacrificing love has little to show, but when it defies death, it celebrates a silent triumph on the cross.

The Other Cheek

There is more than one way of coping with aggression. The first and most natural way is to fight back in self-defense. Parents, whether in the animal or human world, are expected to defend their children and be brave, even in face of overwhelming odds.

Were Christ a father figure, one could have turned to him for help, as the Psalmist did. Being a son, Christ had no power and could not defend anyone. He was as helpless as all other children of Israel and could be as easily victimized as all other persecuted and oppressed people around the world.

Christ's answer to oppression was nonresistance. Perhaps he hoped to disarm them as if saying, "You can't fight against me, for I am goodness and love, and I love all of you. You can fight against those who fight back. You can kill those who want to kill you. But you cannot fight against me who turns the other cheek."

This was Christ's message. This message did not work when the Romans threw Christians to the beasts, as it did not work when the Germans threw Jews to the gas chambers. The Nazis were "civilized," efficient, and systematic, and in a short time murdered, without any interference, six million people. In ancient

Rome, however, the persecution of the innocent and defenseless victims was less efficient and stirred up the conscience of a great many.

The idea of turning the other cheek and nonresistance has, however, a deeper meaning. All living creatures fight for survival, and those armed with stronger jaws and claws usually prevail. Fight against the evil forces raises the question of whether those who fight against the aggressor perpetuate hatred and aggression. To meet violence with violence may foster more violence and more violent antiviolence, and so on. "The other cheek" means a refusal to take part in any violence whatsoever. It is indeed the only possible nonviolent protest.

Being human, we are inclined to respond to violence with violence, and all civilized societies respect those who fight against aggressors. Jewish morality justifies fighting in self-defense; if someone wants to kill you, you have the right to kill him in self-defense. "Thou shalt not kill" applies to aggression, but all civilized societies permit the use of force in self-defense.

There are, however, situations in which an active defense is absolutely hopeless. It is easy to criticize defenseless people who, thrown to beasts or surrounded by a powerful army, did not try to wage a suicidal struggle (Arendt, 1963). One can easily realize that a struggle of starving, emaciated prisoners against beasts of prey or a well-armed animalistic military would only infuriate them, feed their cruelty, and increase the massacre.

A passive surrender to death does not necessarily save people from death, but it may create some chances for reducing cruelty. Eros is the most successful adversary of ares, and the idea of the other cheek is inextricably linked with faith in the human race.

Probably, we are born not as good as Rousseau described us, but perhaps not as bad as Hobbes thought. Even stone age people did not engage in a "war of all against all," and even wild beasts do not attack everything and everybody.

I do not know whether insects are more cruel than birds and birds more cruel than people, but the higher the species the better are the chances for counteracting ares by eros. Even primitive eros, reduced to crude sexuality, nullifies ares, and even wild beasts to not kill each other when they copulate. There are, indeed, pathological cases of sexual murder, especially among human beings, but there are millions of cases of kindness, consideration, and protection in sexual love. In nonsexual, parental love, kindness and protectiveness play a most significant role.

A man hurt by a peer tends to fight back, but a loving parent tends to forgive his aggressive child, and his forgiveness may elicit gratefulness and love. Christ offered forgiveness to his murderers, because they did not know what they were doing. His act of forgiveness elevated him to a level that no swords and shields could. He stood above murder, violence, and anger. There was no contest of arms. His victory was a victory of eros over ares, of love over hate, forgiveness over revenge. He has shown mankind that the only way for stopping violence is nonparticipation in violence. Perhaps it is a very long road, full of victims of persecution, a road paved with bodies of martyrs and marked by crosses. But any other way is swept by never-ending oceans of tears and blood.

It is not easy for a powerful father to forgive aggressors, but is it not more difficult for a sheep to forgive the wolves and pray for their well-being? The love of a powerful father elicits awe; that is, love combined with fear. A love of a hurt child who forgives his oppressors elicits love with compassion.

Only through his own death could Christ evoke compassionate love.

The Voice from the Graveyard

There is also another aspect of Christ's voluntary death. One can rule as a king, dictator, or conqueror, but as long as he is alive, another king may challenge his rule. Rulers can be overthrown, imprisoned, and guillotined by rebels.

The only lasting voice is the voice that comes from the grave. Moses could have been a victorious leader of the disobedient tribes of Israel and a conqueror of the Promised Land, but to become a *symbol* of liberation, he had to transfer his powers to Joshua. *Moses had to die to become Moses.* Moses leading victorious troops in conquest of Canaan would have passed to history as a brave warrior, sort of a Joshua, but not as a man second only to the Lord.

In Freud's *Totem and Taboo* the living father is a source of competition, hatred, and inner strife. As long as the arch-father was alive, he was the sole possessor of all females, causing envy and dismay and provoking parricidal feelings. The rule by the living father was unmistakenly associated with fear and resentment.

Only with his death and through his death could the arch-father put an end to resentment and accomplished a unification of the society. Brothers-in-murder formed a brotherly union based not so much on brotherly love as on admiration of the dead father.

Segal (1950) discovered in pre-Maccabeic documents dating about 200 B.C., the idea of two Messiahs. The first Messiah, called Son of Joseph or Son of Ephraim, was expected to bring victory and redemption to his people, but he himself was supposed to die a martyr's death. His death would pave the road for the arrival of the final Messiah, the Son of David.

Several mythological beliefs have been woven around the story of the second Messiah being the reincarnation of the first one. The story of the two Messiahs has been probably reinterpreted in Christianity as a willing death and resurrection of the same hero.

The idea of resurrection offered the so-much-needed reassurance and promise for reward. Those who suffer now will be compensated later, and those who die will come back to life on the Day of Redemption. The Christian belief in resurrection is tantamount to the belief in immortality. One cannot trust weakness, no matter how beautiful the weakness is. Human beings fear death and forever have sought support in heaven, looking up in hope toward heavenly, superior, immortal beings. Children dread to be left alone, and get panicky at the sight of a sick parent.

But how can one be sure that the admired being is really immortal? The only possible proof is resurrection. If the hero can come back to life, his death was not real. It was a sign of love to die for people, and it was even a bigger sign of love to come back and take care of them.

The dying martyr's voice sounds stronger than the voice of the living. The resurrection of the hero is reassuring, and his voice from the grave speaks louder than life and death, for he has overcome both in the name of love.

The Failure of a Mission

Victor Hugo wrote that no power in the world can stop an idea when the time for this idea has come.

Was the time ripe then?

Messianic hopes come and go, and repeat themselves again and again in religious and secular dreams of a perfect social order and peace on earth. All nations and all eras have had their share in the belief that some day the savior will come.

Whenever men in their perennial struggle for goods they cannot possess forever and in search of a glory that cannot last too long set the earth afire and turn life on earth into a living hell, some of them hope to stay victorious forever, but the victims pray and hope for an early end to their sufferings to be brought about by a messiah.

And there seems no end in sight.

Human history seems to be a nonsensical exercise in repetition compulsion. Great kings and little dictators, famous generals and brave corporals pave the road to nowhere with human bodies killed for nothing. And here and there, a Buddha, a Zarathustra, a Moses, and a Christ break through the gloomy clouds of human history with a ray of light and hope.

Two thousands years have passed since.

Is human life today more human, more noble, more dignified than it was before Christ? Are human beings more kind to one another than they were before? Did they give up violence and turn their swords into ploughshares? Three thousand five hundred years after Mount Sinai and the Ten Commandments, two thousand years after Golgotha and the Gospel, is humanity more human than it was before?

There was a mission of love in man's death on the cross. The mission is still unfulfilled.

BIBLIOGRAPHY

Arendt, H. (1963), *Eichmann: A Report on the Banality of Crime.* New York: Viking Press.

Baron, S. W. (1952), *A Social and Religious History of the Jews.* Second ed., New York: Columbia University Press.

Binet-Sangle, C. (1911), *La Folie de Jesus.* 3 Vols. Paris.

Danielou, J. (1962), *The Dead Sea Scrolls and Primitive Christianity.* New York: Mentor.

Engels, F. (1902), *The Origin of Family, Private Property, and the State,* Chicago: Kerr.

Freud, S. (1913), Totem and taboo. In *Standard Edition 13:* 1–164. London: Hogarth Press, 1953.

——— (1905), Three essays on the theory of sexuality. In *Standard Edition, 7:* 125–243. London: Hogarth Press, 1953.

——— (1920), Beyond the pleasure principle. In *Standard Edition, 18:* 3–66. London: Hogarth Press, 1953.

——— (1922), Group psychology and the analysis of the ego. In *Standard Edition, 18:* 67–144. London: Hogarth Press, 1953.

——— (1924), The economic problem in masochism. In *Standard Edition, 19:* 157–172. London: Hogarth Press, 1953.

——— (1927), The future of an illusion. In *Standard Edition, 21:* 5–56. London: Hogarth Press, 1953.

——— (1932), Why war. In *Standard Edition, 22:* 197–218. London: Hogarth Press, 1953.

——— (1932), *New Introductory Lectures in Psychoanalysis.* New York: Norton, 1933.

——— (1939), *Moses and Monotheism.* New York: Knopf.

——— (1938), *An outline of Psychoanalysis.* New York: Norton, 1949.

Gaster, T. H. (1956), *The Dead Sea Scriptures.* New York: Doubleday.

Greenstone, J. H. (1926), *The Messiah Idea in Jewish history.* Philadelphia: Jewish Publication Society.

Hirsch, W. (1912), *Conclusions of a Psychiatrist.* New York. Norton.

Kanzer, M. (1952), Manic-depressive psychoses with paranoid fiends. *International Journal of Psychoanalysis, 33:* 34–42.

Klausner, J. (1925), *Jesus of Nazareth.* New York: Macmillan.

——— (1946), *The Messianic Idea in Israel* (Hebrew, third ed.). Jerusalem: Mass.

Kraepelin, E. (1921), *Manic-depressive Insanity and Paranoia.* Edinburg: Livingstone.

Kroseber, A. L. (1920), Totem and taboo. *American Anthropologist, 22:* 48-55.

Lacan, J. (1952), *De la Psychoseparanoiaque.* Paris: Payot.

Mendelson, M. (1960), *Psychoanalytic Concept of Depression.* Springfield, Ill.: Thomas.

Murdock, G. P. (1949), *Social Structure*. New York: Macmillan.

Radcliffe-Brown, A. R. and Forde, D., Eds. (1950), *African Systems of Kinship and Marriage*. London: Oxrord University Press.

Renan, E. (1863), *La vie Jesus*. Paris: Alcan.

Scholem. G. G. (1954), *Major Trends in Jewish Mysticism*. New York:

Schweitzer, A. (1961), *Quest of the Historical Jesus*. New York: Macmillan.

Schweitzer, A. (1958), *The Psychiatric Study of Jesus*. Boston: Beacon Press.

Segal, M. H. (1950), The arrival of the messianic king in the testaments of the twelve patriarchs (Hebrew). *Tarbitz, 21:* 129–136.

Standhal, S. et al. (1957), *The Scrolls and the New Testament*. New York: Harper & Row.

Tarachow, S. (1976), St. Paul and early Christianity: A psychoanalytic and historical study. In *Psychoanalysis and Religion*. Vol. 1. *Psychoanalysis and Catholicism,* B. B. Wolman, Ed., New York: Gardner Press.

Werner, H. (1911), Der historische Jesu der liberalen Theologie: Ein Geisteskranker. *Neue Kirchlicke Zeitschrift, 22:* 347–390.

Wolman, B. B. (1965), The Antigone principle. *American Imago, 22:* 186–201.

Wolman, B. B. (1966), Dr. Jekyll and Mr. Hyde: A theory of the manic depressive disorder. *Proceedings of New York Academy of Science,* 28: 1020–1032.

Wolman, B. B. (1973), *Call No Man Normal*. New York: International Universities Press.

DR. SIDNEY TARACHOW *in his study,* St. Paul and Early *Christianity analyzes the personality of St. Paul against the cultural-historical background of the origins of Christianity. The Pharisees and Essenes believed in the idea of Messiah and resurrection. Jesus was but one of many in that period who preached the imminent arrival of the Messiah and the Kingdom of God. The first followers of Christ were Jews; they were never expelled from their communities for their belief in Resurrection and Christ's return, and also Roman authorities did not distinguish legally between Christians from Jews.*

St. Paul was originally a fanatical Pharisee who hated whoever opposed his doctrinal ideas, and he persecuted Christians. According to Tarachow, he was "vindictive, hurt, bitter, jealous, but he craved love." However, on his way to Damascus, when he went to persecute Christians, he had a vision and was converted to Christianity. His vision had led him to identify with both God and Christ. "The inability to separate Christ from God might have an added meaning if we consider the possibility of the conversion experience as also being an unconscious passive homosexual surrender."

To Christ the idea of love took priority over the idea of justice, but St. Paul "changed the merciful father into a strict father demanding atonement and human sacrifice."

According to Gnostics, God chose the man Jesus and made him divine. Christ, the Son, was worshipped but never raised to equal importance with God, the Father. They also tried to retain some vestige of human, sexual origin of Christ. Paul paid no attention to the role of the mother, and supressed any fantasy and mythology about the mother. According to Tarachow St. Paul's "earliest defenses were his strong compulsive drive to fulfill the law in every respect, a task which he felt he could never completely fulfill."

9

St. Paul and Early Christianity
A Psychoanalytic and
Historical Study

by

SIDNEY TARACHOW, M.D.

THIS CHAPTER DEALS WITH THE PERIOD OF THE BIRTH OF THE Christian religion, and particularly with the life of one man, Paul, who had so much to do with setting the ideology of this religion into motion and crystallizing its form. The historical period to be covered begins with the time of Christ and ends with the Council of Nicaea in 325 A.D. Paul, whose exact birthday is unknown, was probably born a few years after Christ and died in 62 A.D., or very close to that time.

At the beginning of this period the Roman Empire was still strong, but facing its declining years. Its official religious dogma was beset by competitors from various directions. Politically, nationalistic aspirations, of the Jews particularly, had to be crushed wherever they appeared. Morally, there were even more serious things afoot, and just as troublesome. Two important religious movements were invading the Roman Empire. The Jews, with their monotheistic ideal, had penetrated the farthest reaches of the empire, amassed millions of converts, and were sufficiently ponderable, ideologically and numerically, to have won important legal and religious concessions from the empire. In many sections, sacerdotally and judicially, they constituted petty states within a state, administering their own justice to their own. The Jewish movement was extremely popular with women, intellectuals, and, in general, people seeking relief from the overpopulated pagan heavens for a simpler and more rational system of belief. The other movement was the spread of oriental mystery religions into the empire. Perhaps the most prominent of these was the cult of Mithra. The Mithraic cult made epecially great strides among certain groups: soldiers, slaves, and certain civil servants and government officials. These groups came from or had contact with the fringes of the empire, and had traveled, in contrast to the large mass of fixed population in the empire. These were the groups exposed to the religions on the borders, and they became the vehicle for bringing the Mithraic cult inward to the center of the empire. The cults of the dying and rising son who will replace the father were not too far removed from the spirit of the messianic movement of the Jews.

It was the historical destiny of Paul to unite these two invading trends into a single form which was long to outlast the Roman Empire. This was Christianity, a religion that owes much more to Paul than it does to Jesus.

Jewish and Pagan Background

The Jahwist religion was an intensely nationalistic one. With each successive calamity the nationalization intensified. This process included a series of psychological adjustments to the successive traumata. The exile, the dispersions, the successive subjugations by the Persians, Greeks, and Romans led to consequences of individual, religious, and nationalistic character. These took both passive and aggressive directions.

The Jews began to look forward to some promise of relief from their present suffering. On a national scale, especially under the Romans, this led to a belief in a Messiah. Donini (1951) makes the interesting point that the Jews had no salvation doctrine of any kind until after the Exile. He also points out that salvation doctrines originated only in slave-holding societies. The original meaning of ''redemption'' is to buy back, in the sense of a slave buying back the freedom from his master. The Jewish Messiah was preponderantly a victorious and not a suffering Messiah (Wunsche, 1870), even though there are some references to a suffering Messiah in portions of the Old Testament which certain apologists make much of.

The prophets predicted the coming of the Messiah, John the Baptist being the one closest to the Christian era. Although the Jews were expected to repent their sins to deserve the favor of God, the successful messianic outcome was to be a nationalistic supremacy of the Jews over the entire world, and the Jewish God was to be victorious over all the gods of other peoples. All other peoples were to be invited to become Jews and worship the Jewish God.

On the personal side the Jews were led to a belief in an afterlife. At the time of Jesus there were fairly well-developed ideas of resurrection among the Jews. Of the three major groups of Jews, Sadduces, Pharisees, and Essenes, resurrection was accepted by the Pharisees and Essenes, most intensely by the latter (Kautsky, 1925). The Sadduces rejected the idea of resurrection. The Essenes were the poor, the Pharisees were the scholars, and the Sadduces were the priests and aristocrats. The Sadduces suffered most during the Babylonian conquest, at which time the intelligent ruling caste was either killed or exiled, leaving but the poor and the agricultural workers; this was not the case under Roman rule. The Romans used the Jewish ruling caste, and, depending on the temper of the Jews as well as the international tensions of the time, even established petty Jewish kings. Thus even under the Romans the Sadduces retained their priestly theocratic position. Their personal need for a happy hereafter was much less pressing than that of the other classes of Jews. The national messianic and personal resurrection drives of the Jews might be classified as the aggressive reactions to their subjugation.

There were also reactions that were passive. There was an intensification of the religious superego function; ethical systems and law reached almost intolerable heights. God became progressively more monotheistic, less magical, more spiritualized, more ethical, and apparently completely masculine. The monotheistic-masculine tendency is the most important. Polytheistic tendencies were supressed, the most important suppression being of mother goddess worship. The ritualized incestuous tie to mother was abandoned, and the mother figure was absorbed into the figure of Jahweh. Although the Jewish God is masculine, it is not too difficult to find concealed in it bisexuality and traces of mother (Roellenbleck, 1949). The god was thus apparently masculine, but really androgynic. The tie to father was emphasized. The submissive, token initiation rite of circumcision permitted identification and masculine aggressiveness. The primacy of a single god, the father, was never questioned. No hostility to father was permitted by the Jews. All rival gods were eliminated. All traces of magic and idolatry were suppressed. The submission to this god required the greatest degree of spiritualization and psychic internalization (Simmel, 1946).

It was during the period of the Second Temple, prior to and including the time of Christ, that the Jews spread massively throughout the Roman Empire. They proselytized actively among the pagans with great success. At the time of Jesus there were millions of Jews outside of Palestine throughout the reaches of the empire (Harnack, 1904; Kautsky, 1925; Guignebert, 1939). Estimates by reliable scholars place the number at three to eight million. There were one million Jews in Egypt alone. There was a certain variety in the character of the proselytes. Many went through a complete acceptance of Jewishness, circumcision and all. There were more women converts than men, many of the women being married to pagans. There were many incomplete (uncircumcised) converts; these were called "God fearers."

The pagan world was at that time in the throes of an intellectual revolution againsg the florid polytheism of the Roman Empire. The other important tendency of the times was the spread of cults of the dying and rising son gods. These were "mysteries" based essentially on mother-son religions. In these the father was destroyed, sometimes the son, too, only to be reborn, often then to possess the mother. The antecedents of Christianity can be seen on the one hand in Jewish Messianism and monotheism and on the other hand in the pagan oriental mysteries of the dying and rising son. The Persian cult of Mithra, of the son who slays the bull, was one of the outstanding cults of that period and was an important antecedent as well as a rival of Christianity up to the fourth century.

Perhaps one could say that because the nationalistic aspirations of the Jews had met such repeated and serious rebuffs, the Jewish energies were deflected in proselytizing activities. A victory that could not be gained by force of arms was sought by conversion. In fact, precisely such complaints were made on the floor of the Roman Senate. The messianic fervor of the Jews and certainly of the early Christians carried a not-too-well-concealed strain of rebellion against the Roman Empire. According to Guignebert (1939):

> The most convincing proof of the practical importance of Messianism about the time of Jesus is the state of emotional upheaval persisting in Israel, a state which would otherwise be quite unmotivated, and which can only be explained by the Messianic hope. During the century which preceded the birth of Jesus, and still more during the two centuries which followed, this state of unrest gave rise to various popular movements of more or less importance which did serious harm to the Jewish nation, and led at last to its final downfall.

There is, nevertheless, a certain paradox. The Roman law, which was so strict in its enforcement of worship of the official imperial gods, contained a legal loophole for the Jews. The Jews could evade worshipping the imperial gods and could worship their own. This might not be surprising in Palestine, where organized military resistance was provoked by any Roman attempt to force the Jews to conform to Roman religious practices, but it is surprising to find this liberality in the scattered cities of the empire. It is possible that certain elements of Judaism were not incompatible with the need of those forces interested in maintaining the Roman status quo, politically and socially. The Romans crushed Jewish nationalism, but not the character of Jewish social and family relations. To the Jews, father was supreme; sexual customs were thoroughly regulated (Epstein, 1948); primogeniture was accepted (Jewish Encyclopedia); religion and religious taxation were absolutely centralized; and theocratic, political stratification was formally accepted. All these tendencies as social attitudes were useful to the highly centralized organization of the Roman Empire. In one important respect Roman society was superior. Women were relatively emancipated and mingled freely with men, and some of them attained high position. In pre-Exilic times, among the Jews men and women had also mingled freely (Epstein, 1948), but after the Exile taboos against women began to be erected. The Jews who returned from the Exile came back with a strengthened monotheism and increased tendencies to suppress all lingering traces of paganism, polytheism, and local god worship (Kautsky, 1925). The movement to stricter monotheism involved suppression of mother worship, since the Jewish God was masculine. Mother was renounced and in effect tabooed. This was carried out in the synagogues by strict separation of the sexes during worship and by erecting various further taboos against women.

Jesus and Primitive Christianity

Jesus was a product of the Messianic era of the Jews. He preached the coming of the Kingdom of God and the need for repentance. His moral ideals came from the Pharisees. He demanded righteousness. However, unlike Paul, he believed man was capable of righteousness without divine aid. Jesus was but one of many in that period who went about preaching the imminent arrival of the Messiah and the Kingdom of God. Although John the Baptist preached the coming of the Messiah, he did not accept Jesus as the Messiah (McGiffert, 1914). In fact, a sect of believers in John existed for a long time after the establishment of Christianity. Jesus' personal followers remained loyal and faithful Jews: they were never expelled for their special belief in the Messiah, resurrection or the expected return of Jesus. This was all compatible with Judaism.

After the execution of Jesus there was a temporary flight of his disciples from Jerusalem. However, they returned and remained as a special sect of Jews who believed that the Messiah had already been there; they awaited his second coming. Although these believers were devout Jews, the death of Jesus perforce added a most important new element which had not been present in the teachings of Christ during his lifetime; that is, the resurrection of Christ was now put in the center of their belief. Otherwise, their overall Jewish ideal remained the same.

The Romans executed Jesus for leading Jewish agitation against Roman rule. The Jews persecuted the Christians and executed their leaders for their excessive veneration of Christ, which had reached the point of his being elevated to equality with God. This offered Paul his first historical role, to participate in the punishment of those Jews who dared say the son was equal to the father.

The original primitive Jewish Christian community in Jerusalem consisted mostly of hellenic Jews, that is Jews who had come from outside Palestine. There was some logic to this. The emphasis on the coming of the Messiah who had died and was to return was very close to the dying and rising son beliefs to which the hellenic Jews had been exposed. There was also a subtle shift away from the original nationalistic fervor of the messianic movement as preached by Jesus himself. Hellenic Jews were perhaps not as nationalistic as Palestinian Jews. Christianity spread into all the hellenic Jewish communities and found its most ready early converts among the pagans who had been partly or completely converted to Judaism.

As is seen later, Paul and the Pauline Christians abandoned the anti-Roman nationalistic aspirations of the Jews and developed a religious system that emphasized personal relationships to the resurrected Christ. Eventually, he almost abandoned the Jews entirely and chiefly sought to convert Gentiles.

Throughout almost his entire career Jesus referred to himself simply as a servant of God. He preached of the Kingdom of God as something to be attained in reality by human beings during their lives. It was only in the last few days of his life, when he was convinced he would be executed, that he proclaimed himself a Messiah (McGiffert, 1947) and proclaimed his return after death. This is not too difficult to understand. Jesus' essential ideal was true sonship to God and repentance to win the favor of God. The translation of the Greek word that is rendered as repentance does not convey the exact meaning. A more accurate rendition is to "change," to "turn about." This could have much more active meanings than the mere passive goal of repentance. This is of importance considering the revolutionary and agitational role of the Jewish prophets during those troubled times as well as the agitational message of the primitive Christians. Jesus, during his lifetime, always emphasized the fatherhood of God. After his death, the accent was shifted to the messiahship of Jesus.

The teaching of Peter was close to that of Jesus and was strictly in keeping with Pharisaic concepts, that is, that it was possible for a man to keep the law and by his own efforts win the blessings of the almighty.

Stephen, after the death of Jesus, threatened the Jewish ideal by his teaching. He held two things. He minimized the importance of the temple and he blasphemed the monotheistic ideology by saying "Behold I see the Heavens spread open and the Son of Man standing on the right hand of God." Even so Stephen considered himself a Jew and made no attempt to abrogate the Law or to turn to the Gentiles.

Jesus never broke with the Jews: he always insisted on fulfillment of the law. To be sure, he excoriated those who fulfilled the letter but not the spirit of the law. Jesus insisted on good works: he was constantly occupied with the conditions of the poor, the sick, the widows, the hungry. Jesus did not care for piety or belief, but for humanitarian behavior.

Pre-Christian Judaism was permeated with messianic hopes. The not-so-remote Maccabean wars and the exaggerated memories of the Hasmonean dynasty were unduly glorified in the minds of the later Jews and assimilated into both national and personal cravings for the coming of a messianic king. Any earlier conflict between the Hasmonean kings and messianism was forgotten. The teachings of Jesus and similar prophets found willing ears. Jesus' emphasis on the Kingdom of God certainly put forward nationalistic strivings the Romans could not afford to overlook. From that standpoint, Paul was no problem to the Roman authorities. He was always on the side of Roman political authority.

Before Paul's execution by the Roman authorities, as a result of the final split between Judaism and its Christian sect, the Christians were not legally differentiated from the Jews by the Roman authorities. The teachings of the early gnostic Christians, especially in Alexandria, led to reprisals by the Romans against the entire Jewish community. Some of these early Roman anti-Jewish edicts were provoked by the Jewish Christian agitation. In its earliest years with its emphasis on the immediate coming of the Messiah it must have been a radical movement potentially dangerous to a slave-holding society such as was the empire. Paul labored hard to get the Christians resigned to the idea that the Messiah would come at some time in the far distant future, that the Messiah was not to be expected imminently. He cooled the fervor of immediate aspirations. The Jews in general thus became the victims of the active messianic hopes of one of its own sects. (Edict of Claudius, Loisy, 1948, p. 131). The early Christian agitation was feverish and had staggering success. The early message was "God and His Christ are on the point of coming." The single factor most facilitating the spread of Christianity was the dispersion of the Jews in all the reaches of the Roman Empire. As Loisy points out, all the synagogues of the Roman Empire were open to the Christian missionaries. Wherever Paul went he always first sought out the synagogue; he always received a hearing. Even though subsequently the Jews might have driven him out of the synagogue or out of the city. "With the way into pagan territory thus opened, Christianity found there an immense clientele of the disinherited" (Loisy, 1948). Their leaders had to restrain them; Peter (I Peter 4:15) was forced to plead, "Let none of you suffer as a murderer, or a thief or an evildoer or as a revolutionary." The Pauline idea of Christian freedom was misused or misunderstood to support the revolutionary temper of the early Christians (Cadoux, 1925, pp. 99–100). Paul abandoned the revolutionary social, ethical, nationalistic ideal altogether and placed in the center of his theology personal salvation, divorced from political or nationalistic considerations.

Paul and Pauline Christianity

The Epistles of Paul are the oldest authentic New Testament writings. Paul, although part of his early life was contemporary with Christ's, never met Christ in person, and his important missionary career did not start until about 20 years after Christ's death. The teachings of Paul, and not the teachings of Jesus, form the basic structure underlying Christian dogma today.

Just as Christianity is a mixture of hellenism and Judaism, so was Paul. A hellenic Jew, with a Greek education and childhood, he had both Greek and Pharisaic elements in him. Originally a fanatical and devout Jew who persecuted the Christians, he suffered his famous conversion to Christ at the height of his persecutory activity. His acceptance by Christians, after his own conversion, was lukewarm, and his conversion was followed by a long, unproductive period. Then, after a series of special circumstances to be described, his career began.

Personality

History records almost nothing about Paul's early development or family. He was a Roman citizen by birth, his family apparently well to do and devout, though hellenic, Jews living outside of Palestine in Tarsus. This is practically all we know, except for a fleeting reference to a nephew who on one occasion in Jerusalem warned him of danger. This suggests that a married sibling lived in Jerusalem. However, Paul makes no mention of members of his family or of his attitudes toward his own family. He did not marry. He never mentions his father or his mother, although he gives a great deal of marital and sexual advice. Although his doctrines deal much with Father and Son, only once did Paul discuss actual father-and-son relations. This is limited to one sentence of advice to fathers, "Fathers, do not vex your sons, lest you break their spirit."

From various meager, scattered (and undoubtedly edited) descriptions of Paul's physical qualities certain impressions can be formed. He was a man of tremendous energy in a small frame. He had a speech defect (he refers to his own "rude" speech); he was small, bowlegged, probably had a slight deformity of his trunk, was most likely blind in one eye, and did not have good vision in the remaining eye. He had recurrent attacks of malaria which he probably contracted on his first missionary journey. Very early paintings of Paul or of Paul in the company of Barnabas indicate these visible characteristics. Later paintings change his appearance, so that nothing of the original man is really portrayed. (Similarly, paintings of Jesus during the first three centuries clearly show dark, Syrian features, but after the romanization of Christianity the Syrian origin of Jesus was concealed and he was turned into a blonde.) So with Paul, about whom there were a number of physical characteristics to be improved. Very early paintings show his small stature and show a ptosis of one eyelid. In some of his letters Paul refers to his poor eyesight. He did not himself write any of his famous epistles; he dictated them. Perhaps this is corroboration of the existence of visual defects. At the end of several of his epistles he writes a special personal greeting in his own hand. According to Greek scholars, Paul's handwriting is in large, irregular lettering, as though written by someone with poor vision, something which he, on one occasion, admits. The question of his having epileptic seizures has been raised by some. Even if this is so, his repeated attacks of hallucinatory revelation can certainly not be taken as evidence of epileptic aurae. These revelations were too closely integrated to reality, and too astute in their solutions of Paul's pressing reality or emotional problems of the moment. Paul's hallucinatory experiences provoked no organic mental confusion in any way. Just the opposite, his revelations always enabled him to embark on new specific courses of action or decision.

Paul was celibate, was constantly enjoining celibacy on others, permitting marriage only as a necessary evil ("It is better to marry than to burn"), and encouraging men and women to remain virgin. Marriage was regretfully recommended to avoid lust (masturbation?). He boasts of the suppression of his flesh, but a famous passage in his epistle to the Romans can be interpreted only as evidence that his own flesh was quite imperfectly suppressed. In fact, this passage reveals that Paul had problems that show vivid similarities to the masturbation struggles of adolescents.

> For we know that the law is spiritual: but I am carnal, sold under sin.
>
> For that which I do I allow not: for what I would, that I do not; but what I hate, that I do.
>
> If then I do that which I would not, I consent unto the law that is good.
>
> Now then it is no more I that do it, but sin that dwelleth in me.
>
> For I know that in me (that is, in my flesh) dwelleth no good thing; for to will is present with me; but how to perform that which is good I find not.
>
> For the good that I would do I do not: but the evil which I would not, that I do.
>
> Now if I do that I would not, it is no more I that do it, but sin that dwelleth in me.
>
> I find then a law, that, when I would do good, evil is present with me.
>
> For I delight in the law of God after the inward man.
>
> But I see another law in my members, warring against the law of my mind, and bringing me into captivity to the law of sin which is in my members.
>
> O wretched man that I am! Who shall deliver me from the body of this death?
>
> I thank God through Jesus Christ our Lord. So then with the mind I myself serve the law of God; but with the flesh the law of sin (Rom. 7:14).

This is in a letter written late in life. His celibacy by no means indicated Paul's freedom from his own flesh. There is some possibility that this problem, which was still troubling him late in life, was especially troubling him as an overt conscious problem when he was on the road to Damascus, that is, immediately prior to his conversion. We do know that the conscious basis for Paul's early fanatic persecution of the Christians lay in his intense religiousness and scrupulosity. He felt he could never completely fulfill the law, and he tolerated no deviation in himself or in others. It is not too difficult an assumption that the struggle with sin was his continuing masturbation problem, with its unresolved attachment to mother and rivalry and hostility to father. However, he was unable to come to terms with his masturbation problem at all. Before his conversion he was fanatically scrupulous about the law, and felt he could never fulfill it completely, and was most zealous in seeing that no one expressed any aggression against father. He is the first-named Jewish persecutor of the Christians. His own aggression against God the father had been put completely at the service of father: his vigorous persecutions of the Christians was probably a defense against his own need to defy father. However, his ambivalence must have heightened to a point he could no longer tolerate. His own suppressed aggression against father and his unconscious sympathy with the Christian elevation of the Son to equality with the Father finally forced him to join the camp of those who would elevate the Son. With his intense masochistic character formation this could only be done through a most violent upheaval, such as his conversion was. He joined those who raised the Son, but he had to accept several most severe temporary castrations. He was blinded and could neither eat nor drink for 3 days.

Paul was constantly referring to his physical infirmities and to the physical hardships and beatings he suffered. He had hysterical spells, spoke with tongues, and probably had states of religious ecstasy in which he was in God and God in him. These states of mutual introjection (Lewin, 1950) with Christ certainly made for complete identification with Christ and also with God, but also has its overtones of latent passive homosexuality.

Paul was doctrinaire and bigoted (Singer, 1919). The synagogue was a tolerant institution; Paul introduced intolerance and bigotry. It should be remembered that the synagogue, in those days, was not the official place of religious worship. Under the Sadduces, after the Babylonian Exile, religious control had become progressively more centralized (Kautsky, 1925). By the time of Christ, though, this process had already undergone a certain degree of reversal. Services were permitted in the various scattered synagogues, but ritual sacrifice was still forbidden, except in Jerusalem. The synagogue was an open forum for discussion, open to all the sects of Judaism. There was a great deal of variation in the beliefs and practices of the various Jewish sects (Friedlander, 1905). Even after Paul was charged by the Sanhedrin with blasphemy and arrived as an accused prisoner in

Rome, the Jewish synagogues in that city remained tolerant and invited Paul to speak. It was Paul who would brook no opposition, "If any man preach any other gospel to you than that ye have received (from me), let him be accursed" (Gal. 1:9).

In evaluating the ambivalent characteristics of Paul's personality, the tender, sensual side of it must not be overlooked. Klausner (1947) classes the following passage as equal to any of the world's greatest poetry, and with this opinion the writer would agree.

> Though I speak in all the tongues of men and angels, if I have not love, I am no better than sounding brass or a tinkling cymbal. And though I have the gift of prophecy, and understand all the mysteries, and all the depths of knowledge; and though I have the fullness of faith, so that I could remove mountains; if I have not love, I am nothing. And though I sell all my goods to feed the poor, and though I give my body to be burned, if I have not love it profits me nothing. Love is long suffering; love is kind; love envies not; love speaks no vaunts; love swells not with vanity; love offends not by rudeness; love seeks not her own; is not easily provoked; bears no malice; rejoices not over iniquity, but rejoices in the victory of truth; foregoes all things, believes all things, hopes all things, endures all things. Love shall never pass away; but Prophecies shall vanish, and Tongues shall cease, and Knowledge shall come to nought. For our Knowledge is imperfect, and our prophecying is imperfect. But when the perfect is come, the imperfect shall pass away. When I was a child, my words were childish, my desires were childish, my judgments were childish; but being grown a man, I have done with the things of childhood. So now we see darkly, by a mirror, but then face to face; now I know in part, but then shall I know, even as I now am known. Yet while other gifts shall pass away, these three, Faith, Hope, and Love abide; and the greatest of these is Love (Cor. I, beginning at 13:1).

Paul was vindictive, hurt, bitter, jealous, but he craved love, as this passage shows. From whom he craved this love is an important consideration, father or mother?

Career and Further Personal Characteristics

The first known fact about Paul is that he killed a man. We hear nothing of him until the stoning of Stephen, an event in which Paul must have had an important part, since he is recorded in Acts as the principal witness. The principal witness, by law, throws the first stone. Acts tells us that the bloodied garments of the dead martyr were laid at Paul's feet. Paul bore the guilt, and there is reason to believe that this guilt was a serious problem to him. To the monotheistic Jew Stephen deserved death for his blasphemy in declaring the Son equal to the Father, yet it is also true that Stephen was executed illegally, before the sentence of death had been officially pronounced by the Sanhedrin. In effect, Stephen was lynched by a mob of infuriated Jews while the court was still in session, and Paul must have been one of the ringleaders of the mob. The intensity of his guilt about this must be measured by his later conversion and other experiences. After the execution of Stephen, Paul spent a number of years in feverish and vindictive persecution of Christians. He set himself up as a sort of informal assistant to the Sanhedrin and became well known to the Christians as their nemesis.

It should be remembered that the original Christians (more correctly, the Jewish sectarian followers of Jesus—the term Christian was used later in Antioch by the Gentile followers of Jesus) were devout Jews, a special sect who believed that the Messiah had come, been killed, resurrected and then vanished, to return at some future time. At worst they deserved contempt for believing in a false messiah, that is, one who had failed in his mission. This sect lived peaceably with their fellow Jews so long as Judaic monotheism remained undisturbed. Stephen, from the academic standpoint, may correctly be called the first Christian. He got into difficulties when he elevated Jesus into a godlike figure to be considered on an equal footing with God. This was more than the Jews could tolerate.

New believers entered the Christian community through baptism, but not so Paul. Paul was not baptized. He became a Christian not through a birth rite from mother but rather through a passive surrender to father.

Paul had established quite a reputation for himself as a zealous Pharisaic persecutor of the Christians. In connection with such activities he asked for and received a letter authorizing him to go to Damascus as the official representative of the Sanhedrin to seek out and bring the Christians to punishment. It was on the road to Damascus that Paul had his famous hallucinatory conversion experience. Christ appeared *in* him in a brilliant blinding vision and asked, "Why dost thou persecute me?" Paul fell to the ground, and could neither eat nor drink for 3 days. He was led, helpless, into Damascus and brought to Ananias, a Christian. Ananias laid hands on him and at that moment his vision was restored and he became a Christian.

A number of interesting problems are raised by the conversion of Paul occurring at the time it did. We must attempt, with the meager factual knowledge of our disposal, to arrive at a rationale for the event and its timing. Paul was acting for the Sanhedrin: he was an official agent. This is the first record of Paul's official relationship to the Sanhedrin. In the first major event, the stoning of Stephen, he certainly was not. We know, from scrutiny of Paul's entire life that he could not tolerate subordination to human authority. It is perhaps a reasonable assumption that so much resistance was provoked in him by this subordinate role, as the agent of the Sanhedrin, that he was driven to overthrow it. We can also be reasonably certain that this ambivalent attitude to the Sanhedrin reinforced his ambivalence about his own opposition to the Christian tendency to elevate the son. The intolerable tension was resolved by the conversion in which the primacy of the Father, as well as the Sanhedrin, was overthrown. True, at a price, but overthrown. Another element is the possibility that, once acting as the official agent of the Sanhedrin, there was no avenue left open for him for his unconscious guilt about the execution of Stephen and the persecution of the Christians. This, too, must have contributed to a heightening of the ambivalent tensions within him. Furthermore, as the official agent of the Sanhedrin, there was no room for ambivalence. He was here a fully committed ally of God, Father, and Sanhedrin. This was more than he was able or willing to do. His elevation of the Son indicates how deeply he was in sympathy with the Christians all the time. Once converted, he had eventually to turn his passive experience into an active one and become a missionary.

Since Christ appeared *in* him, the original conversion experience was an ecstatic identification with Christ and God. Paul does not differentiate clearly between God and Christ, although it is Christ that appears in Paul. This inability to separate Christ from God might have an added possible meaning if we consider the possibility of the conversion experience as also being an unconscious passive homosexual surrender. If so, then perhaps Christ the son *in* him might represent the troublesome penis of father. If so, the conversion goes even farther in resolving Paul's tensions. It makes homosexuality unconsciously tolerable, through the medium of an ecstatic identification with the powerful phallus of father.

The conversion resulted in complete surrender, that is, he gave up his aggression against the Christians, concomitantly accepting a series of genital and oral castrations, being unable to see, eat or drink for three days; nevertheless, he proceeded to put Father in a secondary role; because the Son was equal to God. The Jews recognized intermediaries between themselves and God, even Satan, an adversary of God, a supernatural one. They recognized a Messiah, but one who would only be the agent of God to carry out God's will. To the Jews Paul's position was blasphemy. Stephen and Peter were both executed for this. Later, James, who had reconciled for so many years the Jews and the early Jewish Christians, finally succumbed to the same temptation and was executed by the Jews for daring to consider Jesus as an equal to God. Paul's conversion was a castrative surrender, but his reward was that the Son was put on an equal footing with God.

The Son's characteristics were quite different from the characteristics of a Jewish Messiah. Although here and there in the Old Testament there may be references to the suffering a Messiah might have to undergo, careful students agree that the Jewish Messiah is not a suffering Messiah. He is not a sacrificial victim to God, but the powerful executor of God's will in the reestablishment of the Kingdom of God on the Earth. In this kingdom the Jews would be first, not only people, but the favored ones. True, the Jews would first suffer and be punished for their sins, but the kingdom would be established for the worthy survivors, on this earth. This is exactly what Jesus preached, in the Jewish tradition.

Although Paul preached the most complete submissiveness to God and Christ and insisted that the true believer must always be ready to receive Christ, that Christ dwelt in him (Paul insisted that in his conversion experience Christ appeared *in* him, not *to* him), nevertheless, in his personal dealings with men and institutions, he was markedly ambivalent. On the one hand, he always needed a companion, on the other hand, there was only one disciple, Timothy, who was able to tolerate Paul's temperament consistently over a long period of years. Timothy has been described as gentle and effeminate (Howson, 1873). He was circumcised by Paul's hand. Furthermore, Paul seemed unable to accept the authority of a group. Barnabas, of the Antioch community, had plucked Paul out of 14 years of oblivion and started him on his successful career of missionary tours. One measure of Paul's inability to get along with others was that at the beginning of the second tour he had a quarrel with Barnabas about Mark and refused to work any further with Barnabas or ever again admit the authority of the Antioch community over him. Immediately after his break with Barnabas he idled awhile until he found a new companion, Silas. With Silas he then went forth. After Silas, he added Timothy, whom he circumcised. The castrated became the castrator.

Paul was appreciative of Timothy's loyalty, and showed it in many ways, but in general Paul isolated himself even from the missionary community, felt he was mistreated and persecuted, and over and over again proclaimed his independence of the Twelve Apostles. He made this an important point. He received his commission directly from God, not from man. On the other hand, Paul tried repeatedly to get the group of Apostles in Jerusalem to accept him as one of their number. The reaction of the Twelve Apostles was mixed. They did not prohibit him from preaching his message, but neither did they accept him as one of them.

This must have been a source of bitterness to him throughout his life, since he made so much of the idea that he is, "Paul, an apostle, not of men, neither by men, but by Jesus Christ, and God the Father, who raised him from the dead" (Gal. 1). It was easier for Paul to surrender to the spiritual lord than to his physical representatives on earth. In his later epistles even this spiritual submission acquired physical characteristics. Paul eventually remarked that God is in him, not spiritually, but bodily.

Paul could not work in harmony with the Antioch group either. What Paul would accept from God, he could not accept from man. Paul was isolated, and proud of his isolation, glorying in his uniqueness and in the perpetual bitterness he had to the Twelve Apostles. To quote Loisy (1948), a religious, not a psychiatric, historian, "He sees himself and describes himself as pursued by unrelenting hostility, which he takes pains to discredit by attributing it to a difference of opinion about the essential principles of salvation and to certain unworthy intentions, but which we may suspect was mainly personal, caused by the way in which Paul had created solely for himself a schism from the other missionaries."

Even so, in spite of his bitterness and pride in his lack of subordination and pride in his lack of indebtedness to the elders of Jerusalem, he was nevertheless always eager for an eventual reconciliation with them and hoped for acceptance by them, specifically, as a Jew. During his last visit to Corinth, when he was already planning on Rome as a field for missionary work, he wrote his Epistle to the Romans. This letter was a preliminary piece of spadework intended to precede his arrival there. In it he insisted he was a Jew, "a Pharisee of the Pharisees." Before going to Rome, he planned a trip, which proved to be his last, to Jerusalem. True, this last trip had its degree of political motivation. He brought a collection of money, elaborately gathered throughout the Mediterranean, to the Jerusalem central headquarters of Jewish Christianity. It is interesting and important that at this point in life, Paul, the Apostle to the Gentiles, attempted to make peace with Jerusalem, the headquarters of Jewish Christianity, not with Antioch, the headquarters of Gentile Christianity. He made the trip to Jerusalem as a Jew. He made the Nazirite vow, shaved his head, and entered the Temple to fulfill the vow. This was done with the collaboration and on the advice of the elders in Jerusalem. That this miscarried, when he was recognized as the propagandist to the Gentiles, was fatally unfortunate for Paul. It led to his arrest and eventual death, as discussed elsewhere in this chapter.

It is inconceivable that Paul, who was so sensitive in his appreciation of the sentiments of his opponents, particularly the opposition of Jews and Jewish Christians, would not have known the risks he was running by returning to Jerusalem and entering the Temple. In a sense, Paul knowingly courted death by entering the Temple. He had already, years before, been forced to flee Jerusalem because he had brought an uncircumcised Gentile into the Temple. Perhaps Paul was unconsciously seeking to carry out an identification with Christ and die a martyr's death; perhaps even an identification with Stephen, Stephen who had died an illegal martyr's death at Paul's own hand.

Two remaining outstanding characteristics of Paul are closely interrelated. They are (1) his need for male companions, and (2) his need for revelation at moments of indecision or acute crisis.

We might perhaps recapitulate the important known events in Paul's life as follows: First, he kills a man. Then there is a period of feverish intensification of hostility to believers in the Messiah. At the height of this activity he abruptly explodes in a castrative conversion and a passive, suffering identification with the Son, now a diety.

There then followed an unproductive period of 14 years' duration. His actions during this 14-year period are, briefly, as follows: After the laying on of hands by Ananias in Damascus, he withdrew into the Arabian desert for 3 years. He then returned to Damascus to preach but was forced by the Jews to flee. He came to Jerusalem where he saw Peter and James, elders of the primitive Christian community, and tried to be accepted by them as an Apostle. They refused to accept him as an equal, although they accepted the validity of his conversion. He got into trouble with the Jews and had to flee. This flight was at the instigation of a hallucination. Paul returned to his native province and was lost in obscurity for the next 11 years until Barnabas invited him to be his assistant in Antioch.

The first outstanding event indicating Paul's peculiar relationship to another man is his relationship to Barnabas. At the time Paul was working near Tarsus in obscurity there was an active Christian church at Antioch. Barnabas, a Jew, was one of its leading figures. We do not know how Barnabas came to know of Paul, but, in any event, he invited him to be his assistant in proselytizing work in Antioch. With this invitation from Barnabas his brilliant career as a missionary began. Apparently his active career had to wait until a real conciliation with a father surrogate took place.

Paul had appeared on the stage of history first guilty of murder; only after 14 years of waiting for a reconcilation with a father figure does he then re-enter the stage in a productive way as a missionary. This father-son relationship between Barnabas and Paul is interestingly corroborated by events on the island of Crete. Barnabas and Paul traveled there on a missionary journey. The Greek inhabitants called the two missionaries Zeus and Mercury (father and son). Barnabas was older, tall, handsome, with a beautiful beard. Paul was small and active, even with his physical handicaps.

Within a short time he surpassed his mentor. Paul took the lead. Except for his own father, about whom we know nothing, only this once in his life did Paul accept a man in an overt paternal relationship; this was with Barnabas. Paul turned out to be an aggressive as well as a jealous son. Barnabas apparently helped Paul overcome an inhibition with which he had been left for 14 years after his conversion. Barnabas, an ideal and helpful father figure and a Jew, opened Paul's way to productivity.

There are three large areas of Paul's life that are shrouded in obscurity. One is his early life up to the stoning of Stephen. He was apparently an obsessional, overzealous Pharisee (perhaps the very type Jesus criticized), living away from his parents and family, unmarried, and having nothing to do with women. He keeps us in the dark about his family. It is odd that, in comparing Jesus with Paul, Paul, of whose direct writings and actions we are so much more certain, gives us no data whatever about his family, whereas we do know a little about the family of Jesus.

The second period of obscurity came immediately after his

conversion. Following the laying on of hands by Ananias he isolated himself in the Arabian desert for 3 years. This was probably a period of intense asceticism.

The third period of obscurity is the 11 years he spent in his native province in and near Tarsus. There is no indication in his letters that during this time he had any intimates or co-workers, or that he had any contact with his family. Whatever work he accomplished during this time was apparently not sufficiently important for himself to have made any special mention of in his own later writings.

Thus we can see that Paul remained unproductive for at least 14 years after his conversion. This was partly on account of his own inner reaction associated with his conversion and partly on account of the various real rebuffs. On his return to Damascus from the desert he had to contend not only with the suspicions of the Christians, but with the antipathy of the Jews. As we know, he escaped from Damascus and made his way to Jerusalem. Here he tried to persuade Peter and James that he was one of them. He received only qualified acceptance from them; at the same time he again encountered trouble with the Jews at Jerusalem. He was warned by a hallucination to leave Jerusalem. About this hallucination we might parenthetically remark that from a practical standpoint it was the only conclusion he could safely have come to. He went back to the country of his birth and his family, in and near Tarsus, but he did not live with his family. He produced no work of permanent importance during these 11 years. He had been rejected by all. Perhaps he was sulking, perhaps inhibited. Neither the Jews nor the Christians would have him.

Next is a momentous change. Paul is befriended by a benevolent and kind father figure, Barnabas, of the Antioch community. This center had become, without Paul's help, an important proselytizing center for Christianity among the Gentiles. Paul was invited to be Barnabas' assistant, which he was for several years at Antioch. It was here that Paul recognized the Gentile world as the field for his missionary work, although Paul always made his approach first through the synagogue. At the end of the first period of work at Antioch Paul was selected to go to

Jerusalem with Barnabas and Titus (a Gentile) to iron out the problem of the conversion of Gentiles. Before Paul was able to decide definitely on this trip, he again had recourse to a revelation which told him to go up to Jerusalem. Although in Jerusalem Paul won the right to carry the gospel to the Gentiles, this trip to the elders of the Nazarene community in Jerusalem was essentially a disappointment to him. Paul wanted to be accepted as one of the Apostles, on a par with the elders of Jerusalem. All he received was the "right hand of fellowship." but not equality as an apostle. This was his second rejection at the hands of the elders in Jerusalem.

One most important practical result of this conference must not be overlooked. This conference resulted in the formalization of the split of the Christian movement into a Jewish wing and a Gentile wing. The Jewish wing of the Christian church considered themselves Jews and remained based in Jerusalem. The Gentile wing, of course, did not consider themselves Jews and slowly grew larger in size and farther away in doctrine from their Jewish brethren. Their headquarters were in Antioch. It was Paul who created the final definite split of the Christian movement as a separate religion from Judaism. The Gentile wing of the primitive Christian church eventually became Christianity as we know it today. The Jewish wing disappeared some time after the Bar Kochba revolt.

On his return from Jerusalem the Antioch community planned its first itinerant missionary expedition. Barnabas was to be its leader, and his two assistants were to be Paul and Mark, Barnabas' nephew. Once more Paul needed the intervention of a hallucinatory experience to enable him to embark on this expedition. They set off; the expedition was difficult in many ways; the hostility of the Jews, difficulties of traveling and, to top it all, Paul contracted malaria, from which he probably continued to suffer intermittently for the rest of his life. Because of the difficulties Mark returned to Antioch; Paul never forgave him this desertion. This trip lasted 3 years before they returned to report to Antioch. It is an interesting commentary that Acts records that Barnabas and Paul started their expedition, but by the time of their return they are recorded as Paul and Barnabas.

Barnabas planned a second trip, again inviting Paul and his nephew Mark. This provoked an emotional explosion in Paul. He refused to go if Mark went along. Barnabas refused to drop his nephew. This broke up the relationship between Paul and Barnabas and also between Paul and the Antioch community, to which Paul was never again subordinate. Barnabas went off on his trip into Asian territory.

At this point Paul was adrift and depressed. Without Barnabas he could not get started, and he was unable to get started at all until he met Silas. With a companion his spirits and will revived. He started traveling, added Timothy to his entourage. He circumcised Timothy. Paul tentatively started twice to begin missionary work, but each time was prevented from further missionary work in Asia. Once a vision told him to stay away, the other time he was hindered, probably by a recurrence of his malaria. It is interesting that at this point, after his break with Barnabas, he was unable to work in Asian territory to compete with Barnabas on Barnabas' ground. He could break relations with him, but could not compete with him on his ground.

Finally, still not having accomplished anything, he reached Troas in the Aegean sea, where he met Luke, a Macedonian physician. Perhaps the physician took over the position Barnabas had had for Paul, because the next important event was a vision of a Macedonian pleading for Paul's help. Paul was invited to Europe by a hallucination. This hallucination served several purposes. It kept Paul from infringing on Barnabas' territory, that is, he now turned his back on Asia; it permitted him to deny his passive needs in reference to Luke, who had cared for Paul during his illness; most importantly, he was now able to get back to activity. He was now in working equilibrium; he had accumulated several male companions, including one effeminate companion and one paternal surrogate. The hallucination denied his passivity and reinforced the drive to action and his sense of importance to others. He was now able to get back to work. Paul, Luke, Timothy, and Silas all set sail for Macedonia.

Although Paul had needed the companionship of Silas and Timothy to start his travels on his second missionary journey, he nevertheless had wandered aimlessly from Pisidian Antioch to Troas, where, ill, he met Luke, the physician. This meeting with Luke is what really enabled Paul to get started again. Again Paul had needed a substitute father figure to replace the one he had so recently lost. There was an important difference between Luke and Barnabas. Luke was not an active missionary, as Barnabas was. Rivalry was thus eliminated. Luke was simply a physician and personal companion. It is interesting that it is at Troas that the first of the four famous "we" passages is found in the Acts of the Apostles. The "we" passages are generally attributed to Luke. Students of Acts point out that the four "we" passages are marked by little theological depth, but great richness of description and direct personal experience, in other words, written by a companion of Paul, but by someone who did not engage or compete with him in his religious activities. Under such conditions, Luke remained a lifelong friend of Paul's, although even so he was with him only intermittently. Timothy was the only constant companion.

Paul's conversion was never complete, dramatic and castrative though it was. He was constantly struggling against father figures. In fact, even with Barnabas he probably never really succeeded in overcoming his fear of him. The second missionary trip was planned by Barnabas, not by Paul, and it was Barnabas who invited Paul to accompany him, and not vice versa. Paul finally broke with him. Barnabas was still the victor, when Paul, nursing his hurts, aimless because of the loss of Barnabas, and unable to enter into any competition with him, was in fact unable to get back to work until he found Luke and established a suitable relationship with him.

In his conversion he was helped to master his aggression; in his hallucination of the Macedonian, it was his passivity he needed help with. His supernatural experiences thus helped him handle both sides of his extreme ambivalence. He had been ill and saved by Luke, the physician; in the hallucination, a Macedonian (Luke) is pleading with him for help. He identifies with the aggressor. He became aggressive to save the Macedonian as the Macedonian had saved him. This is both projection and denial. His own passivity was lived out in others.

With all his need for men, Paul nevertheless would not accept the supremacy of any man over him, nor would he accept money from men. He insisted on his practicing his trade as tentmaker to earn his own living, and he cautioned his disciples to do the same. However, he did accept money from a woman, Lydia, the wealthy Macedonian woman who offered her home to Paul and the new converts. He accepted gifts of money from her and from the Phillipian congregation, about which there is evidence to indicate that in it were large numbers of women. Another woman who played an important part in his life was Priscilla, the wife of Aquila. He spent much time in the household of this married couple. When they moved from Corinth to Ephesus, Paul followed them later and lived in their home for a time. The few women in Paul's life seem to be not sexual objects, but persons who cared for Paul and fed and housed him.

By the end of the second missionary journey Paul is without Silas and Luke, but Timothy is with him permanently until the end of his life. Timothy's personality is indicated by Loisy (1948, p. 159): "To remain for long the companion of Paul a docile temper was necessary, like that of the good Timothy." Luke, the physician, is with him from time to time, and probably also with him at the time of his death. On his way to Corinth from Macedonia, during this second missionary journey, Paul stopped in Athens for a short time. Here he was remarkably unsuccessful. One of the reasons for this lack of success was the fact that he was alone. He had sent Timothy and Silas off on errands elsewhere, and he was alone in Athens. He was anxious and depressed. He went on to Corinth and waited there in anxiety and depression until they arrived. Then he went to work, and his work was successful.

In Corinth he ran into a good deal of difficulty with the Jews and was on the verge of fleeing, as he had so often fled other cities when the Jews had turned to the Roman authorities to expel him as a heretic Jew. Again Paul had recourse to a vision which told him to stay. This hallucinatory advice turned out to be remarkably astute, since the Jews at the time were out of favor in Rome, and their pleas to punish Paul would have gone unheeded at that time. This missionary journey included a final short stay at Ephesus and then ended at Antioch.

His third missionary journey was spent largely at Ephesus although he revisited the Macedonian and Corinthian territories. At Ephesus he lived for a time with Priscilla and Aquila, the married couple he had met in Corinth on his previous journey.

It was during his long stay at Ephesus, his third journey, that he decided to tackle the center of the Roman empire, Rome itself. However, he felt it necessary to make it plain that he was doing this as a Jew, and that he was a Jew. He made a long trip gathering money to be given to the Jews in Jerusalem; he made the Nazirite vow, including the shaving of his head. He wanted to get the support of the Jerusalem community, that is, the Jewish party of the Christian Church, for his venture. In Jerusalem James accepted his offering and advised Paul to complete his vow by completing certain prayers in the Temple. Paul did this, and almost completed his vows uneventfully. But he was discovered by the Jews and charged as having been the one who had brought an uncircumcised man into the temple. He was arrested and could have been put to death by the Sanhedrin. At this critical point a vision told him to declare himself a Roman citizen rather than a Jew, and to seek the safety of the Roman court.

The advice dictated by the vision was in effect a maneuver to escape the jurisdiction of the Sanhedrin and to take refuge in his Roman citizenship with its right to a Roman trial. However, although he escaped the Jews, he was now in trouble with the Romans, the only outcome of which could be his death. Although he was removed from the authority of the Sanhedrin, he was now in a fatal conflict with Roman law.

Two and one half centuries later it was precisely Paul's teachings that Rome found useful and used as the mainstay of the reasons why Christianity should become legally acceptable. Rome and the church at that time joined forces to purge Christianity of any anti-Pauline doctrine. However, during first-century Christianity the Roman Empire was strong enough not to need Christianity as an ally. During the first century the Roman Empire had a working arrangement either with the central Jewish authorities in Jerusalem or with the dispersed Jews throughout the empire by which the Jews were permitted to worship their own God and were tacitly excused from having to worship the official Roman gods, who included the Roman rulers. No other group in the entire Roman Empire had such an agreement. The situation that developed late in Paul's life was that his teachings led to a break with Judaism, in fact it was a separate, new religion, with worship of a new deity, Jesus, recognized neither by the Jews nor by the Roman authorities. The Jews who disclaimed any connection with such a religion put Paul in a serious predicament. They claimed jurisdiction over Paul as a blaspheming Jew and could have legally put him to death. Paul, to save his life, sought the protection of the Roman authorities, denying the Jewish jurisdiction. Once outside the Jews, he now faced trial for preaching a religion not officially included among the official Roman deities and not protected by the arrangement between Romans and the Jews. As such, he was subject to the death penalty by the Romans for violating Roman laws governing worship of the official Gods. Paul's case was the official precedent for the punishment of a Christian for violating the Roman laws of religious worship. Fixed, high, Roman policy, not the idle whims of a cruel tyrant, is what touched off the Neronian Christian persecutions.

There is further evidence indicating that Paul was driven by a strong masochistic or even suicidal impulse in returning to Jerusalem to invite the very events which took place, that is, his arrest and eventual execution at the hands of the Romans, a repetition of that which happened to Jesus. The evidence is as follows. The book of Acts gives in great detail Paul's trip to Rome as a Roman prisoner. On this trip through the Mediterranean occurred the well-known storm and hazards to the ship and all its passengers. At the height of the storm, when it seemed that the ship could not possibly survive and all would perish, Paul was visited by an angel of God who said to him, "Fear not, Paul; thou must be brought before Caesar: and lo, God hath given thee all them that sail with thee." Death by drowning, at that point, would have been a tremendous disappointment to Paul. At that moment, facing death, he needed reassurance not merely that his life would be saved, but that it would be saved for a specific purpose, to appear for punishment before Caesar. He was not at all interested in saving his life merely to be alive, or to die in advance and so to cheat the Roman courts of their opportunity to punish him. He welcomed the masochistic experience with Rome; he could not risk losing this opportunity of repeating Christ's experience. The hallucination promised him this gratification. The second half of Paul's message from God is characteristic. In the first half, he is the sacrificial victim; in the second half he is the savior of all. Paul must have been an extraordinarily sadomasochistic individual, because he must have known that by making a test case of himself, he was dooming all other Christians as well to the same punishment. When he exposed himself to the Roman law, he exposed all Christians.

His missionary career is marked by masochistic strivings. He gloried in shipwrecks and floggings, stonings, and punishments visited on him by the Jewish communities, especially in his earlier journeyings. He was provocative, too. In Corinth, for example, where he had a great deal of difficulty with the Jewish congregation and was expelled by them, he set his headquarters up next door to the synagogue, seeking further trouble and embroilments.

Teachings

Curiously, Paul places no emphasis on Jesus' life and work, only on his sacrificial death. The life and teachings of Jesus had certain personal characteristics. Jesus dealt with concrete people, used simple language, and used parables of simple situations. His emphasis was on humane actions. Jesus taught that one served God by serving man. Paul was occupied with a much more subtle kind of teaching.

Paul, who insisted on the elevation and worship of Christ, is nowhere concerned with the actual life of Christ, his family, his birth, his mother, or his teachings. The suppression of the mother and the sexual situation in Pauline theology conflicted with the many contemporary gnostic Jewish–Christian theologies in which

male and female, father and mother were concepts fully treated
and elaborated in their systems. As is noted later, the Gnostics
searched for scientific and sexual explanations of the world. Paul
and later the Catholic Christian church engaged in bitter controversy with the Gnostic sects. In a letter Paul cautions Timothy
against the "endless genealogies," obviously referring to the
Gnostic systems which had almost endless pairs of sexually mated
beings bridging the gap from god to man.

Paul seems to avoid the family and sexual connotations of
Christ's life, just as he avoids giving any biographic family
material about himself. Paul indicates a rather androgynous conception of birth (in this he is closer to the Hebrews): he refers to
his disciples as his sons by his word. Paul is preoccupied with
relations between father and son. Interest in mother or sexual
theories about mother (which the Gnostics had in abundance) or
the physical birth of a son from mother were completely suppressed. The problem of the relation of Christ to Mary was never
even mentioned by Paul. It took awhile for the problem to appear, even after Paul's time. Paul's emphasis was on the relationship to God and a constant readiness to receive him. So far as
heterosexuality is concerned, he railed against it at all times.

Certain aspects of Christ's life, however, did occupy Paul.
These were the Last Supper, the Crucifixion, the Resurrection,
and the problem of the in-dwelling God.

Paul believed man's nature was fleshly and sinful. He traced
the origin of evil to the involuntary transgression of the first man,
the Fall (Rom. v.12–19) (I Cor. 15: 21-22): "For since by man
came death, by man came also the resurrection of the dead" (21).
"For as in Adam all die, so also in Christ shall all be made alive"
(22). God's nature was spiritual. Evil expresses itself in desires or
lusts: all men are slaves of the flesh. Paul struggled with this his
entire lifetime. Sin was death and righteousness was life. He was
constantly searching for some escape from sin. Jesus' continued
spiritual existence was due to his absolute holiness. If he had been
unholy, he could not have escaped the grasp of death. Christ saves
a man by entering and taking up his abode within him, by binding
him indissolubly to himself so it is no longer he that lives but
Christ that lives in him, so that whatever Christ does he does and

whatever he does Christ does. "When it pleased God to reveal his son in me" (Gal. 1:16). "I have been crucified with Christ; yet I live; yet no longer I but Christ liveth in me" (Gal. 2: 20). His union with Christ meant death to the flesh, but life to the spirit. The spirit maintains a constant struggle with the flesh. So long as the attitude of receptivity, openness, and self-emptiness is maintained, Christ dwells in the man, living in him and through him the Christian free life over which the law has no dominion. But if a man fail to keep the atittude of receptivity, Christ will depart, and he will come again under the control of the flesh and will fall under the dominion of the law. The entire Christian life was due to the in-dwelling spirit.

Paul introduced an important shift, from Jesus the Messiah, with emphasis on his life, to Christ the Divine Saviour and Redeemer from sin, with emphasis on his death. His sacrifical death is the center of Paul's teaching. To the Jews and also the Jewish Christians, God the Father was in the center of the theology, but to Paul Christ was in the center. He always approached God through Christ. Paul shifted the center from father to son, but at the same time Christ was a human sacrifice that God commanded to mollify God's wrath (Rom. 3:25). The Jews had finally abandoned animal sacrifice. Paul reintroduced human sacrifice.

Paul's idea of God was quite different from that of Jesus. To Jesus God's love came before his justice, but not so with Paul. For Paul paternal love demanded special atonement. Paul changed the merciful father into a strict father demanding atonement and human sacrifice. Even further, man's fate depended merely on God's will, not on human conduct. "Therefore hath he mercy on whom he will have mercy and whom he will, he hardeneth" (Rom. 9:18). Paul believed that God could hate a man before he was born; for example, he believed God hated Esau before he was born. Jesus believed that God sent certain messengers, angels of love and mercy. To Paul, there were no messengers of love from God. However, there were messengers from Satan. As a direct picture of God or as a projection of his own hostility, this certainly indicates a much greater degree of hatred in Paul than in Jesus. To Jesus, God would forgive a penitent sinner, but not to Paul. Paul assumed God forgave no sins until Christ died.

At the same time Paul rejected circumcision and the law. In fact, he blamed the law for sin. If there were no law, there would be no sin. Paul created the sophist concept of Christian liberty from the flesh and sin, in which there is no law and no sin if one has renounced the flesh and is one with Christ. In a tortured obsessional line of reasoning he blamed the existence of sin on the law. Paul's concept of freedom from the law was used by many Christians in support of sexual and politically revolutionary ideas Paul had not really intended. Paul's verbal bait of liberty was simply liberty to be passive and masochistic.

The ancient Jews practiced baptism as a purification rite; the primitive Christians practiced baptism in the name of Jesus, but without any reference to his death. To Paul, baptism meant a reliving of the death and resurrection of Christ, but a rebirth with freedom from sin and the flesh. Baptism in the name of the Trinity was practically unknown even in the New Testament and is foreign to primitive Christianity and even to Pauline Christianity (McGiffert, 1947). The identification with Christ was then further strengthened through the eucharist. This mystical union with Christ was Paul's important oriental addition to the earlier beliefs of the Judaic Christians. According to Pfister (1920, p. 257) "The idea of an attraction toward and of mystical union with the dead and resurrected God-Saviour is completely lacking in Christian religion before St. Paul. It is, however, found in the cult of Attis and Mithras." In emphasizing the identification with Christ through the meal Paul did have a certain area of Jewish Old Testament belief from which to begin. He could base his ideas to a degree on Jewish tradition. A commemorative meal in which Christ is sacrifice for a new covenant with God corresponds to Exodus 24:3–8, the first covenant between Israel and Jahweh. Thus, broadly considered, the communion is a messianic covenant for Christ to fulfill both the Old Testament and the hopes of the Christians. However, the real derivation of the Christian communion is from the hellenic mystery cults. In these religions the meal is not commemerative, it is direct identification, such as Paul feels; meat, blood, milk, water, even images of the god baked in dough are eaten. The body and the blood of Christ are in this tradition, eating the god. In the seven stages of initiation into the mysteries of Mithras, the identifications proceed up an ascending scale. In the first, the believer is a crow, but by the seventh he is father (Hastings' Encyclopedia, 1910). Another point repeatedly emphasized by Paul was that the church was the body of Christ. This anthropomorphic concept of the church certainly facilitated universal identification with Christ.

Paul did not identify himself with the nationalistic aspirations of the Jews. His doctrine was satisfactory to the Romans and to the rich. He instructed the slave to return to his master; he instructed obedience to constituted legal authority as being so ordained by God. He always referred to the Roman provinces by their Roman not their provincial local names. He also changed his own name from the Hebrew Saul to its Roman counterpart, Paul. His influence was to convert a Jewish, nationalistic, messianic sect into one with emphasis on personal rather than national aspirations. There was a degree of political opportunism in the direction taken by Pauline Christianity. As Klausner (1946) points out (p. 299):

> We are dealing with the end of the period of the Second Temple, when the political fortunes of the Jews were sinking lower and lower. Gentiles in general and Romans in particular at that time felt scorn and contempt for the Jews and Judaism. The powerful of the earth were Gentiles and not Jews. To speak of a Jewish Messiah at that time was very dangerous, since there was a political side in such a Messiah, upon which the Romans looked with suspicion. It was necessary, therefore, to depart more and more from the Jewish Messianic idea, to transform the Jewish Messiah into a pagan "saviour", to compromise more and more with the Gentiles in general and the Roman Empire in particular, to load the sin of the crucifixion of Jesus upon the shoulders of the weak Jews, to blame them and not the Roman authorities for the persecution of the Christians, and to make all sorts of exemptions and lightening of requirements for Gentiles and Gentilism.

The Struggle for Survival

The second, third, and fourth centuries were marked by ferment and struggle. In a way one can say that the contending forces were, on the one hand, struggling attempts to introduce rational thought and science, and, on the other, to develop more irrational, mythological, and magical polytheistic tendencies. On the political side this was the period of the declining Roman Empire, the slave-holding society was disintegrating, and the emperors sought various alliances in their attempts to preserve themselves. Some of these conflicts came to a head at the Council of Nicaea in 325 A.D. Here the rational tendencies were defeated by a coalition consisting of Constantine and the majority of the Christian bishops.

The developing Christian dogma had to contend with tendencies on either side. On one side were the pagan mystery cults, notably of Mithra, which were very close to the instinctual problems that had to be solved. On the other side were the Gnostics, who represented a religious movement struggling in the direction of rationality. They were the intellectuals and rationalists of the time. The church succeeded in crushing both Mithraism and the Gnostics.

The Gnostics might perhaps be characterized as a primitive Protestant movement. Contrary to Paul, who believed in salvation by faith, the Gnostics believed in salvation through knowledge and by conduct (The Catholic Encyclopedia). They considered Christ to have set an example for the human race. Belief was not enough; one had to live according to the teachings of Christ.

The Gnostic attitude to Judaism was in a certain sense hostile, because they believed in Christ and carried their regard for Christ to the point of deifying him, although never for his entire lifetime. They were not as strictly monotheistic as the Pauline Christians.

The Gnostics had a sharply dualistic sense of difference between spirit and matter. The various Gnostic sects had many differences among themselves, but they had even more basic differences with the crystallizing Catholic Christian dogma. Their differences were in the following directions. They based their system on salvation through knowledge. They were the scientific and ethical movement of the period. They set up elaborate systems trying to understand the development of the universe, and they tried to understand Jesus as a human being who had lived to set an example for humanity to follow. Man would be saved not by faith and Christ's sacrifice, but by being enlightened through Christ's example, and man would therefore be able to so live as to be saved. Christ was used as an example for the establishment of an ethical system, and man was not excused from good works. Faith alone was not enough. The Gnostics insisted that the distinction between good and evil was a human work, not divine.

The various sects by no means had the same attitudes about Jesus. Some sects claimed that there never had been a fleshly Jesus who lived and suffered. Jesus was a manifestation of God, unreal in the physical sense and created for the purpose of enlightening humanity. On the other hand, most Gnostic sects insisted on the human, fleshly nature of Jesus, but that he had been made divine by God at some point in his life. He was not of the eternal, preexisting substance of God. The common denominator of both these apparently diverse Gnostic ideas follows. The Gnostics made no attempt to deify the human Jesus completely. They were willing to consider Jesus as a godly idea, a sort of apparition, an attempt on God's part to give man an illumination in ethics. God was simply trying to teach man something; on the other hand, God selected a human being, Jesus, a real man, an exceptional man to be sure, and made him his divine son for the purpose of instructing humanity. Christ's life again was to serve as an example in ethics. They made no attempt to force credulity in accepting absolutely the divine nature of Christ. This was the heart of the famous Arian controversy which led to the establishment of the Nicene Creed concerning the completely divine nature of Christ.

The Gnostics were a series of unsuccessful warriors fighting a rear-guard action against the movement progressively enlarging the divinity of Christ. Jesus originally was a simple Jewish prophet proclaiming the coming of the Kingdom of God. He was still all human. After his death the doctrine of resurrection and his ascension to God opened the way to his divinity. At this first step on the road to divinity Stephen was executed by the Jews for breaching the monotheistic idea. He had proclaimed that the resurrected son was sitting at the right hand of God. In effect he proclaimed two Gods. The Jews reacted with fury, and Paul appears in history at this point, the execution of Stephen. After a time the injection of divinity was moved up to the moment of his baptism, and it was preached that God entered him and so made him divine. The Gnostics were willing to accept this because this still allowed for a human birth and a period of human existence, but the orthodox movement was relentless. It was then taught that Jesus was divine by birth. This provoked the Basilidean struggle. Basilides, a Gnostic, taught that Jesus became divine at baptism, and consequently he celebrated the nativity of Christ as the divine redeemer on the Feast of the Epiphany, January 6. The orthodox Christian, though, with the doctrine of divinity through birth, had to change Christmas Day to the day of his birth. Actually, no one knows Jesus' birthday. Thus the orthodox Christian party proceeded to kill two birds with one stone. They declared anathema the Basilidean heretics for insisting that Jesus had been a human fleshly being at all, and they moved the date of the celebration of Jesus' birth to a day important in many pagan festivals, December 25, the winter solstice when the sun (son?) begins to shine a little longer each day. There the celebration of Christ's birthday has remained to this day in the Western Christian Church. Christ was eventually declared as one, consubstantial with God, and the divinity progressively continued through Mary. Eventually, Mary was deified and her birth was rendered immaculate also.

The Gnostics were denounced for their scientific pursuits. Eusebius' *Ecclesiastic History* (Vol. V, p. 28) quotes an anti-Gnostic tract, "The Little Labyrinth." In this document the author attacks the Adoptionists (Gnostics who believed Jesus was adopted by God at his baptism) for practicing textual criticism and for using a grammatical, literal method of exegesis in their interpretation of the scripture. They are denounced as follows: "Euclid is laboriously measured by some of them and Aristotle and Theophrastus are admired, and Galen perhaps, by some is even worshiped."

To quote McGiffert (1947, Vol. I, p. 241) about the scientific tendencies in gnosticism:

Apparently Theodotus and his followers found the scientists more congenial than religious philosophers like Plato or the Stoics. Their tendency in fact seems to have been rationalistic rather than mystical and because of this the author of the Little Labyrinth thought them no better than heathen....He was moved wholly by rational considerations and by temperamental hostility to mysticism. But it may well be that an ethical motive was also operative and led him to wish to recover the figure of the man Jesus Christ which was largely lost sight of in the common emphasis on his divinity.

There was an acute struggle between the forces contending the divinity versus the humanity of Jesus. On the side of divinity was arrayed the more authoritarian wing of the Christian bishops. Their decisive ally was the Roman emperor Constantine. In those declining days of the Roman Empire, Constantine was using every possible symbol to hold the loyalty of the Roman subjects. He put Jesus on a level equal to all other official Roman gods, but in the process he had to insist that Jesus was also a god. This provoked the violent struggle within the Christian world. Paul, who two and one half centuries before had been executed by the Romans for worshipping a new illegal god, was now welcomed as an ally by a decaying empire. In 325 A.D. the empire was falling, and the Christian hierarchy was rising. They both found it convenient to use one another at that point.

The Gnostics boasted many brilliant intellectual leaders. One of their most important was Paul of Samosata, bishop of Antioch, an Adoptionist who also held political office. To quote McGiffert (1947, Vol. I, pp. 242–243) again:

(Paul of Samosata was moved by) his own profound concern in the real humanity of Jesus which he feared was in danger of being lost sight of altogether as a consequence of the prevalence of the Logos Christology . . . he denied that Christ had come down from above, or was the incarnation of the Logos or any other being and insisted he was only a man. There is indeed no such person as the Logos. The divine Logos or reason is simply an attribute or faculty of God similar to though of course more perfect than the reason of man.

According to Paul (of Samosata) an essential unity of two

persons is impossible. The only unity that has any worth is that of will and purpose. This is in contradiction to the idea of oneness with Christ taught by Paul of Tarsus. Paul (of Samosata) had a lofty conception of Christ, and it was exceedingly difficult to prove he was heretical. Paul was even willing to concede that Jesus should be given the name of God, if it were clearly understood that he was not God in himself but had only been granted the title and the honor that went with it as a reward for his virtue and the constancy of his devotion to the divine will .

His opponents finally succeeded in securing his condemnation at Antioch in 268 for denying the preexistence of Christ. His condemnation was a decisive victory for the Logos Christology.

The various Gnostic sects represented both an extension of and at the same time opposition to Pauline teaching and the developing orthodox dogma. The Gnostic tendencies can be summarized as follows:

1. *There was an attempt to direct Christianity back to monotheism.* Reconciliation with God was emphasized. Christ was worshiped but never raised to equal importance with God—simply an example of the manifestation of the Father. Christ by himself could not redeem man. This was the kernel of the famous Arian controversy.

2. *Both the spirit and flesh were honored equally, at least in some of the Gnostic sects.* Paul's dualism of flesh and spirit was carried through, but with honors to both. This led to some Gnostic sects that practiced extreme asceticism and others that practiced libertinism as a matter of religious duty. Paul's concept of freedom from law was used to justify the libertinism.

3. *Gnostic theology was a more rational system,* really an ethical system. Gnostics insisted on the spiritual character of eternal life; they denied a fleshly resurrection. They tried hard to develop a theology that could explain the distinction between God and man and yet at the same time explain the connection. They pictured an enormous chasm between God and man bridged by aeons of intermediate beings—Christ being one of them. Nevertheless, they insisted on the human nature of Christ.

4. *They rejected totemism.* Their conception of the work of Christ was fundamentally different than Paul's. They did not believe that Christ redeemed man by his sacrificial death. They believed his life was an illumination to man—in other words, not by sacrificial death, but by his life he taught man how to live. This was closer to Judaic belief in the law than Paul's idea of salvation through faith. Jesus was an example of Christian life. They believed in the earthly life of Jesus, but his life illuminated the way to enjoyment of eternal life with God.

5. *Salvation came through knowledge, not faith.* In a sense the Gnostic movement was an attempt to view life from a scientific, intellectual, rational standpoint.

6. *The sexual question was not disguised.* There are innumerable male and female figures in their systems, and much sexual reproduction. One of the early Gnostics, Simon Magus (Loisy, 1948, p. 298) was considered a messiah by his followers. In their theological system he was given a female companion, who for a time had been a prostitute. He rescued her from prostitution (Protestantism). Some sects placed a female aeon beside the Ineffable Being. This was the mother. This led to successive emanations of aeons, sexually paired. Jesus Christ was an aeon appearing in a long chain of aeons. The sexual attitudes of some Gnostics were quite earthy. Epiphanus (Loisy, 1948, p. 305) "poured ridicule on the prohibition of adultery laid down in the Decalogue; the common and equal enjoyment of all things, said he, belonged to all men by divine appointment; human laws had invented the distinction between good and evil, with all kinds of private property, including the marriage bond; thus the law had created the robber and adulterer; but community goods and free love is the law of nature."

In another Gnostic system Valentinus (Loisy, 1948, p. 307) held that in the beginning was Bythos and a female companion. They begot a couple who begot another and so on. The female of the last couple is seized by a desire for the supreme father. There is a further complicated process finally leading to the birth of Christ.

7. *God and matter, and anti-Semitic tendencies.* Some
Gnostics believed that God was spiritual and matter was evil. In
this sense they were Pauline. It is precisely this group of Gnostics
that tended to veer in a somewhat anti-Semitic direction. Mar-
cion, a famous Gnostic, believed that the god of the Jews had
created the material, the evil world. Sex and the material world
(instincts) belonged to the Jewish god. The world creator was the
Jewish god. Christ, however, came from the supreme god. In this
sense the believers of the spirituality of Christ also tended to fall
into anti-Semitic attitudes. To the extent to which they were anti-
instinct, and displaced or projected instinctual impulses, they
were disposed to develop anti-Semitism. It is thus the Pauline tendencies that dispose to anti-Semitism.

Jekels (1936) is certainly correct in pointing out that an ambivalent aggressive feeling toward the father was present in both
the conflicting ideas about Jesus, on both sides of the Arian controversy. On both sides the son was struggling to equal the father
in divine strength. The important element, though, is not the
similarity of the contending ideas but rather the differences. The
Arian faction fought against Constantine and his allied
churchmen. The struggle was How near to us is Jesus? Is Jesus a
human being, is there anything about him that makes us feel equal
to him in some way? The Arian faction was crushed. The
movement to consider Jesus as forever one with God won out.
The transition was now complete. Jesus, who had started as a simple human Galilean, who had been considered as an earthly
Messiah by some Jews, had now, under the impact of Paul's
deification of him and the political necessity of including him with
the other imperial Roman gods, completed the transition. From
now on it was anathema to see any human traits in him at all. He
was God, whose supreme divinity was not to be questioned. True,
the son had won a greater victory than the Arian faction had
wished for him, but the break with reality was complete, and the
son, instead of being a leader of men, was now another God to be
worshiped and obeyed. The issue of monotheism was straddled by
the dogma that Father-Son were, at the same moment, not only
one, but also two (eventually this became three in one). The

monotheistic ideal was clearly smashed.

In connection with his discussion of the Arian controversy Jekels (1936) makes another point. In those earlier days religion was a much more personal and pervasive experience. Religious belief and mythology were part of everybody's constant daily fare. In modern man the development of science and rational thought has narrowed the visible operating area of religious myth; for example, changes of weather are now explained by movement of various types of air masses rather than an act of God, although prayers are still occasionally offered for rain. The Arian controversy provoked the most widespread public discussion of such abstract metaphysical questions as whether Jesus was preceded by nothing or had he always been something. Was he one with God or was he created by God? This involved the masses of the Roman Empire as well as the theologians. The party that won was the party supported by the Emperor Constantine at the Council of Nicaea. This party proclaimed the divinity of Christ. Constantine needed a tractable ideology, and the Christian was moved in the direction of making the believer more passive, of detaching the believer from any tie to natural processes. This was the movement of the Council of Nicaea. A consideration of this is more important than the fact that both factions carried the problem of ambivalence between father and son.

Arius, the leader of the losing faction, fought hard to hold on to a theology that gave some expression to a more rational conception of Jesus, in other words, the last remnant of the Judaic conception of Jesus, that he was human and real and came into history at a certain point, that is, born like any other human. He did not concede the divinity of Jesus. The most that Christ could do to save man was to reveal the will of God and announce the divine judgment and thus lead him to repentance and obedience.

Arius had other activities, indicating his rational character and his attempt to bring religion closer to the people. According to Tunison (1907) who emphasizes the hellenic and Eastern influences in the history of the theater, Arius also had an important part in the church theater and music controversy. Arius permitted a theatrical element and favored singing as part of the services.

This was fought by the orthodox Latin wing of the Church. The Arian singing, dancing, and acting movement suffered severe persecution, even though they eventually influenced the liturgy. Some of his hymns have even remained in use today.

Transformations of Ritual and Dogma.
The Council of Nicaea

The Council of Nicaea (325 A.D.), a coalition of failing temporal and rising hierarchical powers, marks the end of the first important phase of evolution of Christina dogma and practice. The advent of Paul, and especially Paul's death (62 A.D.), mark the embarkation of Christianity as a separate religion from Judaism. It had at that time by no means shed all its Judaic characteristics, which was a slow process, but it was clearly not the Judaism of Palestine. The Council of Nicaea officially sees Christianity embarked on its rising temporal role. During the several centuries leading to this council a number of trends and transformations took place, which are here summarized with varying degrees of brevity.

First, to mention simply the important directions of these trends:

1. The trinity of father, mother, and son was changed to father and son.

2. The human nature of Christ was suppressed;

3. The Gnostic heresies and scientific interests were suppressed;

4. The agape was transformed and divided into the mass and the sodality;

5. There was a shift in emphasis from baptism to communion;

6. There were changes in the Gospels, especially dealing with the life of Christ:

7. There was a shift from the symbolic number four to the number three.

These trends are treated below in varying deatail.

Transformation of the Creeds

The Nicaean Creed, which was the outgrowth of the Arian controversy, is a piece of dogma in which the mother is completely suppressed. It is pretty much a fantasy of the androgynous birth of Jesus. However, many of the creeds before the Nicaean council in the second and third century contained Mary; that is, there was a normal family trinity, father, mother, and son. As it noted in several examples of these ante-Nicaean creeds, there had already been a partial suppression of the sexual situation by eliminating the sexual, sensual human nature of Mary; Mary is already considered a virgin. However, the mother is still present, and the structure at least is still normal. Two of the creeds follow (Warren, 1897, p. 177):

> We believe in one God Almighty,
> Maker of Heaven and earth.
> And in Jesus Christ His Son.
> Born of the Virgin Mary
> He was pierced by the Jews;
> He died and was buried;
> The third day He rose again;
> He ascended into heaven;
> He is about to come to judge.

Another creed, from Tertullian (160–200 A.D.) is:

> I believe in one God Almighty, the Creator of the world.
> Born of the Virgin Mary,
> Crucified under Pontius Pilate;
> On the third day he rose from the dead.
> He was received into heaven,
> He is now seated at the right hand of the Father,
> He will come to judge the quick and the dead,
> Through the resurrection also of the flesh.

Tertullian, a forerunner of the Arians, taught that Mary had other children in addition to Jesus.

The first Nicaean Creed reads as follows:

We believe in one God the Father Almighty, Maker of all things visible and invisible; and in one Lord Jesus Christ, the only begotten of the Father, that is, of the substance of the Father, God of God, light of light, true God of true God, begotten not made, of the same substance with the Father, through whom all things were made both in heaven and on earth; who for us men and for our salvation descended, was incarnate, and was made man, suffered and rose again the third day, ascended into heaven and cometh to judge the living and dead. And in the Holy Ghost. (Later was added the anathema against those who believe that there was a time when He was not, and He was not before He was begotten; and that He was made out of nothing; or who maintain that he is of another hypostasis or another substance (than the Father), or that the Son of God is created, or mutable, or subject to change (them) the Catholic Church anathemizes.

The Gnostics had fought to keep some vestige of natural, sexual origins of Jesus in the religious system, but they lost.

Paul's Judaic androgynic conception reached its victory in this Nicene Creed. The son was born of the father. There is no mention of mother. At the same time the son is absolutely equal to and with God. This was Paul's personal solution, too. The creed mentions the Holy Ghost. This had been interpreted as an expression of the means of fertilization by father; but in the Aramaic, the word for god had also a feminine meaning. So, just as in the Judaic God, which is masculine, there tends to be concealed mother, so is there a trace of the concealed mother in the Nicene Creed.

This creed lent itself precisely to the political needs of Constantine. The believers were separated from their Messiah and forced to venerate him as a God. The elevation of Jesus to equality with the official pagan gods now put Christianity at the service of the empire. Paul's other admonitions—for the slave to return to his master; to obey rulers because they are so ordained by God; the suppression of protest; the disassociation from nationalistic aspirations, the emphasis on his Roman citizenship—all blended into the politico-religious result. There was a mutual strengthening of the powers of the religious as well as the political hierarchy. Events soon proved that the strengthening of the religious hierarchy was a more permanent result than the political. By this time (325 A.D.) the development of the Church hierarchy was quite systemized. By the end of the second century there was already a sharp division between the clergy and laity (Hatch, 1909). Spontaneity in religious expression or experience, for example speaking with tongues, was already being discouraged. The clergy were already becoming a group with vested interests in controlling the laity.

By 381, at the Council of Constantinople, the Virgin Mary was reintroduced into the creed, marking the beginning of an unbroken line of Christian belief in the Trinity. To the original Nicene Creed were added the words, "He was incarnate by the Holy Ghost of the Virgin Mary." By the fifth century, in the Athanasian creed, the Trinity was even more firmly established and developed. "So the Father is God, the Son God, the Holy Ghost God; and yet they are not three Gods, but one God." The persistent problem of the human existence of Christ was annoyingly still present. The two natures were admitted. "He is God, of the Substance of the Father, begotten before the worlds, and He is Man, of the Substance of His Mother, born in the world." The later florid development of Mariolatry is beyond the scope of this study.

Insofar as Mary, the mother of Christ, is concerned, the Nicene Creed represents a temporary Judaic androgynic victory. This phase was both Pauline and Judaic. The original pagan mother worship was temporarily suppressed, shortly to return.

Transformations of the Agape to the Mass and Sodality

The primitive Christians, and especially the first-century Christians, lived out their religious life in a simple and essentially social manner. They met regularly, ate a common meal, exchanged greetings and affection, and then discussed the teachings and sayings and life of Christ as well as the teachings of their early apostles. The food was supplied communally, often by the richest member of the group. The meal served as a thanksgiving, and at the same time the bread and wine were used symbolically to represent the body and blood of Christ. The common meal was called the love feast and was attended by both men and women. An essential part of it was the kiss of peace exchanged between all, men and women, both between opposite sexes and also between men, in brotherly love. With the spread of Christianity in the pagan world, the love feast lent itself to a continuation of certain pagan institutions, notably feasts of orgiastic rites connected with human sacrifice. Jesus was, of course, the human sacrifice offered to appease and to reconcile God. He ensured the salvation of the human race, or at least the believing part of the race, by offering himself as a sacrifice. Being saved was being saved from the wrath of God. As time went on, the idea of the sacrifice of the son to the father became the central idea. This idea was clear to Paul. The pagans took to this religious, sacrificial, orgiastic rite with tremendous enthusiasm. There are no precise descriptions of exactly what took place at the love feasts, but apparently the release from guilt by the sacrifice of the son led to freedom to perform all manner of sexual excesses, homosexual as well as incestuous (Paul's complaint). The kiss of peace was to a degree a homosexual act, because it was exchanged with brotherly greetings.

Paul thundered against the sexual excesses of the agape, and he tried his best to suppress it. The church fathers eventually forbade a second kiss at the agape. Even though the Catholic Church eventually transformed, as will be noted soon, the orgiastic rite into the carefully controlled liturgical ceremony of the mass, the aggressive, sadistic, totemistic aspects were by no means kept a symbolic secret from the Christian believer. The Protestants of Luther's time protested against the emphasis on the crunching of the bones and body of Jesus during the celebration of the eucharist. At the same time, Luther, who protested against the dogma of the wafer being considered the real body of Christ, nevertheless battled strongly to bring the mass back to the people. By the time of the Reformation, the actual mass was slowly being withdrawn from the Christian congregation. Even the architectural construction of churches began to be altered to give the priests more and special space for the conduct of their part of the services, sometimes completely out of sight of the congregation

(Bond, 1910). The chalice of wine was reserved for the priest: it had been completely withdrawn from the Christian, the services were conducted in Latin, a language practically no one knew; often the priests themselves participated in this ignorance. What Luther succeeded in doing was to return the mass to the people, restore the chalice of wine, take it out of the hands of the privileged clergy, and have the services in German. In spite of the Protestant complaint about the barbarity of the custom, they in turn nevertheless fought to have it all, blood as well as body. Parton (1878) describes a thirteenth century church with carvings indicating Jesus being introduced bodily by Mary into the hopper of a meat grinder, with wafers coming out at the other end dropping into the open mouths of the believers. Calvin, too, emphasized the spiritual aspect of the body of Christ in the mass. The Catholics have fought to retain all the aggressive totem aspects of the mass. The Protestants, on the whole, have attempted to spiritualize it.

By the second century the bishops had seized control of the love feast and had succeeded in breaking up the agape and converting it into a liturgical, carefully controlled ceremony (eucharist). It was now treated as a mystery. The rite that had originally been a direct parricidal, sexual, and identification outlet was now being converted into an obsessive religious formula. The communicant today may not even permit his teeth to touch the wafer. It must be swallowed whole, a thoroughly passive oral transformation of the original aggressive-oral meaning of the act. What had originally been an aggressive, communal, instinctual release was now transformed in a highly obsessional manner into the passive opposite.

The agape had provided an orgiastic outlet for orality and sexuality. It should not be overlooked that there are innumerable Christian sects practicing orgiastic means of prayer. These sects are Protestant. Even the Shakers who practiced enforced celibacy had ceremonialized rites of singing and dancing in which the orgiastic nature of these activities can easily be discerned (Andrews, 1940).

The love component of the agape was deflected into a

desexualized direction by the development of the sodality; this became the outlet for the more general social needs of the congregation. The agape was thus split into two. The mass became the ceremonialized outlet for the totemistic oral aggression. The sodality became the desexualized outlet for the component of tender love in the agape.

Shift from Baptism to Communion

Although baptism is still an important rite in Catholic Christianity and is *the* important rite in many Protestant sects, it had been progressively overshadowed by the communion rite. The baptism rite had remained brief and simple and is performed only once; the communion has become an elaborate and florid ceremony which is performed over and over again during the life of the believer. Jesus, the primitive Christian community, and even the testimony of the four evangelists, all considered baptism as the means for entering the Christian community, and then did not require any further rites of renewal of fraternity or renewal of sonship to remain among the group of believers. The Jews, of course, practiced baptism. Jesus was baptized by John.

The baptismal rite has various meanings—it is a purification ceremony; Reik (1946, 1951) notes particularly its initiation usage; it is an intrauterine and rebirth ceremony. The communion is a ceremony of totemistic aggression, oral incorporation, and identification, basically an aggressive identification rite.

In Pauline Christianity there was shift in emphasis away from relationship to mother to the relationship to father. Paul emphasized the totem-meal identification and avoided the relationship to mother. It is perhaps likely that the shift to communion and away from baptism was also one of the results of the Pauline influence. Baptism, with its rebirth implications, is closer to mother; communion is closer to father.

Another reason for the shift away from baptism was undoubtedly to remove emphasis from the baptism of Christ. The problem of Christ's becoming divine upon his baptism was a focus of serious dispute between the church and the heretical

Gnostic sects. Baptism had to be minimized in order to throw the emphasis on Christ's complete godlike nature and also to increase the distance from Judaism.

Changes in the Various Gospels

If we compare the various epistles, the epistle of James and the epistles of the four evangelists, we find conflicting attitudes toward Jesus, not with the result of a compromise position, but with the statement of several varying positions. The reading of the various epistles is like an archaeological expedition into Christian history. James' epistle is almost an Old Testament document thundering against the rich and pleading for the poor. Jesus is mentioned only twice, almost casually, and as a Messiah, not as the Son of God. This is pre-Pauline, almost pre-Christian. Luke is much concerned with Mary, both before and after the birth of Jesus, and he recognizes Joseph. Jesus is given a human origin; his career is given in full detail. Mark simply says Jesus came from Galilee. He disregards his origin almost as completely as Paul does. Mark, however, gives his career in detail. Mark is the oldest of the four Gospels and is pretty much of a Nazarene Christian document. Matthew presents a later idea: Jesus is immaculately conceived through the Holy Ghost. In John (the middle of the second century) the development is complete. We arrive at Logos Christology: the Word was God, and Christ was born of the Word, begotten of Father. Early in the epistle, Christ is already named as the Lamb of God; his sacrificial role is already ordained.

Shift from Four to Three

One of the accessory points of interest in studying the historical movement from Judaism to Christianity is the shift from a religion in which the number four is sacred to one in which the number three has those qualities. The sacred name of the Jahweh is also the Tetragrammaton, four (*Jewish Encyclopedia*). "Four is an age-old symbol always associated with the idea of a

world creating deity'' (Jung, 1938). Jahweh can be shown to consist of two equally androgynic parts, a union of two androgynic
partners. The Christian trinity brings mother goddess worship
more into the foreground, and depending on the extent to which
mother fails to be renounced, there is homosexuality in the
solution. Oddly enough, Christianity, both old and new, also is
still involved with the number four. Four Evangelists were selected, and the number four was heavily involved in the early Gnostic
philosophy.

Cultural Problems

Christianity provided a special stimulus to the development
of Western art. In painting, sculpture and drama, the madonna
and child and Christ's story provided the content and inspiration
for the development of these art forms. The historical and
psychological development of these forms is by no means a simple
one. It might be useful to trace the history of this development,
perhaps somewhat arbitrarily, through three stages: (1) the
Hebrews and early Christians, (2) the Gnostics, and (3) the later
Christians of the fourth century and after.

It is a well-known but rarely discussed fact that the Hebrew
culture up to the Christian era had no sports, no art, no painting,
no sculpture, and especially no theater. A study of ancient
Hebrew arts (Reifenberg, 1950) does more to indicate the paucity
than the wealth of Jewish art. These characteristics of the Hebrew
culture obtained in spite of the fact that Palestine was a small
nation surrounded by a sea of hellenic culture in which sculpture,
the theater as well as games, underwent high development. This
artistic sterility of the Hebrews had as its basic reason the strict
and spiritualized character of its monotheism, especially the
second commandment. However, one may not describe the entire
Hebrew culture as sterile. It was sterile only in its development of
the arts. For certain good reasons, not all of which were outside
pressures, the Jewish culture blossomed in the direction of a
superego culture. The Jewish contribution to the culture of the
world is the Mosaic law, an ethical system that proselytized with

tremendous success. In fact, as Loisy (1948) points out, precisely the wide dispersion of the Jewish ideas facilitated the original speedy dissemination of Christianity.

The Jews, in their development, had imposed on themselves a number of severe renunciations. The most important of the renunciations were (1) the solution of the oedipal problem by the renunciation of mother (goddess) worship and (2) the renunciation of totemistic, aggressive, and all magical practice in connection with father worship.

Nunberg (1949), Barag (1947), and others have pointed out the renunciation of mother in the abandonment of worship of the mother goddess among the Jews. If we look more closely we find that the mother was not absolutely abandoned, since she was absorbed into the figure of Jahweh. Jahweh is recognizably bisexual, showing the latent traces of mother. As Freud (1939), Nunberg (1949), and Barag (1947) point out, it is precisely this suppression of mother worship which is the basis of monotheism.

However, the repressed returns, and once a year the mother worship and the synagogue taboo against women are violated by the Jews. This occurs during the festival of Simchat Torah, during Sukkoth, the harvest festival. During this holiday the men invade the female section of the synagogue; the taboo is violated. The men carry the lulab and ethrog, obvious symbols of the penis and testicles. During this annual invasion, the Torah is also carried in the procession, and there is gaiety and dancing in the synagogue. Barag (1947) has also pointed to the feminine character of the Torah in the Talmud. In olden days, the man honored with the reading from the Torah was called the Groom of the Torah, Chatan Torah. In the modern sects of Judaism the Bridegroom of the Torah as been changed to Kahvod Torah, a title indicating prestige, but desexualized. This is the happiest festival of the year. All this activity and gaiety is an integral part of the ritual. It is precisely at the moment of violation of the taboo, with the (magical) exhibition of the male sex symbols that the sexual excitement is acted out in dancing. Here art, religion, sex, and magical practice are blended into one. This is a breach of monotheism.

The second commandment, against graven images, was a powerful force in the direction of the spiritualization of religion and the renunciation of magical exercise and magical thinking. The ancient Jews found a way of circumventing such a prohibition. The commandment was interpreted to apply to graven images in the round, that is, to sculpture that projected outward from a surface. However, if the image was flat or in a hollow, it was permitted.

The Christians abandoned the relatively pure monotheism of the Hebrews and reverted to a variant of the oriental mysteries of the dying and rising son and mother cults. As the transition toward the divine nature of Christ continued, artistic development also appeared. It was immediately after the Council of Nicaea, at which it was pronounced heresy to question the divine nature of Christ, that Constantine ordered statues of gold and silver made both of Christ and a number of saints. Constantine also ordered that in all reproductions of Christ, the body should be thoroughly covered by folds of clothing. No signs of the fleshly Jesus were to be visible.

It is precisely this breach with monotheism and the unconscious failure to resolve the attachment to mother that provides the focal point of greatest Christian impetus to art. Madonna and child are the Christian subject par excellence. The trinity is a disguised return of mother-son worship, evidence of failure to renounce the tie to mother. The Hebrews, who had renounced mother and even erected taboos against women, such as separating men from women in the synagogue, apparently did this so thoroughly that almost all acting out of the problem was suppressed. The exception is the annual Simchat Torah celebration as described.

The renunciation of magical and incestuous practice by the Hebrews eliminated art and the theater. Perhaps there is a correlation between spiritualized monotheism with suppression of art, on the one hand, and polytheism with mother worship and its associated magical practices and the development of art, on the other. The early Christians, particularly at the eastern end of the Mediterranean, were not the source of Western Christian art.

There was too much of the Judaic and Gnostic influences. In general, Christian art had hard going in the first seven centuries, most particularly in the first three centuries. There were strong protests against violations of the second commandment, even by highly placed churchmen.

The first Roman Christian art was in the catacombs. These productions were feeble copies of Greek style, and the subject matter was mainly resurrection, a logical subject for cemetery art, no matter what the religion. Christ was represented, although there was no agreement with the East as to the portrait. He was Syrian in the East and blonde in the West. For the first six centuries Christ was represented often not by a portrait but by symbols and diagrams, and often by a fish. In general, in the East the decorations of religious buildings tended to diagrams, geometrical designs, and arabesques rather than human figures. Even in the West, Christ was frequently represented by diagrams for about seven centuries.

To recapitulate: on the one hand, we have the Judaic and early Christian tendency to monotheism, with renunciation of mother as object, belief in the human nature of Christ, emphasis on the law, and suppression of magic, art and theater. Mother is renounced, masculine identification is permitted by father and magical gratification is unnecessary. On the other hand, we have a limited kind of polytheism, belief in the divine nature of Christ, abnegation of the Law, failure of resolution of mother as an object, failure of resolution of hostility to father, failure of masculine identification, and a great impetus to magic and art. If mother is not renounced, she must periodically be possessed. This is where magic, ritual, and art are necessary. The periodic instinctual outbursts which even Freud thought might be biologically necessary for man produced dancing, singing, acting. The totem aggression against father produced the passion play, one of the foundation stones of modern theater.

Between these two groups, both theologically and artistically, is the middle group, the Gnostics, whose characteristics have already been described. What was the nature of the artistic products of the Gnostics who were somewhere between the Jews and Christians, between no art whatever and the eventual tendencies to florid artistic development? The contribution of the Gnostics was diagrams for their religious symbols. The diagrams dealt with philosophical conceptions of the relations between the forces of nature and man. These were intermediate between scientific diagrams and theological symbols. There was a small degree of pictorialization, but it was not prominent. The medieval alchemists and cabalists were the later inheritors of some of the Gnostic scientific tradition.

Another factor which might be studied for correlations to artistic development is the shift from baptism to communion. The shift in emphasis from baptism to mass can be conceived of as a regressive shift to a primitive, oral-aggressive exercise. When the instincts are more primitive, more difficult to tolerate, perhaps magic is more necessary. If we turn to Christian art we find the baptismal scenes are rare, but the last supper is one of the great themes of Christian art. It is interesting to note that in the catacomb art, Old Testament scenes are common and the baptism of Christ is common. Certain subjects were rare, the crucifixion and the eucharist.

In the early Christian theater the central topic was the passion play. This concentration on the crucifixion is a dramatic preoccupation with the totemistic aggression against the father. At the moment Christ was impersonated, the totem ritual became theater. Theater supplanted the totem feast. The passion play is, of course, ambivalent. It is passive as well as aggressive. The passive side is given most prominence; the aggressive side is often projected onto Jews. The aggressive side of the totemism was by no means easily suppressed. The ambivalence found other means of expression. As the mystery plays developed, comedy became the vehicle for the expression of the aggressions. The medieval comic characters in the mystery plays were mainly devils and Jews. Their chief comic thrusts were no doubt the virginity of Mary.

To summarize this brief historical discussion, perhaps one can say that the arts were needed as accessory magical practices to overcome the taboos against deeply prohibited acts, such as violation of incest taboos, cannibalistic impulses against the father, unresolved sexual ties to the mother, masochistic homosexual surrender to the father, or even the testing out of identifications with god or father. In connection with the magical practice necessary for identification with god or father, one might recall the totem meal of the oriental Mithra cult. The bull was slain and eaten; the participants who ate wore masks. The identification was carried out by eating and masking. The masking was thus an accessory of a very primitive oral-incorporative type of identification. The magic of the masking is, of course, the first step toward theater. Paul's reference to "putting on Christ" is an indication of the extent to which he had been influenced by Mithraic practice.

Theoretical Problems Concerning Paul and Pauline Ideology

Paul was the vehicle for two sets of transitions, one historical and the other psychological. The historical transition was to realize a compromise union between the monotheistic Judaic system and its pagan contemporaries. The psychological transition was to begin, although not completely, the change from the androgynous Judaic solution of sexuality to the latent passive homosexual Catholic Christian solution.

It should be remembered that the Pauline ideology was not identical with the later and present catholic ideology. Catholic ideology of later centuries is heavily committed to Mary worship. Paul paid no attention to the mother at all. Her role and his attitudes to mother were avoided. This indicated the continuing Jewish influence in Paul. Paul accepted the Judaic repression of mother in the god figure. He went even further than the Jews. His attitude toward women in the synagogue was the same as that of the Jews, but his attitude toward women in sexual relations was not. Paul's central teachings about Christ entirely neglected the aspects of Christ's birth, mother, family, and so on, just as he neglected to tell us these same things about himself.

The attempt to arrive at Christ through a heterosexual mythology, as was done by the Gnostics, met defeat at the hands of the church at Nicaea. This council represents the high point of Pauline teaching, although later Mary was permitted to reappear.

By his suppression of any fantasy or mythology about the mother, Paul continued the Hebrew incest prohibition even more stringently than the Hebrews did. By accepting the sacrificial death of the son, he admitted the original incest guilt, but he was unable to create any conscious fantasy formation dealing with the mother. His fantasy regarding father and son was profuse, but regarding mother was completely repressed. Paul accepted the latent homosexuality, but he repressed the tie to the mother.

As Nunberg (1949) points out, even though Paul accepted the sin and guilt, he nevertheless revolted: Paul never arrived at any solution free of ambivalence. He rejected circumcision and the Mosaic law; he rejected dietary restrictions which Nunberg views as defiance of maternal incest prohibitions. Paul's insistence that the law promotes sin is reminiscent of the attitudes of many obsessional neurotics who must spitefully do precisely that which is prohibited. Nunberg believed that Paul had unconscious insight into his unconscious crime, because he scolded the Corinthians for incest, which probably was part of the celebration of the agape or love feasts.

Nunberg (1949) points out that with the abandonment of circumcision by the Christians, the homosexual tie to father was loosened and the path was opened to worship of the pagan mother and son figures. This is precisely what happened in the evolution of Christianity. However, during the period when Pauline influence was strong, mother-son worship was suppressed. The position of Paul was in a way an unhappy one; he paid the price (latent homosexuality) but did not receive the reward (mother). It took several centuries for the reward, mother, to reappear. Paul had neither mother nor woman, only simply passive gratification from father. If Nunberg is correct, then, the defiance of the dietary laws was the only symbolic incestuous gratification which Paul permitted himself. At this point we might recall Paul's acceptance of money, food, and shelter from women. At the conscious level, of course, Paul thundered against incest and all the gratifications of the agape.

In *Moses and Monotheism* Freud (1939) also discusses the problem of Paul. He believed that Paul had a kind of insight into the father murder which is the basis of the sense of guilt.

> It is quite clear to us now why he could grasp the truth in no other form but in the delusional guise of the glad tidings . . . We have been delivered from all guilt since one of us laid down his life to expiate our guilt . . . Original sin and salvation through sacrificial death became the basis of the new religion founded by Paul.

Paul began the shift to the eventual Catholic passive homosexual solution, but he did not complete it. He was too strongly tied to the androgynous Jewish God. Even in Jesus, he said, "There can be no male and female," a denial of sexuality as well as a denial of sexual differences and a denial of incest. His ethics, his life, and his theology betray a strong, latent, passive homosexuality. The mother is missing in Judaic theology, missing in Paul's record of his own life, in his preoccupation with Jesus, and in his theology. Not only is the mother missing, woman is missing. Paul was celibate and recommended celibacy (Jesus did not). His own human nature kept Paul busy writing against fornication, homosexuality, and incest, but he was by no means able to impose celibacy either on Christians or even on his fellow missionaries. It is well established that the apostles and missionaries traveled about with their wives.

The Judaic (androgynic) component of Paul's theology reached its height of success at the Council of Nicaea, at which the Gnostic heterosexual cults were suppressed and the Nicaean Creed, in which there is no mention of mother, was substituted. The suppression of mother was Paul's link to Judaism. After Nicaea, with the return of mother worship in Christianity, there was an even more complete break with Judaism. At this point Christianity possessed the trinity.

Although Paul's influence toward the deification of the son, identification of the son with God, identification with Christ, and the oral (communion) totem aspects of identification have all permanently remained as his essential contributions to the dogma of Christianity, there is one aspect of his theology that did not remain, his suppression of mother worship. The original interest in mother worship was opposed by Paul's androgynous conception of birth. As noted, Paul's ideas achieved a temporary victory at Nicaea, but receded before the powerful tendency to reinstate mother worship. Jones' discussion of the need for mother worship is given in some detail. Jones (1923) states:

> The transition from Mother to Holy Ghost was not accomplished without a struggle even at the beginning as might be expected in a community accustomed to Goddess worship. Several sects tried to retain the divinity of Mary, the obvious successor to Isis, Hera, Astarte, Aphrodite. The human need for a Mother to worship was too strong, so that she had to be reinstated. Christianity, here, therefore, as in many other respects, effected a compromise between the Hebraic tendency towards an adrogynic conception and the classical tendency towards acknowledgement of the Mother-Goddess as a central figure. [Under Paul's influence the Hebraic androgynic tendency won a complete, though temporary victory. Jones continues:] The replacement of the Mother Goddess by the Holy Ghost is a manifestation of the desirability of renouncing incestuous and parricidal wishes and replacing them by a stronger attachment to the Father—hence the greater prominence in Christianity as compared with Judaism of personal love for God, the Father—the demands of Christianity require homosexuality and effeminacy. The peculiarly Christian solution, which was later adulterated by Catholicism, was the lineal descendant of the Hebraic tendency. The Protestant Reformation was clearly an attempt to reinforce the original (Hebraic) solution (Luther invited the Jews to join him) and to carry it to its logical conclusion by abolishing all traces of Mariolatry from religion; only those who have witnessed the horror with which the "Red Woman" is mentioned among the extreme Protestant sections of the community can fully appreciate the strength of this impulse. It is interesting further to note that the more completely is this process carried out the less necessity is there to adopt a homosexual attitude in religion; the extreme Protestant ministers not only marry, but discard all special costume and other indications of a feminine role, whereas all the self castrating tendencies are more evident where Mariolatry is highly developed. One might say that the Protestant solution of the Oedipus complex is the replacement of the Mother by the Woman, while the Catholic consists in the change of the masculine to the feminine attitude.

Simmel's (1946) evaluation of the specific Jewish contribution to religion and culture is relevant to this discussion. The Jews deprived themselves of the periodic instinctual outlet, the totem feast, by the abolition of all animal sacrifices. In the second commandment, the Jews went even farther and demanded submission, not to a visible God, but to an invisible one, thus effectuating a complete spiritualization of religion. The Jews permitted themselves no aggressions against God; the aggressive strength went into the collective superego formation. Simmel observes that this instinctual renunciation and spiritualization of religion is really a greater sacrifice than the human race can afford. This author would emphasize that Christianity reversed these two Judaic trends by the sacrifice of Jesus and by the violation of the second commandment.

Simmel correctly remarks that the anti-Semitic Christian is still in need of recreating the primitive totem animal and must find it on earth. It was precisely to fill this need that the Christians have needed the devil, the anti-Christ and the malignant Jew. Simmel remarks that it is unfortunate for us that our culture does not possess some institution for the periodic discharge of oral-aggressive totem practices. We are not really without such institutions. This author (1948) has pointed to the useful function annual convention banquets serve in carrying out all the essential psychological needs gratified in totem meal practices. Fenichel (1940) points to the various projections the Jew facilitates for the Christian. Anti-Semitism thus represents a failure of the civilizing process. Complete identification and complete introjection are not attained. To quote Simmel (1946) further: "The anti-Semite accuses the Jew of the crime which he himself unconsciously commits when he eats the holy wafer. It is an act of incorporating which provides him with a discharge of his devouring tendencies of hate and subsequently, enables him to identify himself mentally with Christ in love."

Loewenstein (1947, 1951) asks the important question whether the Christian needs the Jew to prove the reality of Jesus. This writer does not think so. Jesus is real enough to the Christian; after all, the believer is a son. It is the ambivalence, particularly the aggressive side of the ambivalence, that is intolerable to the Christian. The Jew is necessary to prove the reality of the projection. Even so, the Jew is selected not so much out of a need for a scapegoat, but rather because the God is Jewish. Even the Gnostic Christians tended to be anti-Semitic, although some of the sects avoided the paranoia of anti-Semitism by belittling the Jewish God, by considering him simply as an unimportant local deity.

Other Gnostics credited the Jewish God with creating the physical, that is, the evil world, sin. This, too, is a projection, a mild form of the anti-Semitic projection. This writer would not agree with Simmel (1946) that anti-Semitism can appear in normal people. It is a projection, one of the pathological complications of being a Christian. Loewenstein (1951) constructs a most useful formulation, that the Christian is bound to the Jew both by hatred and by loyal indebtedness, that the hatred has been expressed through the centuries, but because of the loyalty, never to the point of the extinction of the Jews. A piece of history that might in a negative way be confirmatory of this is the fact that the fate of Mithraism was entirely opposite to that of Judaism. The only other serious opponent of Christianity, other than Judaism, during the first three centuries was Mithraism. In the fourth century the growing religious and secular strength of the Christians caused the cult of Mithra to be utterly suppressed. The Jews, the actual parents of Christianity, even though they had already begun to be included in the New Testament writings in an unflattering way, particularly being given the blame for the death of Christ, were not exterminated. They were simply loaded with the guilt of the aggression against Christ. It is interesting that in the Mithraic cult the totem animal was openly slain, and the believer became father. In the Jewish religion, all such open aggression had been suppressed. The aggression was out of sight, unconscious, secret, mysterious, and to be feared, an ideal point for projection.

Paul was deeply ambivalent. On the one hand, he was aggressive, hard, driving, and bitter to his enemies. He was not above inviting his Jewish enemies to castrate themselves. He denied the absolute supremacy of the Father God by elevating the son; in fact, in certain passages he names the son before the father. Regarding his apostleship he denied any debt to any living man. He refused to take money except from women. He violated the dietary taboos; he violated the Mosaic law; he denied the necessity of circumcision. On the passive side we note his celibacy, his need for male companions, particularly his need for Barnabas to lift him from obscurity and turn him in a productive and creative direction. We note his need to turn important active decisions into passively experienced hallucinatory commands, his transformation of the son into a suffering Messiah (contrary to Judaic tradition), his emphasis on his perpetual readiness to receive the indwelling lord, and, lastly, his need for love, as shown in the quoted passage from I Corinthinians. One small part deserves repetition here. In this passage Paul seems to mourn the loss of the childhood intimacy with a parent. He writes, "When I was a child, my words were childish, my desires were childish, my judgments were childish; but being grown a man, I have done with the things of childhood. For now we see darkly, by a mirror, but then face to face." Whether this parent whose face he now can see only dimly was his father or mother is a most important question. This writer would suspect it was the father.

His is the classic soil for the genesis of paranoid characteristics. Since Paul's God is a Jewish masculine God, Christian paranoia is directed first to Jews. Anti-Semitism is a peculiarly Christian phenomenon, because the Christian god is a Jew. It was Paul who engineered the break with Judaism, and in this sense he was the first anti-Semite. The primitive pre-Pauline Christians were not anti-Semitic: they were loyal and observant Jews. The persecutory system was started by Paul, by his perpetual conflict between his aggressions and need for surrender to father.

It was Paul's special function in history to introduce the first still partly Judaic step in the migration of Christianity away from Judaism. His chief relationship was, as with the Jews, to an androgynic father, but unlike the Jews, his identification was passive, not active. Paul renounced not only mother but woman as well. He renounced masculine aggressiveness and was capable only of a paranoid, reactive kind of aggression.

Paul's conversion was not a stable solution of his problems. He never resolved his ambivalence. He could tolerate neither his aggressions nor his passivity, and when the tension of either impulse became too strong he had to resort to denial or projection via his behavior of various hallucinatory experiences.

Paul gloried in his physical sufferings and in his masochistic experiences, as can be seen by the following (II Cor. 12: 9): "Most gladly, therefore, will I boast rather in my weakness than in my strength, that the strength of Christ may rest upon me, and dwell in me. Therefore I rejoice in signs of weakness, in outrage, in necessities, in persecutions, in straitness of distress, endured for Christ; for when I am weak, then am I strong."

We can assume that Paul was unconsciously aware of the relationship between masochism, homosexuality, and the need for persecution. When his original, obsessional, character defense against his homosexuality was relinquished in his conversion, the homosexuality was made acceptable and even desirable by being spiritualized into the religious ideals. It was a homosexual surrender to both a father and a brother. The two were always considered as one.

In this study importance is given to the fact that Paul's known career begins with the murder of Stephen, who idealized and elevated Jesus. Stephen and Jesus both were identified with the aspirations of the son to equality with father. Following this line of reasoning, the original murder of which Paul was guilty was not father murder, but brother murder, murder of the brother who was both more ambitious than Paul and closer to God than Paul, a perfect representation of an older brother, both more aggressive and more favored. We know from Paul's letters that he believed that God could favor one brother over another, that God hated Esau, the hairy, the less attractive brother. This certainly suggests the possibility that Paul was working through some such problem of sibling rivalry. Paul's insistent identification drive is not simply to identify with father (Paul never really attained a normal identification with father), but an identification with Christ, the son of God, the son who was so intimately close to

God, eventually one with God. Paul rarely mentions God, the father, alone. He always approaches God through the identification with Christ. Paul insisted on his identification with Christ first. Even in his conversion, it was Jesus who appeared to him and reproached Paul for his persecution of him. One gets the impression from Paul's theology that the son really was the victor, and replaced God.

This suggests the following problem, that Paul, so unprepossessing in his personal appearance, probably unattractive to women, and also feeling unloved by father, might have been very jealous of Jesus, his closeness to father, and have been driven by a need to displace Jesus in the affections of father. Several important things might bear out this supposition. One is that his identifications were with Jesus first, and that Paul was apparently driven to repeat Christ's sacrificial (homosexual) surrender to God. Paul's final drive to be taken a prisoner to Rome was his quest to relive Christ's experience. Paul's final hallucinatory experience would bear this out.

The intense hostility to the siblings (beginning with Stephen, the first known sibling substitute) necessitated some means of atoning or undoing. This must have led him to need to sacrifice himself, thus accomplishing two ends, atone for his sadism and at the same time be closer to God. Particularly in his last hallucinatory experience, on the sinking ship, two ambivalent ends were served; he was saved to be the sacrifice, but in so doing he also saves all the rest, an atonement or an undoing of his own destructive feelings. At the same time, by becoming closer to God his own homosexual fantasies are gratified. Perhaps being taken closer to God also gratifies some incestuous fantasy. This component of Paul's feelings is suppressed, perhaps appearing only in his violation of the dietary taboos.

We do not know the facts of Paul's childhood, but we do know what sort of a young man he was, an obsessionally religious young man, with a great need to carry out the law perfectly, and the feeling that he never was able to do so perfectly. Knowing what we do about his later life, we can assume that this obsessional character must have served as a defense against his two strongest conflicting tendencies, his aggression against father and his unconscious homosexuality. The religious punctiliousness he demanded of himself was the displaced surrender. Pfister (1920, 1948) also looks on Paul's obsessional character as his defense against his great need and desire to love God. The vigor and hostility with which Paul entered the persecution of the Christian indicates his identification with the aggressor, identification with a cruel father. This was a pathological identification process, indicating the difficulties that must have faced Paul in his dealings with his father and family. Paul tried to alter the cruel God to a forgiving one, but this could only be done by means of Christ's sacrifice.

The conversion robbed Paul of his compulsive character defense. He gave up both his old aggression and also his religiously displaced obedience to the law. He was now at the mercy of his aggressions and his homosexuality. Both these tendencies underwent a degree of sublimation in the new religious process taking place in Paul. The son attained equality with the father, but at the same time there was an identification, now not with the aggressive father, but with the crucified son, an identification carrying many masochistic and homosexual overtones. This feminine identification could perhaps also be characterized as an identification with the phallic mother, quite compatible with all Paul's latent homosexual characteristics. Even so, his new religious character formation was not enough to stabilize Paul's character structure. Pfister (1920) also points to the lack of stability in Paul's character after his conversion. Evidence of this is the history of his relationships to men and of the repeated hallucinatory experiences, some of which served as projections of his aggression, whereas others served to project and deny his passive needs. His last hallucinatory experience, during the storm, served to express both his masochism and his grandiose aggression.

The timing of Paul's conversion is a perplexing problem. Perhaps the very fact that he was an official agent of the Sanhedrin was the crux of the problem. It might be remembered that all the members of the Sanhedrin were married men, that is, all fathers. Paul could tolerate a subordinate position to no one. His homosexuality was too easily provoked. Perhaps he had to react with an aggressive defense against the seduction of this relationship to the Sanhedrin. In his conversion he overthrew their authority. The further complications of the conversion are another matter.

Freud (1939) and Nunberg (1949) have both pointed out the basic parricidal and incestuous motives in Paul's life. This present study is concerned with Paul's struggle with his various defensive systems. His earliest defenses were his strong, compulsive drive to fulfill the law in every respect, a task he felt he could never completely fulfill. This compulsive surrender to God reached its height in the attack on Stephen and the Christians. He killed the brother who defied father. However, he soon embarked on a career of replacing the murdered brother, and also atoning for the murder. This career was a grandiose one.

BIBLIOGRAPHY

Encyclopedias and Original Sources

Acts of the Apostles, 2 vols., with Introduction and Notes by Thomas M. Lindsay. Edinburgh: T. and T. Clark, 1884.

Bible, Holy Bible containing the Old and New Testaments, Authorized King James version, with notes especially adapted for young Christians, Pilgrim edition. New York: Oxford University Press, 1948.

The Catholic Encyclopedia, 15 vols., Charles G. Herberman et al., Eds. New York: The Encyclopedia Press, 1913.

A Dictionary of the Bible, 5 vols., edited by James Hastings et al. New York: Scribner's, 1900.

A Dictionary of Christian Antiquities, 2 vols., edited by William Smith and Samuel Cheetham, Eds. Boston: Little, Brown, 1875.

Encyclopedia of Religion and Ethics, 12 vols., James Hastings et al., Eds. New York: Scribner's, 1910.

Eusebius Pamphilus: *The Ecclesiastical History*, translated from the original by C. F. Cruse, and a historical view of the Council of Nice, with a translation of documents by Isaac Boyle. Boston: Rev. R. Davis and Brother, 1836.

The Jewish Encyclopedia, 12 vols., Isidore Singer et al., Eds. New York and London: Funk and Wagnalls, 1901.

Joseph Flavius: *The Life and Works of Flavius Josephus*, translated by William Whiston. Philadelphia: The John C. Winston, nd.

Strabo: *The Geography of Strabo*, 3 vols., translated by H. C. Hamilton and W. Falconer. London: Henry G. Bohn, 1854.

Conybeare, W. J. and Howson, J. S. (1895), *The Life and Epistles of Saint Paul*. Hartford: S. S. Scranton.

Davies, W. D. (1948), *Paul and Rabbinic Judaism*. London: S. P. C. K.

Edman, I. (1936), *The Mind of Paul*. London: Jonathan Cape.

Goodspeed, E. J. (1947), *Paul*. Philadelphia, Toronto: John C. Winston.

Guignebert, C. (1935), *Jesus*, translated from the French by S. H. Hooke. London: Kegan Paul, Trench, Trubner.

Howson, J. S. (1873), *The Metaphors of St. Paul and Companions of St. Paul*. Boston: American Tract Society.

Klausner, J. (1946), *From Jesus to Paul*, translated from the Hebrew by William F. Stinespring. London: George Allen and Unwin.

——— (1947), *Jesus of Nazareth, His Life, Times and Teaching*, translated from the original Hebrew by Herbert Danby. London: George Allen and Unwin.

Knox, W. (1932), *St. Paul*. New York: Appleton.

McGiffert, A. C. (1914), *A History of Christianity in the Apostolic Age*. New York: Scribner's.

Schweitzer, A. (1948), *Paul and His Interpreters*, translated by W. Montgomery. London: A. and C. Black.

Singer, I. (1919), *The Rival Philosophies of Jesus and Paul*. London: George Allen and Unwin.

HISTORICAL REFERENCES

Andrews, E. D. (1940), *The Gift to Be Simple: Songs, Dances and Rituals of the American Shakers*. New York: J. J. Augustin.

Bond, F. (1910), *Wood Carvings in English Churches*, 2 vols. Vol I: Stalls and Tabernacle Work; Vol. II: Bishops' Thrones and Chancel Chairs. London: Oxford University Press.

Burn, A. E. (1906), *The Apostles' Creed*. New York: Edwin S. Gorham.

——— (1912), *The Athanasian Creed*. New York: Edwin S. Gorham.

Cadoux, C. J. (1925), *The Early Church and the World. A History of the Christian Attitude to Pagan Society and the State down to the Time of Constantine*, Edinburgh: T. and T. Clark.

Clemen, C. (1912), *Primitive Christianity and Its Non-Jewish Sources*, translated by Robert B. Nisbet. Edinburgh: T. and T. Clark.

Donaldson, J. (1907), *Woman: Her position and Influence in Ancient Greece and Rome, and among the Early Christians*. London: Longmans, Green.

Donini, A. (1951), The myth of salvation and ancient slave society. *Science and Society, 15*:57.

Epstein, L. M. (1948), *Sex Laws and Customs in Judaism*. New York: Bloch.

Friedlander, M. (1905), *Die religiosen Bewegungen innerhalb des Judentums im Zeitalter Jesu*. Berlin: Georg Reimer.

Gassner, J. (1945), *Masters of the Drama*. New York: Dover.

Gibbon, E. (n.d.), *The Decline and Fall of the Roman Empire*, 2 vols. New York: Modern Library.

Graetz, H. (1919), *Popular History of the Jews*, 6 vols., translated by A. B. Rhine. New York: Hebrew Publishing.

Guignebert, C. (1939), *The Jewish World in the Time of Jesus*, translated from the French by S. H. Hooke. London: Kegan Paul, Trench, Trubner.

Harnack, A. (1904), *The Expansion of Christianity in the First Three Centuries*, 2 vols., translated and edited by James Moffatt. London: Williams and Norgate.

Hatch, E. (1909), *The Organization of the Early Christian Churches*. London: Longmans, Green.

Kautsky, K. (1925), *Foundations of Christianity*. New York: International Publishers.

Kiefer, O. (1933), *Kulturgeschichte Roms*. Berlin: Paul Aretz.

Landon, E. H. (1909), *A Manual of Councils of the Holy Catholic Church*, 2 vols. Edinburgh: John Grant.

Lea, H. C. (1884), *An Historical Sketch of Sacerdotal Celibacy in the Christian Church*. Boston: Houghton Mifflin.

Learsi, R. (1949), *Israel, A History of the Jewish People*. Cleveland and New York: World.

Loisy, A. (1948), *The Birth of the Christian Religion*, translated by L. P. Jacks. London: George Allen and Unwin.

Lowrie, W. (1947), *Art in the Early Church*. New York: Pantheon.

McGiffert, A. C. (1924), *The God of the Early Christians*. Edinburgh: T. and T. Clark.

——— (1947), *A History of Christian Thought*, 2 vols. New York: Scribner's.

O'Brien, J. (1880), *A History of the Mass and Its Ceremonies in the Eastern and Western Church*. New York: The Catholic Publication Society.

Parton, J. (1878), *Caricature and Other Comic Art in All Times and Many Lands*. New York: Harper.

Pfleiderer, D. O. (1905), *Die Entstehung des Christentums*. Munchen: J. F. Lehmann's Verlag.

——— (1907), *Die Entwicklung des Christentums*. Munchen: J. F. Lehmann's Verlag.

Pilcher, C. V. (1940), *The Hereafter in Jewish and Christian Thought, With Special Reference to the Doctrine of Resurrection*. London: Society for Promoting Christian Knowledge.

Radin, M. (1915), *The Jews Among the Greeks and Romans*. Philadelphia: The Jewish Publication Society of America.

Reifenberg, A. (1950), *Ancient Hebrew Arts*. New York: Schocken Books.

Schurer, E. (1890), *A History of the Jewish People in the Time of Jesus Christ*, 5 vols., translated by John Mac Pherson. Edinburgh: T. and T. Clark.

Smith, H. (1831), *Festivals, Games and Amusements, Ancient and Modern*. London: Henry Colburn and Richard Bentley.

Strawley, J. H. (1949), *The Early History of the Liturgy*. Cambridge: The University Press.

Strzygowski, J. (1923), *Origin of Christian Church Art*, translated from the German by O. M. Dalton and H. J. Braunholtz. Oxford: The Clarendon Press.

Trachtenberg, J. (1943), *The Devil and the Jews*. New Haven: Yale University Press.

Tunison, J. (1907), *Dramatic Traditions of the Dark Ages*. Chicago: University of Chicago Press.

van Paassen, P. (1949), *Why Jesus Died*. New York: Dial Press.

Wand, J. W. C. (1937), *First Century Christianity*. London: Oxford University Press.

Warren, F. E. (1897), *The Liturgy and Ritual of the Ante-Nicene Church*. London: Society for Promoting Christian Knowledge.

Williams, N. P. (1927), *The Ideas of the Fall and of Original Sin. A Historical and Critical Study. Being Eight Lectures Delivered before the University of Oxford in the Year 1924, on the Foundation of the Rev. John Bampton, Cannon of Salisbury.* London: Longmans, Green and Co.

Wunsche, A. (1870), *Die Leiden des Messias.* Leipzig: Fues's Verlag.

Young, K. (1933), *The Drama of the Medieval Church*, 2 vols. Oxford: The Clarendon Press.

PSYCHOANALYTIC REFERENCES

Barag, G. G. (1946), The mother in the religious concepts of Judaism. *American Imago, 4*(1):32.

——— (1947), The question of Jewish monotheism. *American Imago, 4*(3):8.

Bunker, H. A. (1951), Psychoanalysis and the Study of Religion. *Psychoanalysis and the Social Sciences, 3:7.* New York: International Universities Press.

Fenichel, O. (1940), Psychoanalysis of antisemitism. *American Imago, 1*(2):24.

Freud, S. (1939), *Moses and Monotheism.* New York: Knopf, 1947.

Glover, E. (1950), *Freud or Jung.* New York: Norton.

Jekels, L. (1936), The psychology of the festival of Christmas, *International Journal of Psycho-Analysis, 17:57.*

Jones, E. (1923), A psycho-analytic study of the holy ghost. *Essays in Applied Psychoanalysis.* London: Hogarth Press.

——— (1944), The psychology of religion. In *Psychoanalysis Today*, S. Lorand, Ed. New York: International Universities Press.

Jung, C. G. (1938), *Psychology and Religion.* New Haven: Yale University Press.

Lewin, B. D. (1950), *The Psychoanalysis of Elation.* New York: Norton.

Loewenstein, R. M. (1947), The historical and cultural roots of anti-Semitism. *Psychoanalysis and the Social Sciences, 1:313.* New York: International Universities Press.

——— (1951), *Christians and Jews.* New York: International Universities Press.

Nunberg, H. (1949), *Problems of Bisexuality as Reflected in Circumcision.* London: Imago Publishing.

Pfister, O. (1920), Die Entwicklung des Apostels Paulus. Eine religions-geschictliche und psychologische Skizze. *Imago, 6:243.*

——— (1948), *Christianity and Fear. A Study in History and in the Psychology and Hygiene of Religion.* London: George Allen and Unwin.

Reik, T. (1946), *Ritual, Psychoanalytic Studies.* New York: Farrar, Straus.

——— (1951), *Dogma and Compulsion, Psychoanalytic Studies of Religion and Myths.* New York: International Universities Press.

Roellenbleck, E. (1949), *Magna Mater im Alten Testament. Eine*

Psychoanalytische Untersuchung. Darmstadt: Claassen und Roether.

Sachs, H. (1948), At the Gates of Heaven. Chap. IV in *Masks of Love and Life*. Cambridge: Sci-Art Publishers.

Simmel, E. (1946), Anti-Semitism and Mass Psychopathology. Chap. III in *Anti-Semitism*. New York: International Universities Press.

Tarachow, S. (1948), Totem feast in modern dress. *American Imago, 5*:65.

Thompson, C. (1940), Identification with the enemy and loss of sense of self. *Psychoanalytic Quarterly, 9*:37.

AUTHOR-SUBJECT
INDEX